CLASSICAL CHINESE PRIMER

# Classical Chinese Primer

# 古文入門

By John C. Y. Wang, Sue-mei Wu,
Shaoyu Jiang, and Frank F. S. Hsueh

王靖宇・吳素美
蔣紹愚・薛鳳生
著

中文大學出版社

***Classical Chinese Primer***
   By John C. Y. Wang, Sue-mei Wu, Shaoyu Jiang,
   and Frank F. S. Hsueh

© The Chinese University of Hong Kong 2007

ISBNs: 978-962-996-339-2
          978-962-996-286-9 (Textbook + Workbook)

First edition        2007
*Fourth printing*     2018

Published by   The Chinese University Press
                    The Chinese University of Hong Kong
                    Sha Tin, N.T., Hong Kong
                    Fax: +852 2603 7355
                    Email: cup@cuhk.edu.hk
                    Website: www.chineseupress.com

Printed in Hong Kong

# Contents

# A Note on Notations and Transliterations

The convention in this reader is to have the Chinese characters followed by *pinyin*, with spaces between the *pinyin* for each character, for example, 然而 rán ér. The exceptions are transliterations, which are written with the *pinyin* followed by the Chinese characters, for example, Zhōu 周. All personal names are written in the conventional format, for example, Wáng Ānshí 王安石. This also includes courtesy names and other honorifics, for example, Zǐlù 子路; Mèngzǐ 孟子. All place names are similarly written in the conventional format, for example, Cháng'ān 長安; Héběi 河北. In cases where the ending of the name indicates a mountain, a water body, or a city, etc., the above convention is maintained, for example, Wǔchéng 武城; Bóhǎi 渤海; Huáshān 華山. Finally, all titles referring to specific persons are written with no spaces between the *pinyin* for the actual title, for example, Lǔ Xiānggōng 魯襄公; Sòng Rénzōng 宋仁宗; Liúhóu 留侯.

# Chronology of Major
# Chinese Dynasties and Periods

| | | |
|---|---|---|
| Xia | 夏 | ca. 2100–1600 B.C. |
| Shang | 商 | ca. 1600–1046 B.C. |
| Zhou | 周 | ca. 1045–256 B.C. |
|   Western Zhou | 西周 | 1045–771 B.C. |
|   Eastern Zhou | 東周 | 770–256 B.C. |
|     Spring and Autumn | 春秋 | 770–403 B.C. |
|     Warring States | 戰國 | 403–221 B.C. |
| Qin | 秦 | 221–207 B.C. |
| Han | 漢 | 206 B.C.–220 A.D. |
|   Western Han | 西漢 | 206 B.C.–24 A.D. |
|   Eastern Han | 東漢 | 25–220 |
| Three Kingdoms | 三國 | 220–280 |
| Jin | 晉 | 265–420 |
|   Western Jin | 西晉 | 265–316 |
|   Eastern Jin | 東晉 | 317–420 |
| Northern and Southern Dynasties | 南北朝 | 420–589 |
| Sui | 隋 | 581–618 |
| Tang | 唐 | 618–907 |
| Five Dynasties | 五代 | 907–960 |
| Song | 宋 | 960–1279 |
|   Northern Song | 北宋 | 960–1127 |
|   Southern Song | 南宋 | 1127–1279 |
| Yuan | 元 | 1279–1368 |
| Ming | 明 | 1368–1644 |
| Qing | 清 | 1644–1911 |

# Introduction

The teaching of Modern Chinese as a foreign language in the United States has advanced by leaps and bounds since the 1950s. One indication of the tremendous progress made in this area is the proliferation of textbooks, teaching aids and tools of all kinds. The same, however, cannot be said about the teaching of Classical Chinese. The total number of published textbooks and reading materials designed specifically to teach Classical Chinese could perhaps be counted on the fingers of just one hand. And up to now, Harold Shadick's *A First Course in Literary Chinese* in three volumes (1968), Michael Fuller's *An Introduction to Literary Chinese* (1999), and *Classical Chinese: A Basic Reader* in three volumes (2004) by Naiying Yuan, Haitao Tang, and James Geiss are the only three textbooks used in the field that are complete with reading selections, annotations, grammatical analyses, and exercises. This is regrettable because, as anyone at all familiar with the history of the development of the Chinese language knows, Classical Chinese functioned as the official medium of written expression all the way down to the beginning of the 20th century when it was finally replaced by a vernacular language based on the everyday spoken language otherwise known as Modern Chinese. Although written Modern Chinese differs from Classical Chinese in many ways, the latter's influence on the former in terms of both vocabulary and syntax is pervasive and profound, so much so that it would not be an exaggeration to say that many of the subtler points and fine nuances in Modern Chinese will be missed unless one also has acquired at least a rudimentary knowledge of Classical Chinese. At the same time, a good and solid foundation in Classical Chinese is a must if one wants to do any amount of reading of just about any text written before the 20th century. The study of Classical Chinese, therefore, is essential not only for a better understanding of traditional Chinese culture, but also for a true mastery of Modern Chinese. Moreover, precisely because Classical Chinese has ceased to be used and a true proficiency in it can only be acquired through extensive reading of classical texts from China's long past, there is all the more reason for more fully annotated and clearly analyzed readers and other teaching aids designed especially for beginning students. The purpose in the compilation of this reader, therefore, is an attempt to address this urgent need in the teaching of Classical Chinese.

Designed for those who have studied Modern Chinese for one or two years, but who have had no exposure to Classical Chinese before, this book contains forty lessons in all. Except for the first two lessons which comprise two sets of well-known Chinese fables or parables taken from an assortment of texts, all the other lessons contain selections from single texts dating mostly to the pre-Han, Han (206 B.C.–220 A.D.), Tang (618–907), and Song (960–1279) periods. This is because the texts from Han and pre-Han times not only constitute the fountainhead of China's cultural tradition, but the language used in these texts was also the Classical Chinese all later writers tried to emulate. Then during the Tang and Song periods, under the leadership of writers such as Han Yu 韓愈 (768–824), Liu Zongyuan 柳宗元 (773–819), Ouyang Xiu 歐陽修 (1007–1072), and Su Shi 蘇軾 (1037–1101), Classical Chinese underwent some transformation and the derivative new style of prose writing with these writers as the chief practitioners became the dominant style that was to last until the turn of the 20th century.

In order not to dampen the spirit of beginning readers of Classical Chinese, the selections in general are short pieces that make interesting reading. In the case of longer ones, only excerpts are included. The teacher is encouraged to have the students read more from the original pieces as a sort of exercise. As the basic grammatical features of Classical Chinese are more readily seen in prose rather than poetry, except for a few supplemental poems on the same subject matter as the main texts, which were included to increase the students' interest, all the texts included here are prose pieces and they represent the three most common discourse types — narrative, descriptive, and deliberative.

Each lesson is accompanied by an annotation section for words and terms. Needless to say, the annotations are meant primarily to elucidate the text on hand; they are not designed to be like the entries found in a dictionary. In other words, only the definitions most relevant to the context are provided. This is also why some words are glossed again when they appear to have different or slightly different meanings than before. A comprehensive Vocabulary Index is included at the end of the reader for the convenience of the student. Similarly, a Grammar Summary is appended (Appendix I). For those interested in reading the reader in simplified characters, a simplified character version accompanied by *pinyin* is also appended (Appendix II).

Since this textbook is designed for those who may have had some basic knowledge of Modern Chinese but are studying Classical Chinese for the first time, a special section on grammatical analyses is provided at the end of most selections, where sentences from the selection that may appear unusual to beginning readers of Classical Chinese are analyzed, explained, and, when appropriate, compared with their modern counterparts. Our interest here, however, is not so much in introducing arcane linguistic theories as in helping the reader understand the particular text on hand. Our own experience as teachers of Classical Chinese has shown that too much specialized linguistic discussion can be confusing to especially a beginning student: it actually dampens rather than encourages the student's spirit in learning the language.

We have therefore tried our best to avoid linguistic jargon except such commonly used terms as syntax, sentence, clause, subject, predicate, object, modifier, noun, pronoun, verb, adjective, adverb, conjunction, etc. We have also decided not to draw analytical diagrams in the form of either "immediate constituents" or "tree-branching", because we believe that simple verbal explanations are better, or more readily understandable, to our readers. The purpose of the analysis is not to demonstrate that a certain sentence is or is not "grammatical". Of course, all the sentences we have analyzed are grammatical. So the sole and only purpose of the analysis is to explain why a certain sentence means what it is supposed to mean. In other words, the justification for the analysis of a sentence lies in its ability to determine the semantic interpretation of that sentence.

Like sentences in English (maybe all languages), sentences in Chinese can also be conceived as consisting of two fundamental components, subject and predicate, but the similarity almost seems to end there. This is because the two languages differ very much in terms of what can serve as subject and what can serve as predicate. It happens that there are some seemingly "strange" but common features in the way sentences are formed for both Classical and Modern Chinese, perhaps due to the dialogic or conversational style even in writing. Following are some of the "strange" features which must always be kept in mind when we try to understand or analyze a Classical Chinese sentence, because they may help free us from the preconceptions, or "biases", about sentence formation that we have subconsciously acquired through the European languages.

**(1) Words can play different grammatical roles without overt marking.**

This is not something completely unknown to English. For example, a stone can be used "to stone" someone, and to call someone means to give him a "call". But, by and large, English distinguishes different parts of speech by prefix or suffix. For example, "large" becomes "enlarge" as a verb, and "beauty" becomes "beautiful" as an adjective. Chinese, however, ignores any overt marking. Thus, when we see a "noun" in a Classical Chinese sentence, we cannot assume that, as a noun, it serves as subject or object, because it may be a modifier (adjectival or adverbial), or the verb (i.e., "center" of the predicate). Similarly, verbs, adjectives, or adverbs should not be automatically assumed to be such. It all depends on the context. So it must be remembered that "parts of speech" do not always match with their supposed corresponding grammatical roles. (Incidentally, many people have the tendency to interpret Chinese sentences word by word. This practice does not work well with Modern Chinese, but it works well, almost perfectly, with Classical Chinese, which is said to be "analytical".)

(2) **"Word order" is the most crucial grammatical feature of Chinese grammar.** Chinese grammar is most strict in demanding that proper word order be kept. This means that modifier must always come before the modified, and the object must follow its verb. Therefore, "I will come tomorrow" must be rendered into Chinese as something like "I tomorrow come", and "something new" as "new something". It is also true that the relative clause must come before the noun it modifies, and the subordinate clause before the main clause. When this rule is consistently observed, it will help us determine accurately the role a word or a phrase plays in a given sentence.

(3) **Grammatical particles, especially conjunctions, are sometimes omitted.** Again, this is not absolutely unique for Chinese. The same is sometimes true with less formal English. For example, in certain places (especially restaurants), we may see a sign like "No shirt, no shoes, no service". What it means, presumably, is something like "If you are barefooted and barebacked, we won't serve you." "Sentences" like that are, of course, very rare and are considered to be "pidgin" English, but they are very common in even formal Classical Chinese writings. For proper interpretation of any Classical Chinese texts, this must always be kept in mind. Normally, the context helps us determine what the omitted particles are.

(4) **There are many modal particles which can help us understand the structure of a sentence.** Perhaps due to its dialogic ("colloquial") style, Classical Chinese has many modal particles, such as sentence-initial particles like 夫, 蓋, 且 or sentence-end particles like 也, 矣, 哉, etc. Though some of them cannot be easily

defined, the modal particles, together with interrogative and exclamatory particles, as well as conjunctions, often serve as clues to the grammatical structure of the expressions which include them. We will have a better chance of making an accurate analysis of any expression when we take this function of the particles into serious consideration.

**(5) Subject means "topic" and predicate means "comment" on the topic.**

This is a very crucial discovery for Chinese grammar by Dr. Y. R. Chao, and the next two features can be regarded as corollaries of this one. What it means is that, unlike the "subject" in English grammar which generally means the "actor" of the "action" represented by the "predicate", "subject" in Chinese grammar means literally the "subject-matter" or "topic" while "predicate" means literally the "predication" or "comment" on that topic. When "subject" and "predicate" are so defined for Chinese grammar, we will be able to see the logic behind all the seemingly "strange" sentences in Chinese and realize that they are in fact quite normal.

**(6) The predicate may appear in various forms, even simply a noun phrase or a "sentence".**

If the predicate of a sentence means the "comment" a speaker makes on the subject or the "topic", it follows that it need not be a "verb phrase" as it normally is in English. In fact, any expression (including "verb phrase") that can serve as a comment will do. For example, if you don't like somebody, you can simply say: "He, stupid", or "He, big-mouth", or "He, I couldn't care less", and naturally "He, doesn't like me". Except for the last one, none of these sayings qualify as a sentence in English because they do not include a "verb" for the subject. In Chinese, however, all (including the last one) will be accepted as normal sentences, because the predicate in each sentence is a "comment" on the subject. Sentences like these are very common in Chinese. So, it is not to be surprised when we claim that an adjective, or a noun, or a "sentence" (i.e., a clause) serves as the predicate of a sentence.

**(7) Sentences without a subject are extremely common (but no sentence can be without a predicate).**

Since the subject of a sentence in Chinese means the "topic", speakers naturally have a tendency to avoid repeating it, or even mentioning it, when they feel that the person or persons they speak to already know it, or when it is something as general as the weather. (In the latter case, English grammar requires, nevertheless, a subject in the form of an expletive "it", as in, "It may snow tomorrow".) Consequently, subjectless sentences are extremely common in Classical Chinese. Sometimes it may be difficult to recognize a subjectless sentence, especially when its predicate happens to be a noun phrase or a clause. It can thus be mistaken for something else, leading inevitably to inaccurate grammatical analysis and semantic interpretation of the sentence, as well as improper definition of the grammatical particles involved.

Clearly, accurate interpretation of any Classical Chinese texts depends heavily upon a good understanding of its grammar. Hopefully, the seven features discussed above may help our readers acquire such an understanding. A sentence may be formed when several of these features are involved simultaneously, and thus becomes very complex. One example can be given here to illustrate this point.

In the *Shijing*《詩經》(*Classic of Poetry*), we can find 人而無儀, 不死何為 (《鄘風‧相鼠》). Practically, all scholars say that it is a conditional sentence which means something like, "If people have no manners, why don't they die?" Several questions can be raised. (1) How do we know this is a conditional sentence? Many scholars have tried to explain this by asserting that the conjunction 而 here means 若 "if". This explanation is not acceptable (see discussion below). Our explanation is rather that, because 人而無儀 comes before 不死何為, it can only be the subordinate clause (Feature 2), serving as the condition for the main clause, even though conjunctions for conditional sentences such as 若 "if" and 則 "then" are not included (Feature 3). (2) Is 人 really the subject? Since subject means "topic" (Feature 5), it often implies something specific or "definite". Therefore, to regard 人 as the subject would be a violation of that general rule. Besides, that assumption would mean the poet (or speaker) was philosophizing about human behavior, which is highly unusual. More likely, he was bitterly complaining about some person or persons without mentioning names. If so, the sentence has to be accepted as one without subject (Feature 7). (3) What is the function of the conjunction 而? Because of sentences like this where 人 was assumed to be the subject, 而 was never properly defined. Some have said it means "if" here, which is merely ad hoc. Others have said it is simply a "connective" between subject and predicate, which makes us wonder why subject and predicate need a connective. Moreover, that also would imply 人無儀 and 人而無儀 mean the same thing, which we know is not true. If we remember that 人, though a noun, can also serve as a predicate (Feature 6), we shall be able to see that it actually stands here as the predicate of a clause without a subject. Then we shall also be able to see that 而 is, here and everywhere else, a conjunction which always comes between two clauses, indicating that the one before it is the subordinate clause and the one after it is the main clause. After all the factors mentioned above have been considered, we can now see that 人而無儀 means actually "(That person) is a human and yet (he) has no manners." This then serves as the conditional clause to 不死何為, the main clause which is also subjectless, and together they form a conditional sentence, which can now be rendered into more idiomatic English as, "Since he, being a human, does not behave like one, why doesn't he drop dead?"

More examples can be found in the Grammar Note(s) sections for the selected texts. Those sentences have all been similarly analyzed in accordance with the seven grammatical features discussed above, though a bit more briefly. Although we have tried to be thorough in annotating words and terms and clear in explaining the syntax and grammar involved, there must still be details that have escaped our attention. Feedback from users of this set of textbook would be much appreciated for possible future revisions.

Finally, a word about the exercises that are provided for each lesson. Bound as a separate volume from the reader itself, the exercises appear in the form of filling in the blanks, rearranging word order in a sentence to make grammatical sense, punctuating, translating into English both studied and new passages, explaining the usage of particles or function words in sentences, or, in one case, even doing a crossword puzzle. Although quite varied, the prerequisite for being able to do the exercises right is a thorough familiarity with the texts already studied. The more familiar one is with the text or texts involved, the easier and faster one can finish the exercises. As said earlier, since Classical Chinese is no longer a living language, to become proficient in it the student has to become so familiar with what s/he has read that s/he can almost recite the texts studied from memory. (Surely, this must be why in the old days memorization formed such an important part of classical education.)

This Classical Chinese reader is truly the result of collaborative work of the four people whose names appear on the cover. The idea of compiling a reader in Classical Chinese came from John C. Y. Wang and Frank F. S. Hsueh. Shaoyu Jiang selected most of the readings as well as prepared a list of vocabulary with preliminary annotations when he was visiting Stanford University and The Ohio State University during 1989 to 1990. As the reader was taking shape, Frank Hsueh began working on the grammar analyses of sentence structures, and selected several more readings. The work on the project received a much needed push when Sue-mei Wu joined the team. She contributed to the annotations, translations, and grammar analyses, and designed all the exercises. She also typed all the materials on the computer and designed the layout of the volumes. John Wang then did the overall checking and editing, and wrote the Introduction with input from Frank Hsueh. A note of thanks goes to Janice Foong Kam, a Ph.D. student in Chinese literature at Stanford, for her conscientious and effective assistance during the final stages of the compilation of this reader, and for her valuable input after using a draft version of this reader to teach a Classical Chinese class at Dartmouth College. Thanks are also due to Mark Haney for proof-reading the English and Chris Yuan-ching Lin who provided the lively computer-generated illustrations for the reader.

Last but not least, we would like to thank Steven K. Luk, Director of The Chinese University Press, for his encouragement and support throughout and Flo Chan, Project Editor, and her colleague, Wai-keung Tse for their patient, meticulous, and expert editing. The reader is a much better product as a result.

# 一.寓言選（上）

## （甲）揠苗助長[1]

## 📖 課文 (Text)

宋人有閔其苗之不長而揠之者，²芒芒然歸，³謂
其人曰：⁴「今日病矣，⁵予助苗長矣！⁶」其子趨而往視
之，⁷苗則槁矣。⁸天下之不助苗長者寡矣！⁹以為無益
而舍之者，¹⁰不耘苗者也；¹¹助之長者，揠苗者也；非
徒無益，而又害之。¹²

《孟子‧公孫丑上》¹³

*(handwritten annotations: "worried" above 閔 circled, "pull" above 揠 circled)*

## 📋 註釋 (Annotations)

| | | | |
|---|---|---|---|
| 1. | 甲 | jiǎ | the first of the ten so-called Heavenly Stems (天干 tiāngān): 甲 jiǎ, 乙 yǐ, 丙 bǐng, 丁 dīng, 戊 wù, 己 jǐ, 庚 gēng, 辛 xīn, 壬 rén, 癸 guǐ. Among other things, they are used as serial numbers. |
| | 揠 | yà | to pull up. |
| | 苗 | miáo | seedlings; sprouts (of grains). |
| 2. | 宋 | Sòng | the name of a feudal state during the Spring and Autumn (春秋 Chūnqiū) period (ca. 770–403 B.C.) of the Zhōu 周 Dynasty (ca. 1045–256 B.C.), located in the eastern part of present-day Hénán 河南 province. (See Chronology of Major Chinese Dynasties and Periods.) |
| | 閔 | mǐn | to feel sorry for; to commiserate with. (Written as 憫 in later times.) |
| | 其 | qí | his. (A general third-person possessive pronoun, hence, "his; her; its; their", depending on the context.) |
| | 之 | zhī | somebody's; something's. (A possessive marker after a nominal expression.) [See 文法闡釋 I (1).] |

| 而 | ér | a conjunction of verb phrases or clauses. [See 文法闡釋 I (2).] |
| 之 | zhī | them. (A general third-person pronoun only for the objective case, hence, "him; her; it; them", depending on the context.) |
| 者 | zhě | a particle. (It generally nominalizes the verb or verb phrase to which it is attached.) [See 文法闡釋 I (3).] |
| 3. 芒芒然 | máng máng rán | looking tired. (The duplicative 芒芒 means "blank and inactive"; 然, as a suffix, means "in such a way or manner".) |
| 歸 | guī | to return; to go back to where one belongs. (Normally, one's home.) |
| 4. 謂 | wèi | to speak to; to address. |
| 其人 | qí rén | his people, i.e., his folks at home. |
| 曰 | yuē | to say. (This word often serves to indicate a quotation from direct speech in Classical Chinese.) |
| 5. 病 | bìng | exhausted; suffering badly. (Note that in Classical Chinese this word means "to be in a severe condition [for any reason]", unlike in Modern Chinese where it means "to have some medical problem [or disease]".) |
| 矣 | yǐ | sentence-end particle, indicating that what the sentence describes is a new situation. (It is an equivalent to the sentence-end particle *le* 了 in Modern Chinese.) [See 文法闡釋 I (4).] |
| 6. 予 | yú | I. (A pronoun.) |
| 7. 趨 | qū | to walk fast. |
| 往 | wǎng | to go to. |
| 視 | shì | to look at. |

8. 則　　　zé　　　another conjunction for verb phrases or clauses. [See 文法闡釋 I (2) for the difference between 而 and 則.]

槁　　　gǎo　　　withered.

9. 天下　　　tiān xià　　　the whole world. (Literally, "[all] under the sky".)

寡　　　guǎ　　　rare; few.

10. 以為　　　yǐ wéi　　　to regard (someone or something) as. (The full form is 以 A 為 B. Note that the object of 以 here is implied. Also note that these two words have separate functions in Classical Chinese, whereas in Modern Chinese they have become the compound "to think".)

無益　　　wú yì　　　of no help; without avail; useless.

舍　　　shě　　　to give up; to ignore; to discard. (Written as 捨 in later times.)

11. 耘　　　yún　　　to weed.

也　　　yě　　　sentence-end particle, indicating confirmation. [See 文法闡釋 I (4).]

12. 非徒⋯　　　fēi tú ...　　　not only ..., but also .... (Similar to 不但⋯
而又⋯　　　ér yòu ...　　　而且⋯ in Modern Chinese.)

害　　　hài　　　to harm.

13. 孟子　　　Mèngzǐ　　　*Mencius.* Title of a work collecting the sayings and activities of Mencius 孟子 (ca. 372 B.C.–289 B.C.) whose fame is only second to that of Confucius in the Confucian school of thinkers.

公孫丑　　　Gōngsūn Chǒu　　　name of a person; here, the title of a chapter from *Mencius.*

上　　　shàng　　　part one.

## ☀ 文法闡釋 (Grammar Notes)

## I. Some most commonly-used grammar particles

Though very short in length, this extract contains quite a few of the most commonly-used grammar particles. To grasp the specific functions of these particles is most important for understanding Classical Chinese texts. As function words, they are, however, very complex. In the following, we can, therefore, only give each of them a definition specifically used for understanding the context of the extract.

### (1) The character 之

The character 之 is used to denote two unrelated meanings in Classical Chinese. The first is a pronoun, as in 揠之, 視之, 舍之, 助之, and 害之, and it serves as the object of a verb. The other is a possessive marker to be attached to a noun (or pronoun), as in 苗之不長 "the seedlings' not growing" and 天下之不助苗長者 "those of the world who do not assist the seedlings in growing". However, when the object of this possessive marker is a verb phrase, as in 苗之不長, we can say for practical purposes that it turns the whole phrase into a noun clause (i.e., "the seedlings' not growing" is the same as "that the seedlings are not growing") serving as the object of its preceding verb (閔 in this case).

### (2) The conjunctions 而 and 則

Both 而 and 則 are conjunctions used to join clauses to form compound sentences. However, since sentences (hence, clauses) are often without subject (omitted or implied) in Chinese, these conjunctions may seem to connect verb phrases (when the predicates are verb phrases) or even nouns (when a noun serves as predicate). Syntactically, both 而 and 則 indicate that what precedes them is the subordinate (adverbial) clause, while what follows them is the main clause. Semantically, the relationship between the two clauses (events) connected by 而 is somewhat ordinary and matter-of-fact, therefore, 而 can be translated as "and (thus)", as exemplified by 閔其苗之不長而揠之 "(he) felt sorry that his seedlings did not grow, and thus pulled at them"; 其子趨而往視之 "his son walked in a hurry and went to see them"; and 以為無益而舍之 "(someone) regards it to be of no avail and thus gives it up". (To better reveal the subordination of the clause in front of 而, it can be translated with such words as "when" or "because".) On the other hand, the semantic relationship between the two clauses connected by 則 seems to be rather contrastive, conditional, or contradictory. The only example we have in this extract, 苗則槁矣, is not typical enough, because 則 is proceeded only by the noun 苗. Nevertheless, the sentence should be understood as, "As for those seedlings (he pulled at), well, they have all withered!"

## (3) The particle 者

The particle 者 is generally defined as a nominalizer. That is, when being attached to the end of a verb or a verb phrase, it turns the whole phrase into a nominal expression. Such an expression usually means, in a concrete sense, "one who does (or those who do) something", as exemplified by expressions in this extract such as 閔其苗之不長而揠之者 "one who felt sorry that his seedlings did not grow, and thus pulled at them". Note that 者 can, sometimes, also be used in a more abstract sense for emphasis, transforming a verb or a verb phrase into "a certain action", like an infinitive phrase ("to do something") or a gerund phrase ("doing something"). For such usage, it can even be attached to a name, changing its meaning to "a certain person (or thing) that people call by that name". For example, 韓信者, 淮陰人也 "The person known as Han Xin was a man from Huaiyin".

## (4) The sentence-end particles 矣 and 也

矣 and 也 are the two most frequently-used sentence-end particles in Classical Chinese. When attached to a sentence, 矣 implies that what the sentence describes is a new situation. The meaning and function of 矣 is very similar to the sentence-end particle *le* 了 in Modern Chinese. For example, 今日病矣! can be translated into Modern Chinese as 今天累死了! And 苗則槁矣! can be rendered as 原來好好的苗現在都枯槁了! On the other hand, 也 implies that the sentence to which it is attached is merely a statement describing a plain or static situation, with an undertone of assertion, as if to say "and that's it". Since Classical Chinese does not have a copular verb, a sentence like "A is B" in Classical Chinese would simply be "A, B" to which 也 is often added as a sentence-end particle (A, B 也). But 也 should not be equated with the verb "be", though it often marks equational sentences. For example, 助之長者, 揠苗者也 "Those who hasten it are people who pull at their seedlings".

## II. 揠苗助長

The title of this Mencian fable is a typical four-character compound which has become a common Chinese idiom. It is a condensed form derived from 揠苗以助之長 "to pull at a young plant in order to help it grow". It means metaphorically "to cause damage to somebody or something from overzealousness or impatience".

## III. 宋人有-VP-者

In the Chinese story-telling tradition (and historical writings), this sentence pattern is frequently used to introduce a character (person). 宋人 "(of) the Song people" is the topic, which, therefore, should be followed by a slight pause when reading aloud. 者, the nominalizer, turns the VP into a nominal which serves as the object of the verb 有 "there is; there are".

## IV. 以為無益而舍之者，不耘苗者也。

This is an equational sentence of the "A, B 也" type, with both its subject and predicate represented by a phrase nominalized by 者. An equational sentence does not necessarily always mean "A is B". It may also imply "A means B", or "A is just like B", which is what it does in this metaphorical saying. The sentence means, therefore, "Those who neglect it because they regard it to be without benefit to them are like people who do not weed their seedlings". (Note that the pronoun 之 does not refer to 苗. In the original text from *Mengzi*, it refers to the 浩然之氣 hào rán zhī qì, the mysterious qì of a righteous mind. But it can also be taken to refer to any work or business one is undertaking, if this metaphor is quoted as a warning against overzealousness or impatience.)

# 一. 寓言選 (上)

## (乙) 濫竽充數[1]

## 📖 課文 (Text)

齊宣王使人吹竽，²必三百人。³南郭處士請為王吹竽，⁴宣王説之，⁵廩食以數百人。⁶宣王死，湣王立，⁷好一一聽之，⁸處士逃。

《韓非子·內儲説上》⁹

## 📑 註釋 (Annotations)

1. 乙    yǐ    second of the Heavenly Stems.

   濫    làn    to handle improperly; to misuse.

   竽    yú    a kind of pipe-like musical instrument popular in ancient China.

   充數   chōng shù    to make up the numbers, i.e., to fill a vacancy in a team (in the derogatory sense of "as a dummy").

2. 齊    Qí    a state during the Zhou Dynasty, located on the Shāndōng 山東 peninsula.

   宣王   Xuānwáng    King Xuan, a king of Qi.

   吹    chuī    to blow; to play (a wind instrument).

3. 必    bì    must; always. (An adverb.)

4. 南郭   Nánguō    a family name.

   處士   chǔ shì    a scholar in retirement; a private individual; a gentleman.

   請    qǐng    to ask; to beg for permission.

   為    wèi    for. (A preposition.)

5. 説    yuè    to be delighted with. (Written as 悦 in later times.)

| | | |
|---|---|---|
| 6. 廩食 | lǐn sì | to give (someone) grain from the government granary. When 食 means "to feed", it is pronounced sì. |
| 7. 湣王 | Mǐnwáng | King Min, the son of King Xuan. |
| 立 | lì | to be enthroned; become established. |
| 8. 好 | hào | to like. (A verb.) |
| 一一 | yī yī | one by one. |
| 9. 韓非子 | Hán Fēizǐ | title of a work collecting the writings of the Warring States period thinker Han Fei. |
| 內儲說 | Nèi chǔ shuō | "Inner Collected Sayings". Title of a chapter from the *Han Feizi*. |

## ☀ 文法闡釋 (Grammar Notes)

## I. 濫竽充數

This is a four-character idiomatic expression still frequently used in Modern Chinese. Grammatically, this VO + VO construction is a condensed form of 濫竽以充數 which means literally "to pretend to play the *yu* so as to make up the requisite numbers". Figuratively, it is now used to criticize a person for occupying a certain position without the necessary qualifications. However, in a typically Asian way, it is also often used as a humble expression for oneself, meaning "being a stand-in for the lack of a more qualified person".

## II. 必三百人

This is a sentence without a subject. Unlike English in which sentences like this often have "it", or "there", as their subject, Chinese simply leaves such sentences with no subject. Adverbs like 必 can also be used without a verb (or function as a verb, comparable to 會 in Modern Chinese, as in 他會中文). The sentence means, therefore, "there must be three hundred people", or "it always required three hundred people". This sentence serves as the main clause for the compound sentence, while its preceding sentence 齊宣王使人吹竽 serves as the subordinate clause.

## III. 廩食以數百人

廩 "government granary" functions here as an adverb modifying the verb 食 "to feed". The phrase means, therefore, "to let (someone) receive food from the government", or in modern terminology, "to put him on the government payroll". The minimum amount of grain paid to one worker was counted as one unit, and higher officials were paid more on that basis. So 以數百人 means "with several hundred (basic) units". The understood ("omitted") subject of the sentence is the king. So a fairly close translation of the sentence is "(the king) paid him several hundred units (of grain)".

# 一. 寓言選(上)

## (丙) 守株待兔[1]

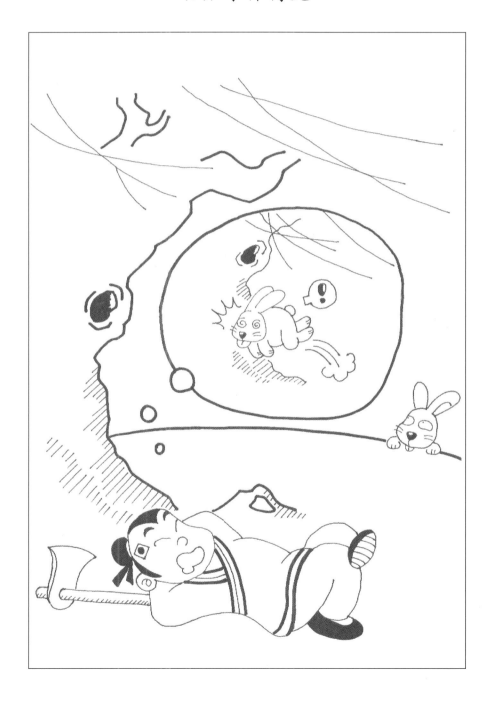

## 📖 課文 (Text)

宋人有耕者，<sup>2</sup>田中有株，兔走觸株，<sup>3</sup>折頸而死。<sup>4</sup>
因釋其耒而守株，<sup>5</sup>冀復得兔。<sup>6</sup>兔不可復得，而身為宋
國笑。<sup>7</sup>

《韓非子・五蠹》<sup>8</sup>

## 📝 註 釋 (Annotations)

| 1. | 丙 | bǐng | third of the Heavenly Stems. |
| | 守 | shǒu | to watch; to guard. |
| | 株 | zhū | the trunk of a tree. |
| | 待 | dài | to wait for. |
| 2. | 耕 | gēng | to plow. |
| 3. | 走 | zǒu | to run. (Note that the meaning of 走 in Classical Chinese is "to run", but in Modern Chinese it means "to walk".) |
| | 觸 | chù | to touch; to bump against. |
| 4. | 折 | zhé | to bend (and break). |
| | 頸 | jǐng | neck. |
| 5. | 因 | yīn | for that reason; subsequently. |
| | 釋 | shì | to let (something) go; to put down; to set free. |
| | 耒 | lěi | a plow. |
| 6. | 冀 | jì | to hope. |
| | 復 | fù | again. (An adverb.) |

|  | 得 | dé | to get. |
|---|---|---|---|
| 7. | 身 | shēn | oneself. |
|  | 為 | wéi | to be; to become. (See 文法闡釋 III.) |
|  | 笑 | xiào | to laugh at (somebody). |
| 8. | 五蠹 | Wǔ dù | "Five Vermin". Title of a chapter from the *Han Feizi*. |

## ☀ 文法闡釋 (Grammar Notes)

### I. 守株待兔

This is a shortened form of 守株以待兔, and it literally means "to stay at a tree stump to wait for a rabbit". This is also an idiomatic expression still commonly used, meaning figuratively "to wait passively for luck to strike again".

### II. 兔走觸株

Grammatically, the sentence should be 兔走而觸株, but the conjunction 而 was often omitted for stylistic purposes. This explains why the said sentence does not use 而 while the succeeding one does—in order to maintain a series of balanced four-syllable utterances. So this compound sentence means: "When a rabbit was running, it bumped against a tree stump".

### III. 身為宋國笑

The word 身 is often used in the sense of "(one)self", as it is in this case. 宋國笑 is a noun clause, meaning "what (the people of ) Song laughed about". It serves as the object of the verb 為 "to become". So the whole sentence means: "and he himself became a laughing stock in Song". However, the construction 為 + N + Vt, and its full form 為 + N + (所) + Vt, often seems to denote a passive sense. So, for practical purposes, this sentence can also be translated as: "and he was laughed at by (the people of) Song".

# 一．寓言選（上）

## （丁）畫蛇添足[1]

## 📖 課文 (Text)

楚有祠者，[2] 賜其舍人卮酒。[3] 舍人相謂曰：[4] 「數人飲之不足，[5] 一人飲之有餘。[6] 請畫地為蛇，先成者飲酒。[7]」一人蛇先成，引酒且飲之，[8] 乃左手持卮，[9] 右手畫蛇曰：「吾能為之足。[10]」未成，[11] 一人之蛇成，奪其卮曰：[12] 「蛇固無足，[13] 子安能為之足？[14]」遂飲其酒。[15] 為蛇足者，終亡其酒。[16]

《戰國策‧齊策》[17]

## 📑 註釋 (Annotations)

| | | | |
|---|---|---|---|
| 1. | 丁 | dīng | fourth of the Heavenly Stems. |
| | 添 | tiān | to add; to increase. |
| | 足 | zú | foot. (A noun.) |
| 2. | 楚 | Chǔ | a state during the Zhou Dynasty, located in present-day Húběi 湖北. |
| | 祠 | cí | a place of worship; temple. (A noun.)<br>to worship or offer sacrifice. (A verb.) |
| 3. | 賜 | cì | to give (from a superior to an inferior); to grant. |
| | 舍人 | shè rén | a retainer; a houseguest. |
| | 卮 | zhī | a goblet; a large cup. |
| 4. | 相 | xiāng | to each other; mutually. (An adverb.) |
| 5. | 數 | shù | several. |
| | 飲 | yǐn | to drink. |

| | 足 | zú | sufficient; adequate. (An adjective.) |
|---|---|---|---|
| 6. | 餘 | yú | excess; abundance. |
| 7. | 為 | wéi | to do; to make. (But in different contexts it may indicate various different actions, for example, 為國 means "to govern a state"; 為學 means "to do research"; etc.) |
| | 先 | xiān | first. |
| | 成 | chéng | to complete; to finish. |
| 8. | 引 | yǐn | to draw or pull (toward oneself). |
| | 且 | qiě | to be about to. (An adverb.) |
| 9. | 乃 | nǎi | then. (An adverb.) (The adverb 乃 means far more than simply "then". It implies that the speaker himself feels, or the people he speaks to may feel, that the expression it modifies represents a rather unexpected turn of events. So it should be translated here as "then, unexpectedly, …".) |
| | 持 | chí | to hold; to grasp. |
| 10. | 為 | wèi | for. (A preposition.) |
| 11. | 未 | wèi | not yet. |
| 12. | 奪 | duó | to grab; to seize (something from others, usually by force). |
| 13. | 固 | gù | solidly; absolutely. (An adverb.) 本來 in Modern Chinese. |
| 14. | 子 | zǐ | sir. (An honorific form for "you".) |
| | 安 | ān | how; by what; from where? (An interrogative particle.) |

15. 遂        suì              then; subsequently. (An adverb.)

16. 終        zhōng            finally; in the end.

    亡        wú               to lose.

17. 戰國策    Zhànguó cè       *The Intrigues of the Warring States*. Title of a book. It is
                              a collection of anecdotes dealing with events in the
                              Warring States period. It is classified by state.

    齊策      Qí cè            "Intrigues of Qi". Title of a chapter from the
                              *Zhànguó cè*.

## ☀ 文法闡釋 (Grammar Notes)

### I. 畫蛇添足

This is a frequently quoted idiomatic expression. Its full form should be 畫蛇而
添足 "when (somebody) drew a snake, (he) added feet (to it)". Figuratively, it
means "to do something absolutely redundant and unnecessary".

### II. 賜其舍人卮酒

The meaning of the sentence is "(he) bestowed upon his houseguests a goblet of
wine". (Note that in the syntax of Classical Chinese, the direct object of verbs like
賜 is always the intended recipient, while the thing handed over is the indirect
object which is sometimes introduced with the particle 以. Also note that when a
measure word or a container [or a "classifier" in later Chinese] does not have a
number in front, "one" is always implied as the amount.) The sentence reflects the
social hierarchy of the fedual (or "class") Chinese society. Different verbs can be
used in the same sentence structure so as to convey the same meaning of "giving".
For example, 賜, 與, 獻 ... all these verbs mean "to give". The main difference
among these verbs is in terms of their implication of the relative social status of the
people involved in the action. Take the verb 賜 used in the sentence as an example.
It is used when a person of higher status gives something to a person of lower
status. Besides, it can also be used as a courtesy word, when the speaker tries to be
humble and assumes himself a lower status. Since 舍人 means "people who stay

in a house under the patronage of its owner", they are considered to be of lower status, hence the verb 賜.

## III. 數人飲之不足

This sentence consists of two clauses. The main clause 不足 does not have a subject and it means "(it) is not sufficient", while 數人飲之 is the subordinate clause, meaning "when (or if) several persons drink it". (Normally, the conjunction 則 is required between the two clauses.)

## IV. 請畫地為蛇

Unlike in Modern Chinese where it is a simple polite term like "please" in English, the word 請 in Classical Chinese is a courtesy verb, meaning: "beg for your permission (or approval) to do (something)". So "I" is normally its implied subject. 畫地為蛇, as a clause, serves as the object of that courtesy verb. The implied subject of this clause is "we". The focus of the predicate is on the second VO phrase "to make a snake". So the whole sentence means literally, "(I) beg for your permission to suggest that (we all) make a snake by drawing on the ground", or idiomatically, "with your permission, I would like to propose that we each draw a snake on the ground". (In later Chinese usage, the implied subject of the clause which serves as the object of 請 changed from the speaker [or a group including the speaker] to the people spoken to, i.e., "you". This is why 請 in Modern Chinese can be translated simply as "please".)

## V. 子安能為之足

The word 安 here is an interrogative like 焉, "in what (way)" or "how". It therefore turns the sentence into a rhetorical question. 足, a noun by itself, functions in this sentence, however, as a verb, "to add a foot or feet". So the sentence means: "how can you, sir, add feet to him?"

# 二. 寓言選（下）

## （甲）狐假虎威[1]

## 📖 課文 (Text)

　　虎求百獸而食之，[2] 得狐。[3] 狐曰：「子無敢食我也！[4] 天帝使我長百獸，[5] 今子食我，是逆天帝命也。[6] 子以我為不信，[7] 吾為子先行，[8] 子隨我後，[9] 觀百獸之見我而敢不走乎？[10]」虎以為然，[11] 故遂與之行，[12] 獸見之皆走，[13] 虎不知獸畏己而走也，[14] 以為畏狐也。

*Qiú  Shòu  Shí*

*wéi rán*

《戰國策・楚策》

## 📋 註釋 (Annotations)

*Lǎo Hǔ yǐ Wéi Zhè Shì Shì Shí*
*Suó yǐ Tā Gēn Hú Lì Zǒu Le    tāmén*
*Yě Shòu kàn Dào ~~XXXX~~ de Shí hòu*
*dōu pǎo le*
*Lǎo Hǔ Bù Zhī Dào*
*Tā Mén wèishén me*
*pǎo le*
*Qí Shí Shì Yīn Wèi*
*Tāmen pà Lǎo Hǔ*

1. 假　　jiǎ　　　　to make use of.

　　威　　wēi　　　prestige; majesty; fearsomeness.

2. 求　　qiú　　　　to seek; here, to look for.

3. 得　　dé　　　　to get; here, to capture.

4. 無　　wú　　　　here used as 毋 "not".

5. 天帝　tiān dì　　the Thearch of Heaven, the supreme being.

　　長　　zhǎng　　to be the chief of.

6. 逆　　nì　　　　to disobey; to oppose.

　　命　　mìng　　order.

7. 信　　xìn　　　　trustworthy; honest. (Note that the original meaning of 信 is "the speech is true".)

8. 吾　　wú　　　　I; me. (A first-person pronoun.)

　　行　　xíng　　　to walk.

| 9. | 隨 | suí | to follow. |
| 10. | 觀 | guān | to watch; to observe. |
| | 敢 | gǎn | to dare. |
| | 乎 | hū | particle indicating a question. |
| 11. | 然 | rán | thus; to be so. |
| 12. | 故 | gù | therefore. (A conjunction.) |
| | 與 | yǔ | with. (A preposition.) |
| 13. | 皆 | jiē | all. |
| 14. | 畏 | wèi | to fear. |

## 文法闡釋 (Grammar Notes)

### I. 子以我為不信

This is the conditional clause for the long sentence that ends with 敢不走乎？ Normally, such kind of clause would be introduced by a conditional conjunction such as 如 or 若, but it is common to omit the conjunction. 以 A 為 B means "to regard A as B", hence, "to think of A as B". So this clause can be translated as, "If you, sir, think I am not trustworthy, …".

### II. 觀百獸之見我而敢不走乎？

This is the main clause of a longer, complete sentence. The subject of it is 子 which appears earlier. The verb is 觀 which takes an interrogative sentence (a clause by definition) as its object. The possessive particle 之 is placed between the subject and the predicate of that interrogative sentence to indicate that it is no longer an independent sentence. Note that, unlike English where an indirect question is introduced by "if" or "whether", Chinese does not modify the question form but uses it as a clause/object directly. So the said sentence can be rendered literally as: "(you) watch, if the various animals see me, dare they not run away?"

# 二. 寓言選（下）

## （乙）刻舟求劍[1]

## 📖 課文 (Text)

　　楚人有涉江者，²其劍自舟中墜於水，³遽契其舟曰：⁴「是吾劍之所從墜。⁵」舟止。⁶從其所契者入水求之，⁷舟已行矣，⁸而劍不行，求劍若此，⁹不亦惑乎?¹⁰

《呂氏春秋・察今》¹¹

## 📑 註 釋 (Annotations)

1. 刻        kè        to carve (a mark).

     舟        zhōu        boat.

2. 涉        shè        to wade (through shallow water); to cross (a river).

     江        jiāng        the Yangtze River. (江 was later used as a generic term for "river".)

3. 自        zì        from. (A preposition.)

4. 遽        jù        hurriedly; hastily. (An adverb.)

     契        qì        to cut (a mark).

5. 是        shì        this; these; that; those. (A demonstrative pronoun.)

     所        suǒ        a nominalizer of the verb or verb phrase that follows it. (A particle.) (See 文法闡釋 II and III.)

     從        cóng        from. (A preposition.)

6. 止        zhǐ        to stop.

7. 入        rù        to enter.

8.　已　　　　　yǐ　　　　　already. (An adverb.)

　　行　　　　　xíng　　　　to move.

9.　若　　　　　ruò　　　　　to be like. (Same in meaning as 如.)

10.　不亦…乎　　bú yì … hū　isn't it …? (An idiomatic pattern, expressing a rhetorical question.)

　　惑　　　　　huò　　　　　confused; foolish.

11.　呂氏春秋　　Lǚshì chūnqiū　an encyclopedic work compiled during the late Warring States period under the patronage of and named after Lǚ Bùwěi 呂不韋, a prime minister of the state of Qin.

　　察今　　　　Chá jīn　　　"Investigating Contemporary Matters". A chapter title of the *Lüshi chunqiu.*

## ☼ 文法闡釋 (Grammar Notes)

### I. 刻舟求劍

Syntactically, this is a short form for 刻舟以求劍 "carving a mark on the boat in order to search for the (lost) sword", a metaphor for lacking the wisdom or ability to adjust to a changing situation.

### II. 是吾劍之所從墜

This is an equational sentence, though not marked by 也. Its subject is 是 and the rest is the predicate. 所 is a nominalizer for the verb or verb phrase that follows it, and is the implied object of the verb, if there is only one verb; or the object of the co-verb ("preposition") when one exists, as in the present example 從. Thus, the phrase 所從墜 can be literally translated as "that from which (something) fell off". 之 is here a possessive particle. So the whole sentence means literally, "This is my sword's place from which it fell off", and idiomatically, "This is where my sword fell off".

## III. 其所契者

The structure of this nominal phrase is similar to the predicate of the sentence analyzed above. 其 means "his". 所契 means "that which (somebody) marked" (or "that which was marked"). 者, also a nominalizer, is used here in coordination with 所. As such, its use is optional and semantically secondary to 所. The whole phrase means, therefore, "the place that he marked".

## IV. 不亦惑乎?

不亦…乎? is a commonly-used form for rhetorical questions, always carrying a tone of courtesy. That tone comes from the word 亦 which implies other possibilities or alternatives, therefore, suggesting an attitude of non-assertion on the part of the speaker. So the sentence can be translated as: "Isn't it rather confused?"

# 二. 寓言選（下）

## （丙）塞翁失馬[1]

## 📖 課文 (Text)

　　近塞上之人有善術者，[2] 馬無故亡而入胡，[3] 人皆弔之。[4] 其父曰：「此何遽不為福乎？[5]」居數月，[6] 其馬將胡駿馬而歸，[7] 人皆賀之，[8] 其父曰：「此何遽不能為禍乎？[9]」家富良馬，[10] 其子好騎，[11] 墜而折其髀，[12] 人皆弔之。其父曰：「此何遽不為福乎？」居一年，胡人大入塞，丁壯者引弦而戰。[13] 近塞上之人，死者十九。[14] 此獨以跛之故，[15] 父子相保。[16] 故福之為禍，[17] 禍之為福，化不可極，[18] 深不可測也。[19]

《淮南子・人間訓》[20]

## 📝 註釋 (Annotations)

| | | | |
|---|---|---|---|
| 1. | 塞 | sài | a fortress; a pass along the Great Wall. |
| | 翁 | wēng | old man. |
| | 塞翁 | sài wēng | an old man who lived near the frontier. |
| | 失 | shī | to lose. |
| 2. | 善 | shàn | to be good at. |
| | 術 | shù | skill, referring especially to divination and magic power. |
| 3. | 故 | gù | reason; cause. |
| | 亡 | wáng | to run away. |
| | 胡 | Hú | the northern nomadic tribes in ancient times; here, referring to the area where they lived. |

4. 皆     jiē     all. (An adverb.)

   弔     diào     to offer condolences; to express sympathy to.

5. 何     hé     what; which? (An interrogative pronoun.)
how; why? (When used adverbially.)

   何遽     hé jù     why. (See 文法闡釋 I.)

   福     fú     good fortune.

6. 居     jū     to live; to stay. (A verb.) When used before a time word, it has a derived meaning of "after (a period of time)" from the sense of "staying (on for a period of time)".

7. 將     jiāng     to lead; to escort. (A verb.)

   駿     jùn     fine (horse).

8. 賀     hè     to congratulate.

9. 禍     huò     misfortune; disaster.

10. 富     fù     abundant; to be rich in.

11. 騎     qí     to ride.

12. 墜     zhuì     to fall down.

   髀     bì     thighbone.

13. 丁壯者     dīng zhuàng zhě     those who are able-bodied among the young males.

   引     yǐn     to draw; to pull toward oneself.

   弦     xián     bowstring.

   戰     zhàn     to fight.

14. 死者     sǐ zhě     those who died.

|  | 十九 | shí jiǔ | nine out of ten. (Abbreviated from 十之九.) (See 文法闡釋 III.) |
|---|---|---|---|
| 15. | 獨 | dú | only; alone. |
|  | 以…之故 | yǐ…zhī gù | because of; for the sake of. |
|  | 跛 | bǒ | lame; crippled. |
| 16. | 相保 | xiāng bǎo | to mutually protect; to take care of each other. |
| 17. | 為 | wéi | to be; to become. (A verb.) Here, it means "to transform into". |
| 18. | 化 | huà | change; transformation. |
|  | 極 | jí | to reach the ultimate end; to exhaust. |
| 19. | 深 | shēn | depth; mystery. |
|  | 測 | cè | to fathom. |
| 20. | 淮南子 | Huáinánzǐ | a work compiled during the Western Han Dynasty under the patronage of the Prince of Huainan. |
|  | 人間訓 | Rén jiān xùn | "In the Human World". A chapter title from the *Huainanzi*. |

## ☀ 文法闡釋 (Grammar Notes)

### I. 此何遽不 (能) 為…乎？

From the context, this can be clearly regarded as a rhetorical question. It can be simplified as 此不能為…乎？ "Can't this be … ?" With the insertion of 何 "how？" and 遽 "suddenly; quickly", the question becomes more challenging. The inserted phrase is probably a short form for 何遽知 "How do (we, you) know so quickly that … ?" Normally, the yes-or-no question marker 乎 is not needed when the sentence contains an interrogative like 何, but its inclusion here seems to add a certain degree of emphasis.

## II. 入塞

This phrase does not mean simply "to enter a fortress". It means rather "to enter the territory inside the Great Wall". Similarly, 出塞 means "to go out into the territory beyond the Great Wall". (These two terms appear frequently in historical writings and poetry.) 塞 as a verb means "to seal; to block". As a noun, it refers to any of the gates along the Great Wall, which can be readily closed against invaders. (Interestingly, since the Chinese are traditionally defenders, their thinking is reflected in their language. So what is called a *pass* in English is called 塞 *seal* in Chinese or 關 *shut* in Modern Chinese, as in 山海關 "the Shanhai Pass".)

## III. 死者十九

十九 is ambiguous. It may mean "nineteen" (十有九 "ten plus nine") or "nine out of ten" (十之九 "ten's nine"). The latter is the case in this context. The sentence may seem to be strange in that its predicate does not contain a verb, but actually it is quite normal to have numbers alone serving as predicates in Classical Chinese. So this sentence means: "Those who died numbered nine out of ten".

# 二.寓言選（下）

## （丁）葉公好龍[1]

## 📖 課文 (Text)

葉公子高好龍，<sup>2</sup> 鉤以寫龍，<sup>3</sup> 鑿以寫龍，<sup>4</sup> 屋室雕文以寫龍，<sup>5</sup> 於是天龍聞而下之，<sup>6</sup> 窺頭於牖，<sup>7</sup> 施尾於堂。<sup>8</sup> 葉公見之，棄而還走，<sup>9</sup> 失其魂魄，<sup>10</sup> 五色無主。<sup>11</sup> 是葉公非好龍也，好夫似龍而非龍者也。<sup>12</sup>

《新序·雜事第五》<sup>13</sup>

## 📄 註 釋 (Annotations)

| | | | |
|---|---|---|---|
| 1. | 葉 | Shè | name of a small state during the Zhou Dynasty. |
| | 公 | gōng | duke; ruler of a state. |
| 2. | 子高 | Zǐgāo | name of the Duke of She. |
| 3. | 鉤 | gōu | hook; buckle. |
| | 寫 | xiě | to draw; to imitate. |
| 4. | 鑿 | záo (zuò) | chisel; here probably used as a loan word for 爵 (jué), a wine vessel. |
| 5. | 室 | shì | room. |
| | 雕 | diāo | to carve. |
| | 文 | wén | to decorate. |
| 6. | 於是 | yú shì | at this point; thereupon. |
| | 天龍 | tiān lóng | the dragon in Heaven. |
| | 聞 | wén | to hear. |
| | 下 | xià | to come down. (A verb.) 下之 is the same as 下於之, meaning "descend upon him". |

| | | |
|---|---|---|
| 7. 窺 | kuī | to peep. |
| 牖 | yǒu | window. |
| 8. 施 | yì | to drag; to extend. |
| 尾 | wěi | tail. |
| 堂 | táng | hall. |
| 9. 棄 | qì | to desert. |
| 還 | huán | to turn back. |
| 走 | zǒu | to run; here, it means "to run away". |
| 10. 魂魄 | hún pò | soul and spirit. (Chinese folklore has it that each person has three 魂 and seven 魄.) |
| 11. 五色 | wǔ sè | five (i.e., various) colors; here, referring to the full facial complexion. |
| 五色無主 | wǔ sè wú zhǔ | to lose color; frightened. |
| 12. 夫 | fú | this; that. |
| 似 | sì | to appear similar to. |
| 13. 新序 | Xīnxù | a work containing historical anecdotes complied by Liú Xiàng 劉向 (79–8 B.C.) of the Western Han. |
| 雜事 | Zá shì | "A Miscellany". Title of the first five chapters in the *Xinxu*. |
| 第五 | dì wǔ | (chapter) number five. |

## ☀ 文法闡釋 (Grammar Notes)

### I. 鉤以寫龍, etc.

This sentence and the two immediately following it share the same syntactic structure. 以 functions here as a co-verb ("preposition"), with the basic meaning of "using", and can, therefore, be translated as "with " or "by". Its implied object is the noun before it. This change in word order puts emphasis on that noun, making it almost a separate clause. The author repeated the same pattern three times for intensification, to the effect of: "With everything and on all things he had, he drew dragons". The three sentences can be translated into Modern Chinese as: 鉤也拿來寫龍；鑿也拿來寫龍；屋室雕文也拿來寫龍。

### II. 是葉公非好龍也，好夫似龍而非龍者也。

This is syntactically a complex equational sentence with two clauses as predicates. The subject is 是 "this", referring to the moral of the story, and an equational sentence of this type often implies "This means that …", or "This shows that …". The predicative clauses are "equational sentences" too, both with an implied subject (i.e., "it"). The first clause is marked by the negative particle for equational sentences 非, and means, therefore: "It is not (true) that the Duke of She is fond of dragons". The second clause is affirmative, meaning: "It is rather that he is fond of those things which look like dragons but are not really dragons". Note that the nominalizer 者 covers the verb phrase 似龍而非龍, and the nominalized phrase serves as the object of the verb 好. (When the implied subject of a negative equational sentence is the "it", the subject of the predicative clause is always moved to the front of the negative particle 非.)

# 三. 《論語》選（上）

# 三.《論語》選（上）

## （甲）學而[1]

### 📖 課文 (Text)

　　子曰[2]：「學而時習之，[3] 不亦説乎？有朋自遠方來，[4] 不亦樂乎？[5] 人不知而不愠，[6] 不亦君子乎？[7]」

〈學而〉[8]

### 📑 註釋 (Annotations)

| | | | |
|---|---|---|---|
| 1. | 論語 | Lúnyǔ | the *(Confucian) Analects*, a collection of the sayings and activities of Confucius (孔子 Kǒngzǐ) and his disciples. Confucius (551–479 B.C.) was a great thinker and teacher in ancient China. |
| 2. | 子 | zǐ | an honorific form of address meaning "The Master". In the *Lunyu*, it always refers to Confucius. |
| 3. | 時 | shí | on time; from time to time. (An adverb.) |
| | 習 | xí | to review and practice. |
| 4. | 朋 | péng | a friend. |
| | 遠方 | yuǎn fāng | a distant place. |
| 5. | 樂 | lè | happy; delightful. |

6. 人　　rén　　　people; others (in contrast to 己 "oneself").

　　知　　zhī　　　to know; to acknowledge.

　　慍　　yùn　　　to be irritated; to be angry.

7. 君子　jūn zǐ　　a noble-minded man. (See 文法闡釋 II.)

8. 學而　Xué ér　　a chapter title. Chapter titles in the *Lunyu* consist typically of two or three characters taken from the beginning of the main text that may or may not make semantic sense.

## 文法闡釋 (Grammar Notes)

### I. 學而時習之

This is a clause without an overt subject. The implied subject is understood to be "anybody". The clause then serves as the subject of the sentence with 不亦說乎 as its predicate. The whole sentence means, therefore, "Isn't it delightful that one, after learning something, practices it from time to time?" Note that the pronoun 之 does not have an overt reference, but since Confucius was speaking to his disciples, we can assume it refers to the Master's teaching.

### II. 人不知而不慍

Syntactically, this expression consists of two clauses with different subjects. The conjunction 而 indicates that 不慍, the second clause with an understood subject ("you; we; anyone"), is the semantic focus. The first clause 人不知 has an overt subject 人 "any other people". The verb 知 "to know" was frequently used in Classical Chinese to mean "to recognize (somebody's) talents". So the sentence means: "you do not become unhappy (or bitter) when others do not understand you (i.e., when your talents are not recognized)". This sentence then becomes a clause serving as the subject of a larger sentence with 不亦君子乎 as its predicate. Note that the noun 君子 is adjectival here ("gentlemanly"), as it is determined by the formula 不亦…乎?

# 三.《論語》選(上)

## (乙) 學而

### 📖 課文 (Text)

　　曾子曰：¹「吾日三省吾身：²為人謀而不忠乎？³與朋友交而不信乎？⁴傳不習乎？⁵」

〈學而〉

### 📋 註釋 (Annotations)

| | | | |
|---|---|---|---|
| 1. | 曾子 | Zēngzǐ | a well-known disciple of Confucius named Zēng Shēn 曾參. |
| 2. | 日 | rì | day; used here adverbially to mean "daily" or "every day". |
| | 三 | sān | three. (In Classical Chinese, 三 often means "several times" in a general sense.) |
| | 省 | xǐng | to examine; to reflect upon. |
| | 身 | shēn | oneself. |
| 3. | 為 | wèi | for. (A preposition.) |
| | 謀 | móu | to plan. |

| | | |
|---|---|---|
| 忠 | zhōng | devoted. (Note that in Classical Chinese, the primary meaning of 忠 is "devoted" or "assiduous", not "loyal".) |
| 4. 交 | jiāo | to associate; to have mutual contacts. |
| 信 | xìn | faithful; trustworthy. |
| 5. 傳 | chuán | to pass on; here used as a noun, meaning "teachings passed down by one's teacher". |

# 三. 《論語》選 (上)
## (丙) 公冶長

### 📖 課 文 (Text)

　　子貢曰：[1]「孔文子，何以謂之文也？[2]」子曰：「敏而好學，[3]不恥下問，[4]是以謂之文也。[5]」

〈公冶長〉[6]

### 📑 註 釋 (Annotations)

| 1. | 子貢 | Zǐgòng | a disciple of Confucius, particularly known for his business talents. |
|---|---|---|---|
| 2. | 孔文子 | Kǒng Wénzǐ | a lord of the Wèi 衛 state. 文 is his posthumous epithet (諡號 shì hào). (In ancient China, when a king or a lord died, he was given a posthumous epithet in accordance with his character.) |
| | 何以 | hé yǐ | what for; why? |
| | 謂 | wèi | to call. |
| 3. | 敏 | mǐn | intelligent. |
| 4. | 恥 | chǐ | shame; disgrace. Here used as a transitive verb, meaning "to feel ashamed of". |

| 下問 | xià wèn | to ask for advice or instruction from subordinates. (In this phrase, 下 is used as an adverb for the verb 問, indicating the direction of the action.) |

5. 是以    shì yǐ    therefore. (The normal word order for this phrase is 以是 "for this (reason)", which is reversed to give greater emphasis to 是.)

6. 公冶長    Gōngyě Cháng    name of a disciple of Confucius. Here, it also functions as a chapter title.

## ☀ 文法闡釋 (Grammar Notes)

## I. 孔文子，何以謂之文也?

This is a good example of the topic-comment type of sentence. 孔文子 is first mentioned as the topic, and a specific question is then raised about him. As a general rule in standard Classical Chinese grammar, when an interrogative noun serves as the object of a verb or co-verb, it is always put before the verb or co-verb, as 何 is here before 以. The main verb is 謂 which has two objects, 之 "him" and 文 "civility". Note that 謂 does not have a subject but has 之 as its object referring to 孔文子. Since Classical Chinese does not have a specific formula for the "passive voice", subject-omission is actually one way to express passivity. The sentence can thus be translated as: "As to Kong Wenzi, why do (people) call him (i.e., why is he called) Mr. Civility?"

## II. 不恥下問

Most nouns in Classical Chinese can also function as transitive verbs, in the sense of "to regard (or assume) [the object] as the noun itself". Thus, the present phrase means literally "not to regard [下問] as a shame". A noun functioning in this way is called a "putative verb".

# 三.《論語》選 (上)

## (丁) 述而

### 📖 課文 (Text)

子曰：「若聖與仁，¹則吾豈敢？²抑為之不厭，³誨人不倦，⁴則可謂云爾已矣！⁵」公西華曰：⁶「正唯弟子不能學也。⁷」

〈述而〉⁸

### 📑 註釋 (Annotations)

| | | | |
|---|---|---|---|
| 1. | 若 | ruò | as to. |
| | 聖 | shèng | sageliness; the ultimate level of personal cultivation. |
| | 與 | yǔ | and. (A conjunction.) |
| | 仁 | rén | perfect virtue (of which the main feature is humanity). |
| 2. | 則 | zé | then. (A conjunction.) (See 文法闡釋 I.) |
| | 豈 | qǐ | how could it be that … ? (An adverb.) (This is a particle for rhetorical questions, with an emphatic negative implication.) |
| | 敢 | gǎn | to dare; to be daring. |

3. 抑　　　　yì　　　　or; rather. (This is a particle to express possible alternatives to what was just mentioned.)

　　為　　　　wéi　　　　to do (something).

　　厭　　　　yàn　　　　satisfied; tired (of something).

　　為之不厭　wéi zhī bú yàn　to practice them (referring to 聖 and 仁) without being tired.

4. 誨　　　　huì　　　　to teach.

　　倦　　　　juàn　　　　tired; weary.

　　誨人不倦　huì rén bú juàn　to teach other people without weariness.

5. 云爾　　　　yún ěr　　　to say that; to call it such. (An idiomatic form.)

　　已　　　　yǐ　　　　just this and nothing more. (A particle of limitation.)

6. 公西華　　Gōngxī Huá　a disciple of Confucius. Gongxi is his family name (姓 xìng).

7. 正　　　　zhèng　　　exactly. (An adverb.)

　　唯　　　　wéi　　　　always placed between the subject and the nominal predicate. (A particle.)

　　弟子　　　dì zǐ　　　disciple. (The term here means "this disciple of yours", i.e., "I".)

8. 述而　　　Shù ér　　　chapter title.

## ☀ 文法闡釋 (Grammar Notes)

## I. 若聖與仁，則吾豈敢？

若 and 則 are two conjunctions often used in coordination to form what is generally called a conditional sentence, and can thus be translated as "If … , then … ", though sometimes one of them (more often 若) is omitted. Sometimes what comes after

若 may seem to be nothing but a noun, rather than a clause, but syntactically it should be understood as the predicate of a clause without a subject. 豈 is an adverb for a rhetorical question, strongly implying the negative answer to the question. It can, therefore, be conveniently translated as "how could it be that … ?" The present sentence can thus be translated literally as: "If it were 聖 and 仁 (that you would call me), then how could it be that I would dare (to accept it)?" But in a more idiomatic way, it can be translated simply as: "As to 聖 and 仁, how could I possibly dare accept such honor?"

## II. 正唯弟子不能學也

This is an equational sentence without a subject which must be restated as "that" in the English translation. (English grammar requires that a sentence must normally have a subject, but Chinese grammar does not.) It refers to the description or image that Confucius accepted for himself. So the sentence means: "That is exactly what I, your student, cannot imitate".

# 四.《論語》選（中）

# 四.《論語》選(中)
## (甲)公冶長

### 📖 課文 (Text)

　　顏淵季路侍，¹ 子曰：「盍各言爾志？²」子路曰：「願車馬衣輕裘與朋友共，³ 敝之而無憾。⁴」顏淵曰：「無伐善，⁵ 無施勞。⁶」子路曰：「願聞子之志。」子曰：「老者安之，⁷ 朋友信之，⁸ 少者懷之。⁹」

〈公冶長〉

### 📑 註釋 (Annotations)

| | | | |
|---|---|---|---|
| 1. | 顏淵 | Yán Yuān | the most beloved disciple of Confucius. |
| | 季路 | Jì Lù | the oldest disciple of Confucius. |
| | 侍 | shì | to wait on; to accompany. |
| 2. | 盍 | hé | why not? (A phonetic fusion of 何 + 不.) (See 文法闡釋 I.) |
| | 言 | yán | to speak about. |
| | 爾 | ěr | you or your; here, it means "your". (A second-person pronoun.) |
| | 志 | zhì | ideal (of life); goal. |

3.  子路   Zǐlù    courtesy name (字 zì) of 季路.

    願    yuàn    to wish.

    輕    qīng    light.

    裘    qiú    fur coat.

    共    gòng    to share. (A verb.)
                  together. (An adverb.)

4.  敝    bì      to wear out; here used as a causative verb.

    無憾   wú hàn  to have no regret.

5.  無    wú      same as 毋 wú, the imperative negative "don't!"

    伐    fá      to boast of; to brag about.

    善    shàn    merit; good qualities.

6.  施    shī     to boast of; to make a show of.

    勞    láo     merit; achievement.

7.  安    ān      to be at peace (or ease) with.

8.  信    xìn     to trust.

9.  少    shào    young.

    懷    huái    to remember with care and affection.


## ☀ 文法闡釋 (Grammar Notes)

### I. 盍各言爾志？

One character may represent two words, as a result of the fusion of two syllables into one in casual speech (e.g., 了 ＋ 啊 ⟶ 啦 in Modern Chinese). 盍 in the present sentence is the fusion of 何 and 不, meaning "why not". The sentence means, therefore, "Why don't (you) each talk about your goal?"

**II.** 老者安之，朋友信之，少者懷之。

This is what Confucius said he himself wished to be. The omission of 願 at the beginning can thus be assumed. The pronoun 之 refers to "such a person". The whole sentence means, therefore, "(I wish to be such a person whom) older people feel comfortable with, friends trust, and young people will have a good memory of".

# 四.《論語》選 (中)
## (乙) 先進

## 📖 課文 (Text)

　　子路問：「聞斯行諸？[1]」子曰：「有父兄在，如之何其聞斯行之？[2]」冉有問：[3]「聞斯行諸？」子曰：「聞斯行之。」公西華曰：「由也問：[4]『聞斯行諸？』；子曰：『有父兄在。』求也問：[5]『聞斯行諸？』；子曰：『聞斯行之。』赤也惑，[6] 敢問。[7]」子曰：「求也退，[8] 故進之。[9] 由也兼人，[10] 故退之。[11]」

〈先進〉[12]

## 📝 註釋 (Annotations)

| | | | |
|---|---|---|---|
| 1. | 斯 | sī | then. (A conjunction.) (Used in this sense, it is equivalent to 則.) |
| | 行 | xíng | to practice. |
| | 諸 | zhū | phonetic fusion of the pronoun 之 and the question particle 乎. |
| 2. | 如之何 | rú zhī hé | how is it that … ? (An idiomatic phrase.) |

3. 冉有      Rǎn Yǒu      a disciple of Confucius. 冉 is his family name.

4. 公西華    Gōngxī Huá   another disciple of Confucius.

   由        Yóu          the formal name (名 míng) of 子路. (See 文法闡釋 III.)

   也        yě           used in the middle of a sentence to indicate a pause. (A particle.)

5. 求        Qiú          the personal name of 冉有 (有 is his courtesy name). (See 文法闡釋 III.)

6. 赤        Chì          the personal name of 公西華. (See 文法闡釋 III.)

   惑        huò          confused.

7. 敢問      gǎn wèn      may I ask; allow me to ask? (An idiomatic expression of courtesy, used when questioning somebody.)

8. 退        tuì          withdrawing; hesitant; indecisive.

9. 進        jìn          to encourage; to push forward. (A causative verb derived from its ordinary meaning of "to advance".)

10. 兼人     jiān rén     to outdo others.

11. 退       tuì          to discourage; to pull back. (A causative verb derived from its ordinary meaning of "to withdraw".)

12. 先進     Xiān jìn     chapter title.

## ☼ 文法闡釋 (Grammar Notes)

### I. 聞斯行諸？

This sentence consists of two clauses, both with an implied subject "one" (or "I; you; we; anybody"). The first clause is represented by the single character 聞 "hear", meaning "when one learns (a lesson)". 斯 is used as 則, the conjunction for conditional sentences. The second clause 行諸 is a question, because 諸 is the fused form of the pronoun 之 and the question particle 乎. So the whole sentence means: "Should one practice a lesson upon hearing it?"

## II. 如之何其聞斯行之？

The phrase 如之何 is an idiomatic way of challenging something. Together with the modal particle 其 which suggests "uncertainty" (hence, "courtesy"), the phrase always comes before a clause representing the issue in question. So the sentence is a rhetorical question: "How is it, if I may ask, that one should practice it upon hearing it?"

## III. (子) 路 versus 由

Both names refer to the same person. The second name 由 is the 名 "formal name", to be used by one's seniors, superiors, and officials, as well as by oneself as a pronoun when speaking to one's superiors (also by one's equals, but only when speaking to common superiors). Pronouns like 吾 "I" and 爾 "you" were used only when one spoke to one's equals or people of lower status. The first name 子路 is the 字 "courtesy name", adopted for the convenience of other people when they cared to show courtesy (子 was an honorific prefix added by the narrator of the conversation). Other examples are (冉) 有 versus 求, and (公西) 華 versus 赤. Note how these names were used in the present story. Note also that there is always some semantic connection between the courtesy name and the formal name, as can be seen from the examples above.

# 五.《論語》選（下）

## （甲）陽貨

# 五.《論語》選（下）

## （甲）陽貨

### 📖 課文 (Text)

　　子之武城，¹ 聞弦歌之聲。² 夫子莞爾而笑。³ 曰：「割雞焉用牛刀？⁴」子游對曰：⁵「昔者偃也聞諸夫子曰：⁶『君子學道則愛人，⁷ 小人學道則易使也。⁸』」子曰：「二三子，⁹ 偃之言是也。¹⁰ 前言戲之耳。¹¹」

〈陽貨〉¹²

### 📝 註釋 (Annotations)

| | | | |
|---|---|---|---|
| 1. | 之 | zhī | to go to. |
| | 武城 | Wǔchéng | name of a place, in present-day Shandong province. |
| 2. | 弦 | xián | string (of a musical instrument). |
| | 弦歌之聲 | xián gē zhī shēng | the sound of singing accompanied by string music. |
| 3. | 莞爾 | wǎn ěr | smiling. (爾 is a suffix for an adverb or adjective.) |
| 4. | 焉 | yān | for what; why? (An interrogative particle, always used before a verb.) |

5.  子游    Zǐyóu    a disciple of Confucius, who was serving as magistrate of Wucheng.

    對    duì    to reply (to a senior or superior).

6.  昔者    xī zhě    in the past.

    偃    Yǎn    formal name of 子游.

    諸    zhū    phonetic fusion of 之 and 於. (之 refers to the ensuing quote from Confucius.)

7.  君子    jūn zǐ    a man of noble birth. (This is the literal and original meaning, as it is used here. The term is also used in the sense of a noble-minded man, as in Lesson 3, p. 42.)

    道    dào    the original meaning of 道 is "road". The derivative meaning is "way" or "method". In the Confucian Classics, 道 often refers to 先王之道 xiān wáng zhī dào, namely, the doctrines of the ancient sage kings.

8.  小人    xiǎo rén    a person of humble birth. (This is the literal and original meaning, as it is used here. It is also used in the sense of a small-minded person.)

    易使    yì shǐ    easy to use; obedient.

9.  二三子    èr sān zǐ    you fellows! (An intimate way of addressing one's friends or disciples, here referring to those who accompanied Confucius to Wucheng.)

10. 是    shì    right. (In contrast to 非 "wrong".)

11. 前言    qián yán    the words I said just now. (Referring to 割雞焉用牛刀.)

    戲    xì    to jest; to play a joke on.

    耳    ěr    that is all. (A particle expressing limitation.)

12. 陽貨          Yáng Huò        name of a person; here, it also functions as a
                                 chapter title.

---

### ☀ 文法闡釋 (Grammar Note)

## 割雞焉用牛刀？

This rhetorical question consists of two clauses, 割雞 and 焉用牛刀, which share
the same implied subject ("anyone"). The interrogative 焉 always comes before a
verb, meaning "in what way" or "why". The sentence can thus be translated literally
as: "When one cuts up a chicken, why does one need a knife for an ox?" (用 "to
use" also means "to need", even in Modern Chinese, e.g., 不用來 "no need to
come".) This metaphor, with its first word 割 changed to 殺, has survived into
modern times, with, however, a slightly different implication, namely, "Such a small
job doesn't need a big man!" It can be used either as a humble expression ("You
don't have to bother. A small person like me can do it".), or as a joke ("Don't bother
me with such trivialities!").

# 五.《論語》選 (下)
## (乙) 子張

### 📖 課文 (Text)

　　叔孫武叔語大夫於朝曰：[1]「子貢賢於仲尼。[2]」子服
景伯以告子貢。[3] 子貢曰：「譬之宮牆，[4] 賜之牆也及
肩，[5] 闚見室家之好。[6] 夫子之牆數仞，[7] 不得其門而
入，[8] 不見宗廟之美，百官之富。[9] 得其門者或寡矣。[10]
夫子之云，[11] 不亦宜乎？[12]」

〈子張〉[13]

### 📒 註釋 (Annotations)

| 1. | 叔孫武叔 | Shūsūn Wǔshū | a minister of the Lǔ 魯 state. |
|---|---|---|---|
| | 語 | yù | to speak to. |
| | 大夫 | dà fū | a rank of the nobility in the Zhou Dynasty. It is lower than 卿 qīng, but higher than 士 shì; normally translated as "minister". The old reading for 大 here is dài. |
| | 朝 | cháo | the ducal court. |
| 2. | 子貢 | Zǐgòng | a disciple of Confucius. |

|   | 賢 | xián | virtuous; worthy. |
|---|---|---|---|
|   | 於 | yú | "adjective + 於" expresses comparison. (A preposition.) |
|   | 仲尼 | Zhòngní | the courtesy name of Confucius. |
| 3. | 子服景伯 | Zǐfú Jǐngbó | a minister of the Lu state. |
|   | 以 | yǐ | with. (A preposition.) (The object of 以 is omitted.) |
|   | 告 | gào | to tell; to report to. |
| 4. | 譬 | pì | to make an analogy; to compare to. |
|   | 宮 | gōng | house. (Note that in the pre-Qin period, 宮 refers generally to "house", rather than "palace" in particular.) |
| 5. | 賜 | Cì | the formal name of 子貢. |
| 6. | 闚 | kuī | to peep. (Same as 窺 in Lesson 2, p. 38.) |
|   | 室家 | shì jiā | a house in an enclosure. |
| 7. | 仞 | rèn | a measure of length, usually defined as around seven or eight 尺 chǐ. (One 尺 is equivalent to around 1.1 feet.) |
| 8. | 得 | dé | to get; here, it means "to find". |
| 9. | 宗廟 | zōng miào | ancestral temple. |
|   | 官 | guān | office. (Note that the earliest meaning of 官 is "office", later, 官 means "official".) |
|   | 富 | fù | abundant. |
| 10. | 或 | huò | perhaps. (An adverb.) |
| 11. | 夫子 | fū zǐ | here it refers to 叔孫武叔. |

| 云 | yún | to say. |
| 12. 宜 | yí | proper; appropriate. |
| 13. 子張 | Zǐzhāng | name of a disciple of Confucius; here, it also functions as a chapter title. |

## ☀ 文法闡釋 (Grammar Note)

### 子貢賢於仲尼

Comparison in Classical Chinese can be expressed simply by implication (i.e., without any marking), but it is also expressed by certain patterns, and the example in question is one of them. This pattern can be formulated as A + Adj. + 於 + B, meaning "A is more (Adj.) than B". So the present sentence means "Zigong is worthier than Confucius".

# 六.《孟子・梁惠王上》(節)[1]

## 📖 課文 (Text)

孟子見梁惠王。² 王曰：「叟！³ 不遠千里而來，⁴ 亦將有以利吾國乎？⁵」

孟子對曰：「王何必曰利？⁶ 亦有仁義而已矣。⁷」王曰：「何以利吾國？」大夫曰：「何以利吾家？⁸」士庶人曰：⁹「何以利吾身？¹⁰ 上下交征利而國危矣。¹¹ 萬乘之國，¹² 弒其君者，¹³ 必千乘之家；千乘之家，弒其君者，必百乘之家。萬取千焉，¹⁴ 千取百焉，不為不多矣。苟為後義而先利，¹⁵ 不奪不饜。¹⁶ 未有仁而遺其親者也，¹⁷ 未有義而後其君者也。王亦曰仁義而已矣，何必曰利？」

## 📑 註釋 (Annotations)

| | | | |
|---|---|---|---|
| 1. | 孟子 | Mèngzǐ | *Mencius.* |
| | 梁惠王 | Liáng Huìwáng | King Hui of Liang. Liang was a state during the Warring States period, also known as Wèi 魏. Here, 梁惠王 also functions as a chapter title. |
| | 節 | jié | short for 節錄 (jié lù)—excerpt, extract. |
| 2. | 見 | jiàn | to visit; to go to see. |
| 3. | 叟 | sǒu | old man. |
| 4. | 遠 | yuǎn | to consider (it) a long distance. (A putative verb derived from its ordinary meaning of "far; distant".) |

| 5. | 亦 | yì | maybe; perhaps. (An adverb.) |
| | 利 | lì | to profit; to benefit. |
| 6. | 必 | bì | must; necessarily. (An adverb.) |
| 7. | 義 | yì | righteousness. |
| | 而已 | ér yǐ | and that's all. 已 here is the same as 止 "to end". (An idiomatic expression indicating finality.) |
| 8. | 家 | jiā | noble house or clan. (In the ancient feudal system, each minister had his own fief which was like a small state within the state.) |
| 9. | 士 | shì | descendants of nobles, who had lost the status of nobility, but remained as a class of people above the other common men. (In later times, this term referred to a distinguished person or a scholar, regardless of his origin.) |
| | 庶人 | shù rén | the common people other than the 士. |
| 10. | 身 | shēn | oneself (and one's immediate family). |
| 11. | 上下 | shàng xià | those above and those below. |
| | 交 | jiāo | with each other. (An adverb.) |
| | 征 | zhēng | to get; to collect. |
| | 危 | wéi | to be in danger. |
| 12. | 乘 | shèng | a measure word for chariots and carriages. |
| | 萬乘之國 | wàn shèng zhī guó | a first-rank state. (Literally, a state that possesses ten thousand chariots.) |
| 13. | 弒 | shì | to murder (one's own sovereign or parents). (See 文法闡釋 II.) |
| | 君 | jūn | sovereign. |

14. 萬取千焉    wàn qǔ qiān yān    to take a thousand from ten thousand. (It means in a state which possesses ten thousand chariots, a minister possesses a thousand chariots, i.e., his force constitutes one tenth of the state's military force.)

15. 苟    gǒu    if. (A conjunction.)

後    hòu    to put behind.

先    xiān    to put in front.

16. 饜    yàn    to be satisfied; to have enough.

17. 遺    yí    to abandon; to desert.

親    qīn    parents. (Note that in Classical Chinese 親 often means parents, not relatives.)

## ☀ 文法闡釋 (Grammar Notes)

### I. 亦將有以利吾國乎？

The basic elements of this sentence are represented by 有以利吾國 "(You) have (something) with which to benefit my state", and the particle 乎 turns the sentence into a question. Note that, when the verb 有 does not have a specific object, it always implies an unspecified one ("something"). (So does its counterpart 無 "to have nothing".) 亦 and 將 are adverbs used to soften the tone of the question. The former suggests possible alternatives (hence, "perhaps; maybe; also"), and the latter implies what is about to happen (hence, "will; may"). Thus, the whole sentence means: "Could you possibly have something (therewith) to benefit my state?"

### II. 萬乘之國，弒其君者，必千乘之家。

This is a simple equational sentence, with 弒其君者 as its subject and 千乘之家 as its predicate. Since the noun phrase 千乘之家 serves here as the predicate, it can thus be directly modified by the adverb 必. The word 家 means a clan (or noble house) which has its own territory and armed force within a state ("a state within a state", hence, the Modern Chinese compound 國家 "country"). The number of chariots (乘) each state might have was specified by Zhou rules, with ten thousand as the largest number allowed for the big states. That limitation was later ignored, but 萬乘之國 became a term for "a big state of the first rank". The verb 弒 "to kill" indicates that the killer is of lower status (thus, without the authority to kill), while the killed is of higher status. So the sentence means: "In a big state, the one who [can possibly] murder its ruler can only be the head of a powerful clan that possesses one tenth of its armed force". The succeeding sentence has the same structure.

## III. 苟為後義而先利，不奪不饜。

苟 is the conjunction marking the subjunctive clause 為後義而先利. So the clause means: "if it were (or should it be) that (people) put profit before justice, … " (後 and 先 are both causative verbs here). The main clause is 不奪不饜 which is a conditional sentence by itself, meaning, "if (people) don't grab (from each other), (they) won't feel satisfied". The whole sentence can thus be translated as: "Should it be that everybody puts profit ahead of justice, no one would be content without grabbing".

## 📖 課文 (Text)

　　齊人伐燕，² 勝之。³ 宣王問曰：⁴「或謂寡人勿取，⁵ 或謂寡人取之。以萬乘之國伐萬乘之國，⁶ 五旬而舉之，⁷ 人力不至於此。⁸ 不取，必有天殃。⁹ 取之何如？¹⁰」孟子對曰：「取之而燕民悅，則取之。古之人有行之者，武王是也。¹¹ 取之而燕民不悅，則勿取。古之人有行之者，文王是也。¹² 以萬乘之國伐萬乘之國，簞食壺漿以迎王師，¹³ 豈有他哉？¹⁴ 避水火也。如水益深，¹⁵ 如火益熱，亦運而已矣。¹⁶」

## 📝 註釋 (Annotations)

1. 下　　　xià　　　part two.

2. 齊　　　Qí　　　a state during the Zhou Dynasty located on the Shandong peninsula.

　　伐　　　fá　　　to attack openly.

　　燕　　　Yān　　　a state in the present-day Beijing (北京) area.

3. 勝　　　shèng　　　to win a victory over.

4. 宣王　　Xuānwáng　　King Xuan, a king of Qi.

5. 或　　　huò　　　someone. (Note that in Classical Chinese 或 is a pronoun, not a conjunction.)

　　謂　　　wèi　　　to tell.

　　寡人　　guǎ rén　　this humble person. (A term used by rulers to refer to themselves.)

| | | |
|---|---|---|
| 勿 | wù | don't + verb + it. (A phonetic fusion of the imperative 毋 and the pronoun 之.) |
| 取 | qǔ | to take possession of. |
| 6. 以 | yǐ | with. (A preposition.) |
| 7. 旬 | xún | ten days. |
| 舉 | jǔ | to take over (a territory) by force. |
| 8. 人力 | rén lì | human capability. |
| 至 | zhì | to reach; to arrive. |
| 9. 天殃 | tiān yāng | calamity from Heaven. |
| 10. 取之何如 | qǔ zhī hé rú | what do you think if I keep it? |
| 11. 武王 | Wǔwáng | King Wu. The first king of the Zhou Dynasty, who overthrew the Shāng 商 Dynasty. |
| 是 | shì | this. (A demonstrative pronoun.) |
| 12. 文王 | Wénwáng | King Wen, King Wu's father, who laid the basis for the founding of the Zhou Dynasty. |
| 13. 簞 | dān | a bamboo utensil for holding cereal foods. |
| 食 | sì | solid cereals. (Note that when 食 means food in general, it is pronounced shí, but when it means cereals, or used as a verb meaning "to feed", it is pronounced sì.) |
| 漿 | jiāng | a kind of beverage. |
| 簞食壺漿 | dān sì hú jiāng | baskets of food and pitchers of drink. |
| 以 | yǐ | therewith. (Syntactically it helps to connect two verb phrases, the second of which indicates the purpose of the first.) |
| 迎 | yíng | to welcome; to go forward to meet. |

| 王師 | wáng shī | the King's army; here referring to the army of the King of Qi. |
| 14. 他 | tā | other. (Note that in Classical Chinese, 他 does not mean "he" or "she".) |
| 哉 | zāi | particle used at the end of a sentence as an exclamation. |
| 豈有他哉 | qǐ yǒu tā zāi | how could there be any other reason? |
| 15. 益 | yì | more. (An adverb.) (Used before an adjective, the word is like 更 in Modern Chinese.) |
| 16. 運 | yùn | to move; to turn around. |

## 文法闡釋 (Grammar Notes)

### I. 不取，必有天殃。

This is a conditional sentence without a marker (such as 則 between its two clauses). The conditional clause 不取 has neither subject nor object, but the context makes it clear that it means: "if I do not take it (the Yan territory)". The verb 有 in the main clause 必有天殃 may be taken in either a general sense ("there will be") or in a more specific sense ("someone will have"). So the sentence can be translated as: "If I do not annex it, there will certainly be some natural disaster (as an indication of Heaven's curse)".

### II. 豈有他哉？避水火也。

The rhetorical question marker 豈 implies forcefully that the opposite of what the question says is the truth. It often, but not always, comes together with the sentence-end particle 哉 which indicates exclamation. It can thus be conveniently translated as: "How can there be such a thing that … !?" The understood subject of the sentence is "the reason why the Yan people came forward to welcome the Qi army". So the sentence means, literally, "How can there be such a thing that there is some other (reason)!?" 避水火也 is an equational sentence which functions as an answer to the question. Its implied subject is "it (the real reason)". For a more idiomatic translation, the two sentences can be combined as: "How could there be any reason other than that they merely wished to move away from flood and fire (i.e., disaster)!?"

# 八.《孟子・滕文公下》(節)[1]

## 📖 課文 (Text)

孟子謂戴不勝曰：[2]「子欲子之王之善與？[3] 我明告子。[4] 有楚大夫於此，欲其子之齊語也，[5] 則使齊人傅諸？[6] 使楚人傅諸？」曰：「使齊人傅之。」曰：「一齊人傅之，眾楚人咻之，[7] 雖日撻而求其齊也，[8] 不可得矣；[9] 引而置之莊嶽之閒數年，[10] 雖日撻而求其楚，不可得矣。子謂薛居州善士也，[11] 使之居於王所。[12] 在於王所者，[13] 長幼卑尊皆薛居州也，[14] 王誰與為不善？[15] 在王所者，長幼卑尊皆非薛居州也，王誰與為善？一薛居州，獨如宋王何？[16]」

## 📝 註釋 (Annotations)

1. 滕文公　Téng Wéngōng　Duke Wen of the state of Teng; here functioning as a chapter title.

2. 戴不勝　Dài Búshèng　a minister of the state of Song.

3. 與　yú　question particle. (See 文法闡釋 I.)

4. 明　míng　clearly.

5. 齊語　Qí yǔ　dialect of Qi; here used as a verb, i.e., to speak the dialect of Qi. The ensuing (求其) 齊 and (求其) 楚 are the same.

6. 傅　fù　to tutor; to teach.

   諸　zhū　phonetic fusion of 之 and 乎. (See 文法闡釋 I in Lesson 4, p. 58.)

| | | |
|---|---|---|
| 7. 眾 | zhòng | a lot of. |
| 咻 | xiū | to chatter. |
| 8. 雖 | suī | even if. (Note that in Modern Chinese, 雖 means "although", but in Classical Chinese 雖 means both "although" and "even if".) |
| 撻 | tà | to beat with a stick; to whip. |
| 9. 得 | dé | to obtain; here, it means "to achieve the goal". |
| 10. 引 | yǐn | to pull (close to oneself). |
| 置 | zhì | to place. |
| 莊嶽 | Zhuāngyuè | name of a district in the heart of the capital of Qi. |
| 閒 | jiān | a space (or time) within certain limits. (Same as 間 .) |
| 11. 薛居州 | Xuē Jūzhōu | name of a person. |
| 善士 | shàn shì | good man. |
| 12. 居 | jū | to reside. |
| 所 | suǒ | place; location. |
| 13. 在 | zài | to be present. (A verb.) |
| 14. 長 | zhǎng | old (in age); here used as a noun, referring to those who are old. |
| 幼 | yòu | young; those who are young. |
| 卑 | bēi | low; humble; those in low positions. |
| 尊 | zūn | high; honorable; those in high positions. |
| 15. 為 | wéi | to do. (A verb.) |
| 善 | shàn | good; here, 不善 is used as a noun, meaning "evil things". |
| 16. 如…何 | rú … hé | an idiomatic pattern. (See 文法闡釋 III.) |

## ☀ 文法闡釋 (Grammar Notes)

### I. 子欲子之王之善與？

The sentence-end particle 與 (sometimes written as 歟) represents the compound 也乎. So it turns the sentence into a question of the form "Is it (true) that … ?" The word 之 in both its occurrences is a possessive marker. So 子之王 means "your king", but since the second 之 occurs between a noun and an adjective, it can be seen as a marker for the subordination of the simple sentence 王善 "that the king is good". Thus, the sentence can be translated as: "Is it true that you, sir, wish your king to be good?" (If 與 is replaced by 乎, the sentence would mean simply, "Do you wish your king to be good?")

### II. 王誰與為不善？

The interrogative pronoun 誰 is the object of the co-verb 與, and because it is an interrogative, it occurs before the co-verb. 為 is here an action verb ("to do; to act"), with 不善 as its object. So the sentence can be rendered as: "With whom will the king do what is not good?"

### III. 一薛居州，獨如宋王何？

"如 somebody 何?" is an idiomatic expression, meaning "What can one do about that somebody?" The number 一 before the proper name 薛居州 turns the latter into a common noun, "a person like him". So this sentence can be rendered as: "What can a single person like Xue Juzhou alone do about the King of Song?"

# 九.《禮記》選

## (甲) 有子之言似夫子[1]

📖 **課文 (Text)**

　　有子問於曾子曰：[2]「問喪於夫子乎？[3]」曰：「聞之矣。『喪欲速貧，[4] 死欲速朽。[5]』」有子曰：「是非君子之言也。」曾子曰：「參也聞諸夫子也。[6]」有子又曰：「是非君子之言也。」曾子曰：「參也與子游聞之。」有子曰：「然。然則夫子有為言之也。[7]」

　　曾子以斯言告於子游。[8] 子游曰：「甚哉，[9] 有子之言似夫子也！昔者夫子居於宋，見桓司馬自為石椁。[10] 三年而不成。夫子曰：『若是其靡也！[11] 死不如速朽之愈也。[12]』死之欲速朽，為桓司馬言之也。南宮敬叔反，[13] 必載寶而朝。[14] 夫子曰：『若是其貨也，[15] 喪不如速貧之愈也。』喪之欲速貧，為敬叔言之也。」

〈檀弓上〉[16]

📑 **註釋 (Annotations)**

| | | | |
|---|---|---|---|
| 1. | 有子 | Yǒuzǐ | a disciple of Confucius. 子 is an honorific form of address. |
| 2. | 曾子 | Zēngzǐ | a disciple of Confucius. (See Lesson 3, p. 45.) |
| 3. | 喪 | sàng | to lose; here, meaning "to leave one's office". |
| 4. | 速 | sù | quick; quickly. |
| | 貧 | pín | poor. |
| 5. | 朽 | xiǔ | to rot; to decompose. |

| | | | |
|---|---|---|---|
| 6. | 參 | Shēn | the formal name of 曾子. |
| 7. | 然則 | rán zé | if so, then …. |
| 8. | 斯 | sī | this. (A demonstrative pronoun.) |
| 9. | 甚 | shèn | excessive; extreme. |
| 10. | 桓 | Huán | a family name. |
| | 司馬 | sī mǎ | an official title. |
| | 自 | zì | for oneself. (An adverb.) |
| | 槨 | guǒ | outer coffin. |
| 11. | 若是 | ruò shì | like this. |
| | 靡 | mǐ | extravagant; wasteful. |
| 12. | 愈 | yù | better. |
| 13. | 南宮敬叔 | Nángōng Jìngshū | a lord of the Lu state. |
| | 反 | fǎn | to return. (南宮敬叔 once lost his office and left the state, but returned later. 反 was later replaced by 返.) |
| 14. | 載 | zài | to carry in a vehicle. |
| | 寶 | bǎo | treasure. |
| | 朝 | cháo | to have an audience with the prince. |
| | 載寶而朝 | zài bǎo ér cháo | to go to court with treasures (as bribes in order to get his post back). |
| 15. | 貨 | huò | to bribe; to present gifts. |
| 16. | 檀弓 | Tán Gōng | name of a person. Here, it functions as a chapter title from the *Lǐjì* 《禮記》 (*Book of Rites*), one of the classics of the Confucian canon. |

## ☀ 文法闡釋 (Grammar Notes)

## I. 然則夫子有為言之也

The two words 然 and 則 often appear together as a compound in Modern Chinese, but they actually serve separate functions in Classical Chinese. 則 indicates the sentence is conditional, and 然, a verb, represents the conditional clause. Together they mean "If it is so, then …." 有, the verb in the main clause, implies an object ("something"; see 文法闡釋 I in Lesson 7, p. 78) which in turn serves as the understood object of the co-verb 為 in the verb phrase 為言之. So the whole sentence means: "If (it is) so, then the Master has (a reason) therewith to say that".

## II. 甚哉，有子之言似夫子也！

This is an inverted sentence, with its predicate 甚哉 put before its subject which is a complex clause. The possessive particle 之 turns 有子言 into a nominal ["(the way) Youzi talks"] which then serves as the subject of the clause with 似 as its verb. The sentence can, therefore, be rendered as, "It is extraordinary indeed, how Youzi talks just like the Master!"

## III. 若是其靡也！死不如速朽之愈也。

We actually have here two independent sentences, which are, however, closely related semantically. The first is an inverted sentence with its predicate 若是 appearing before its subject 其靡 "It's like that, his extravagance!" (Note that 若 is here a verb, just like 如 in the following sentence, not a conjunction for conditional clauses.) Then, with the first sentence as its implied conditional clause, the second sentence becomes the conclusive clause of a conditional sentence, "(If it is to be like that, then) when one dies, it is not as good as decomposing quickly". Note that 死 is not the subject of the verb 如, but a point of reference ("in death" or "when one dies"). Note also that, in the "A 不如 B" type of comparative sentences, 之愈 is mostly omitted, rather than spoken out as it is here.

# 九.《禮記》選

## （乙）苛政猛於虎[1]

## 📖 課文 (Text)

孔子過泰山側，²有婦人哭於墓者而哀。³夫子式而
聽之。⁴使子路問之曰：「子之哭也，壹似重有憂者？⁵」
而曰：「然。⁶昔者吾舅死於虎，⁷吾夫又死焉，⁸今吾
子又死焉。」夫子曰：「何為不去也？」曰：「無苛政。」
夫子曰：「小子識之，⁹苛政猛於虎也。」

〈檀弓下〉

## 📝 註釋 (Annotations)

1. 苛　　　kē　　　　　harsh; cruel.

   政　　　zhèng　　　government.

   猛於虎　měng yú hǔ　fiercer than a tiger.

2. 過　　　guò　　　　　to pass by.

   泰山　　Tàishān　　　name of a mountain in Shandong.

   側　　　cè　　　　　　side.

3. 哀　　　āi　　　　　　sad.

4. 式　　　shì　　　　　crossbar in the carriage (this character is written as 軾 later); here used as a verb, meaning "to bow and lean on the crossbar". This is a gesture of respect.

5. 壹似　　yī sì　　　　to be very much like.

   重　　　chóng　　　　doubly; repeatedly. (An adverb.)

   憂　　　yōu　　　　　sorrow.

6. 而曰　　ér yuē　　and (she) said. (The use of 而 here is rather unusual. Some scholars say it is a substitute for 乃 nǎi.)

　　然　　rán　　it is so; yes.

7. 舅　　jiù　　father-in-law. (Note that in Classical Chinese 舅 means both uncle (mother's brother) and father-in-law (husband's father).)

8. 夫　　fū　　husband.

　　焉　　yān　　equivalent to 於 + 之 here. 之 refers to the tiger; 於虎 means "(killed) by the tiger".

9. 小子　　xiǎo zǐ　　young fellows. (A term elders may use when addressing youngsters.)

　　識　　zhì　　to remember; to mark.

## ☼ 文法闡釋 (Grammar Notes)

### I. 子之哭也，壹似重有憂者？

The phrase 子之哭 means literally "your crying", but it can also be taken as a subordinate clause, "that you cry", or "the way you cry". Marked by 也, it serves as the topic of the sentence. (Note that the honorific 子 can also be used for women.) The following clause 壹似重有憂者, with "you" as its implied subject, serves as the comment on that topic. 壹 is here an adverb, meaning "wholly; very much", and the nominalizer 者 covers the verb phrase 重有憂. So the sentence can be rendered as: "(Judging by) the way you cry, (I would say) you seem very much like one who has suffered repeatedly from some sorrows".

### II. 何為不去也？

The interrogative pronoun 何 is the object of the co-verb 為, so the phrase means "what for" or "why". The verb 去 in Classical Chinese does not mean simply "to go". It means rather "to leave" or "to move away (from some place)". So the sentence means: "Why don't you move away (from this place)?"

# 十.《老子》選[1]

## 📖 課文 (Text)

大道廢，[2] 有仁義。慧智出，[3] 有大偽。[4] 六親不和，[5] 有孝慈。[6] 國家昏亂，[7] 有忠臣。[8]

## 📝 註釋 (Annotations)

| | | | |
|---|---|---|---|
| 1. | 老子 | Lǎozǐ | a book attributed to Lǎo Dǎn 老聃, the leading philosopher of the Daoist School. The Daoist School advocates going along with nature and is against artificial contrivance. |
| 2. | 大道 | dà dào | the ultimate Way. |
| | 廢 | fèi | to abolish; here used in the passive sense. |
| 3. | 慧智 | huì zhì | intelligence. |
| | 出 | chū | to emerge. |
| 4. | 偽 | wěi | falsehood; hypocrisy. |
| 5. | 六親 | liù qīn | the six kinds of closest relatives. (Interpretations differ on the specific relations. Some possible groupings include 父子 fù zǐ; 夫婦 fū fù; 兄弟 xiōng dì "father and son; husband and wife; elder brother and younger brother".) |
| | 和 | hé | harmonious. |
| 6. | 孝 | xiào | filial piety. |
| | 慈 | cí | parental love. |
| 7. | 國家 | guó jiā | state. |
| | 昏 | hūn | dark; confused; disorderly. |
| 8. | 臣 | chén | minister. |
| | 忠臣 | zhōng chén | a loyal minister. |

## ☀ 文法闡釋 (Grammar Note)

大道廢，有仁義。

This is a compound sentence with two clauses. The first clause should, therefore, be translated with "if" or "when". The verb 有 in the Daoist texts generally means the coming into existence of something that did not exist before. So the sentence should be translated as: "When the great Dao was neglected, (the concepts of) *Ren* and *Yi* then came into existence". The three sentences following this one share the same structure.

## 📖 課文─續 (Text — Continued)

天下莫柔弱於水，⁹ 而攻堅強者莫之能勝，¹⁰ 以其無以易之 。¹¹ 弱之勝強，柔之勝剛，¹² 天下莫不知，莫能行。¹³ 是以聖人云：¹⁴「受國之垢，¹⁵ 是謂社稷主；¹⁶ 受國不祥，¹⁷ 是為天下王。」正言若反。¹⁸

## 📑 註釋 (Annotations)

| | | | |
|---|---|---|---|
| 9. | 莫 | mò | no one; nothing; nobody. (A pronoun.) |
| | 柔 | róu | soft. |
| 10. | 堅 | jiān | hard. |
| | 強 | qiáng | strong. |
| 11. | 其 | qí | its. (A possessive pronoun.) |
| | 易 | yì | to replace. |
| 12. | 剛 | gāng | hard. |
| 13. | 行 | xíng | to practice; to do. |

| 14. | 聖人 | shèng rén | the Sage. |
|---|---|---|---|
| 15. | 受 | shòu | to receive; to be subjected to. |
|  | 垢 | gòu | humiliation. |
| 16. | 社 | shè | deity of land. |
|  | 稷 | jì | deity of grain. |
|  | 社稷 | shè jì | in ancient China, the ruler of every state must offer sacrifice to the local deity of land and deity of grain. So 社稷 means "national altars" in a general sense, and represents "state sovereignty" figuratively. |
| 17. | 不祥 | bù xiáng | bad luck; disaster. |
| 18. | 正言若反 | zhèng yán ruò fǎn | positive words may sound like negative ones. |

## ☀ 文法闡釋 (Grammar Notes)

### I. 天下莫柔弱於水

莫 is a general negative pronoun ("none; nothing; nobody") and serves as the subject of this sentence. When an adjective is followed by 於 and a noun, it is generally read in the comparative sense. So the sentence should be translated as: "Under the sky, nothing is softer and weaker than water".

### II. 以其無以易之

The expression 無以易之 is syntactically a sentence by itself, meaning "There is nothing (with which) to replace it". When used, as it is here, as a description for something, it means that thing is irreplaceable. The 以 at the beginning means "due to" or "because of". 其 is a possessive pronoun. So this sentence is an explanation for the preceding sentence, and can be translated as: "This is because of its being irreplaceable".

## 📖 課文—續 (Text — Continued)

　　小國寡民，[19] 使有什佰之器而不用，[20] 使民重死而不遠徙。[21] 雖有舟輿，[22] 無所乘之；[23] 雖有甲兵，[24] 無所陳之；[25] 使人復結繩而用之。[26] 甘其食，[27] 美其服，[28] 安其居，[29] 樂其俗。[30] 鄰國相望，[31] 雞犬之聲相聞，[32] 民至老死不相往來。[33]

## 📝 註 釋 (Annotations)

| | | | |
|---|---|---|---|
| 19. | 小國寡民 | xiǎo guó guǎ mín | make the state small, make the people few. (小 and 寡 are used as causative verbs.) |
| 20. | 什佰 | shí bǎi | ten times and a hundred times. |
| | 器 | qì | tool. |
| | 什佰之器 | shí bǎi zhī qì | tools which are tenfold or a hundred-fold more efficient than the normal ones. |
| 21. | 重死 | zhòng sǐ | to take death seriously. (重 is here a putative verb.) |
| 22. | 輿 | yú | chariot; carriage. |
| 23. | 乘 | chéng | to mount; to ride on. |
| 24. | 甲 | jiǎ | armor. |
| | 兵 | bīng | weapon. |
| 25. | 陳 | chén | to display. |
| 26. | 結繩 | jié shéng | to keep a record by making knots with a rope. (A primitive method to keep records before the invention of writing.) |

| 27. | 甘 | gān | sweet; here used as putative verb, meaning "to regard something as sweet". |
|---|---|---|---|
| 28. | 服 | fú | clothes. |
| 29. | 安 | ān | to feel comfortable with. |
|  | 居 | jū | dwelling place. |
| 30. | 樂 | lè | to feel happy with. |
|  | 俗 | sú | customs. |
| 31. | 鄰國相望 | lín guó xiāng wàng | (people of ) neighboring states can see each other. |
| 32. | 雞犬之聲相聞 | jī quǎn zhī shēng xiāng wén | the crowing of roosters and the barking of dogs can be heard mutually (by the people of either state). |
| 33. | 至 | zhì | till. (A preposition.) |
|  | 往來 | wǎng lái | to visit each other; to have contact. |

## ☀ 文法闡釋 (Grammar Notes)

### I. 小國寡民

The two adjectives 小 and 寡 are here causative verbs, and 民 does not merely mean "people", but "subjects" or "the ruled" (versus "the rulers"). So this sentence must be translated as "make your state small and your subjects few". (Note that this extract advises rulers how to rule. In interpreting this piece of writing, this undertone must be kept in mind.)

### II. 甘其食，美其服，安其居，樂其俗。

Unlike the previous sentences, this one is not preceded by either 使民 or 使人, but it must, nevertheless, be understood as such. This means that the adjectives 甘, 美, 安, and 樂 here are all putative verbs, so we have to understand their respective objects as having such qualities. So the sentence should be interpreted as, "(Make your subjects) regard their food as delicious, their clothes as beautiful, their homes as comfortable, and their way of living as enjoyable". That is, to make them feel satisfied with what they have.

.

# 十一.《墨子・公輸》：

## 墨子說公輸盤[1]

## 📖 課文 (Text)

公輸盤為楚造雲梯之械，² 成，將以攻宋。子墨子
聞之，起於齊，³ 行十日十夜而至於郢。⁴ 見公輸盤。公
輸盤曰：「夫子何命焉為？」子墨子曰：「北方有侮臣
(者)，⁵ 願藉子殺之。⁶」公輸盤不說。子墨子曰：「請獻
十金。⁷」公輸盤曰：「吾義固不殺人。」子墨子起，再拜
曰：「請說之。⁸ 吾從北方，聞子為梯，將以攻宋。宋何
罪之有？荊國有餘於地，⁹ 而不足於民。殺所不足而爭
所有餘，¹⁰ 不可謂智；¹¹ 宋無罪而攻之，不可謂仁；知
而不爭，¹² 不可謂忠；爭而不得，不可謂強。¹³ 義不殺
少而殺眾，不可謂知類。¹⁴」公輸盤服。¹⁵

## 📑 註釋 (Annotations)

1.  墨子　　Mòzǐ　　　　a book about Mò Dí 墨翟 compiled by his disciples. Mo Di (480–420 B.C.) was the founder of the Mohist School, which was very influential in its time. Impartial love (兼愛 jiān ài) and against attacking (非攻 fēi gōng) are the basic propositions of the Mohist School.

　　　說　　shuì　　　　to persuade.

　　公輸盤　Gōngshū Pán　a famous craftsman from the state of Lu, hence also known as Lǔ Bān 魯班. He was revered by carpenters as the patron saint of their profession. 盤 is also written as 般 in some texts. Gongshu, the family name of Gongshu Pan, also functions here as a chapter title from *Mozi*.

2. 雲梯　yún tī　scaling ladder.

　　械　xiè　tool.

3. 子墨子　Zǐ Mòzǐ　the Master, Mozi.

　　起　qǐ　to set out; to get up.

4. 行　xíng　to walk.

　　郢　Yǐng　the capital of Chu.

5. 侮　wǔ　to insult.

　　臣　chén　servant. (Humble form used when a speaker refers to himself.)

6. 藉　jiè　to borrow (same as 借); here, to rely on.

7. 獻　xiàn　to offer respectfully; to present.

　　十金　shí jīn　ten units of gold.

8. 再　zài　twice. (Note that in Classical Chinese, 再 means "twice", not "again".)

　　拜　bài　to bow.

　　說　shuō　to explain.

9. 荊　Jīng　another name for Chu.

10. 爭　zhēng　to contend (for).

11. 智　zhì　wisdom.

12. 爭　zhēng　to remonstrate against. Cf. 爭 in (10).

13. 強　qiáng　strong (in will).

14. 知　zhī　to know.

　　類　lèi　analogy.

15. 服　fú　to be convinced.

## ☀ 文法闡釋 (Grammar Notes)

### I. 夫子何命焉為？

This sentence exemplifies a very unique type of question. 為 at the end is a particle used for emphasis. Without the particle, the sentence is just a polite question. "What does the Master (i.e., you) want him (i.e., me) to do?" Or, in more idiomatic English, "What can I do for you, sir?" With the particle, the question acquires a flavor of surprise, puzzlement, or even sarcasm, "What could I possibly do for you, sir?" 命 is the verb ("order", hence "want", or "demand"), with 何 as its object. Note that the post-verbal 焉 is not an interrogative, but stands semantically for 於之, "of him" or "from him".

### II. 吾義固不殺人

Both the noun 義 "righteousness" and the adjective 固 "solid" function as adverbs in this sentence. So the sentence can be translated as: "I, on principle, absolutely won't kill people!"

### III. 宋何罪之有？

之 is a pronoun referring back to 何罪 which is the object of the verb 有. It helps to put more emphasis on that object by way of repetition. The sentence can thus be translated as: "What offence (or crime), for that matter, has Song committed?"

# 十二.《莊子・秋水》(節) [1]

## 📖 課文 (Text)

秋水時至，[2] 百川灌河。[3] 涇流之大，[4] 兩涘渚崖之間，[5] 不辯牛馬。[7] 於是焉河伯欣然自喜，[7] 以天下之美為盡在己。[8] 順流而東行，[9] 至於北海；[10] 東面而視，不見水端。[11]

於是焉河伯始旋其面目，[12] 望洋向若而歎曰：[13]「野語有之曰：[14]『聞道百，以為莫己若』者，我之謂也。且夫我嘗聞少仲尼之聞，[15] 而輕伯夷之義者，[16] 始吾弗信，[17] 今我睹子之難窮也，[18] 吾非至於子之門，則殆矣，吾長見笑於大方之家。[19]」

## 📑 註釋 (Annotations)

| 1. | 莊子 | Zhuāngzǐ | a book attributed to Zhuāng Zhōu 莊周, an important thinker of the Daoist School. The work is known for its charming prose style. |
|---|---|---|---|
| | 秋水 | qiū shuǐ | autumn flood. Here, it is also the title of a chapter from *Zhuangzi*. |
| 2. | 時 | shí | on time. (An adverb.) |
| 3. | 川 | chuān | stream. |
| | 灌 | guàn | to pour into. |
| | 河 | Hé | the Yellow River. (Note that in the pre-Qin period, 河 was the proper noun for the Yellow River.) |
| 4. | 涇 | jīng | to flow unimpeded. |
| | 流 | liú | currents; flow. |

5. 涘    sì    bank (of river).

渚    zhǔ    islet.

崖    yá    steep bank.

6. 辯    biàn    this character means "to debate"; here, it is a substitute for 辨, meaning "to distinguish".

7. 焉    yān    a particle syntactically redundant here but with the effect of a pause.

欣然    xīn rán    gladly; in a cheerful manner.

8. 盡    jìn    altogether. (An adverb.)

9. 順流    shùn liú    to go downstream.

東行    dōng xíng    to go east.

10. 北海    Běihǎi    the North Sea, now called the Bohai Sea (Bóhǎi 渤海).

11. 端    duān    end.

12. 始    shǐ    only then. (An adverb.) (Similar to 才 in Modern Chinese.)

旋    xuán    to turn around.

面目    miàn mù    face and eyes; look; color.

13. 望洋    wàng yáng    with an admiring and awestruck look. (A disyllabic word.)

向    xiàng    to face. (A verb.)

若    Ruò    name of the god of the North Sea.

14. 野語    yě yǔ    common saying.

15. 且夫    qiě fú    moreover; furthermore. (A conjunction.)

嘗    cháng    once (in the past). (An adverb.)

| 少 | shǎo | to belittle; to consider (something) as being unimportant. (A putative verb.) |
| 聞 | wén | what one hears; learning. (A noun.) |
| 16. 輕 | qīng | to consider (something) negligible; to despise. (A putative verb.) |
| 伯夷 | Bó Yí | name of a worthy man in the Shang Dynasty who died of starvation rather than subject himself to the rule of the Zhou Dynasty. |
| 17. 始 | shǐ | in the beginning; at first. (A noun used as an adverb.) |
| 弗信 | fú xìn | not believe it. (弗 is the equivalent to 不之. The object 之 is put in front of the verb 信 because this is a negative sentence.) |
| 18. 難窮 | nán qióng | difficult to reach the bottom; hard to measure. |
| 19. 見笑於 | jiàn xiào yú | to face the mockery of; to be laughed at by (somebody). |
| 大方之家 | dà fāng zhī jiā | a man of great learning. (家 here indicates a person, as it does in such Modern Chinese terms as 教育家 "educator", 作家 "writer", etc.) |

## ☀ 文法闡釋 (Grammar Notes)

**I. 『聞道百，以為莫己若』者，我之謂也。**

One rhetorical technique frequently employed in Classical Chinese is to quote some ancient saying and then declare that it is a fitting description of the case at hand. What we have here is such an example. First, the saying is quoted, with 者 attached to its end. The particle 者 here is a nominalizer in a more abstract sense, as a sign of confirmation, so that the quote can now serve as the subject of the sentence. 我之謂也 is the predicate of the sentence wherein 謂 is the verb and 我 is its object. The object is put before the verb for emphasis, and, as if it were not enough, the pronoun 之 is added to intensify it ("me, this person!"). So the sentence can be translated literally as, "That saying, 'After learning about a hundred lessons, (he) took it to be (i.e., assumed) that no one was as good as himself', talks about (i.e., describes) me, this person!"

## II. 吾非至於子之門，則殆矣。

Because of the particle 則, we know this is a conditional sentence, and a subjunctive one. 殆矣 represents the consequential clause, with 吾 as its implied subject. 非 in the conditional clause does not negate the verb 至. As a negative particle for equational sentences, it negates instead the whole clause, though the subject of that clause is, more often than not, placed before it. Therefore, the sentence should be translated as: "If it had not been that I came to your door, I would have been finished".

## III. 吾長見笑於大方之家

見笑 means literally "to meet (or encounter) laughter (or jeering)", but, for practical purposes, it can be translated as "be laughed at". This is why, when 見 is followed by a transitive verb (sometimes with 於 + N after them), the pattern is called a "passive construction" by some scholars. This sentence actually shares the same conditional clause with the last sentence, and is, therefore, subjunctive too. So it should be rendered as: "(If it had not been that I came to your door,) I would have always been laughed at by the great enlightened masters".

# 十三.《莊子・徐無鬼》：
## 運斤成風[1]

## 📖 課文 (Text)

莊子送葬，<sup>2</sup> 過惠子之墓。<sup>3</sup> 顧謂從者曰：<sup>4</sup>「郢人堊慢其鼻端，<sup>5</sup> 若蠅翼。<sup>6</sup> 使匠石斲之。<sup>7</sup> 匠石運斤成風，聽而斲之，盡堊而鼻不傷。<sup>8</sup> 郢人立不失容。<sup>9</sup> 宋元君聞之，<sup>10</sup> 召匠石曰：<sup>11</sup>『嘗試為寡人為之。<sup>12</sup>』匠石曰：『臣則嘗能斲之，雖然，<sup>13</sup> 臣之質死久矣。<sup>14</sup>』自夫子之死也，吾無以為質矣！吾無與言之矣！」

## 📑 註釋 (Annotations)

| | | | |
|---|---|---|---|
| 1. | 徐無鬼 | Xú Wúguǐ | name of a person; here functioning as the title of a chapter. |
| | 運 | yùn | to brandish; to swing. |
| | 斤 | jīn | axe. |
| | 運斤成風 | yùn jīn chéng fēng | brandishing the axe so swiftly that a small whirlwind is produced. |
| 2. | 送葬 | sòng zàng | to accompany a deceased friend to the cemetery for burial. |
| 3. | 惠子 | Huìzǐ | Huì Shī 惠施, a famous logician and a friend of Zhuangzi. |
| 4. | 顧 | gù | to turn one's head and look at. |
| 5. | 堊 | è | plaster. |
| | 慢 | màn | to stain. (A substitute for 漫.) |
| | 端 | duān | tip; end. |
| 6. | 蠅翼 | yíng yì | wings of a fly (which are very thin). |

| 7. | 匠石 | Jiàng Shí | 匠 (carpenter) is his occupation; 石 is his name. |
|---|---|---|---|
| | 斲 | zhuó | to cut; to chop. |
| 8. | 聽 | tīng | to leave the axe take its own course. |
| | 盡堊 | jìn è | to clean off the plaster completely. |
| 9. | 失容 | shī róng | to lose one's countenance. |
| 10. | 宋元君 | Sòng Yuánjūn | Prince Yuan of Song. |
| 11. | 召 | zhào | to summon. |
| 12. | 嘗試 | cháng shì | to try. |
| 13. | 雖然 | suī rán | though (it is) so. |
| 14. | 質 | zhì | the original meaning is "target"; here, it means "partner". |

## 🜲 文法闡釋 (Grammar Notes)

### I. 臣則嘗能斲之

Since 臣 appears before the conjunction 則, we can see that it is not syntactically the subject of a simple sentence, but represents a clause by itself, in the sense of "if it's me", or more idiomatically, "as far as I am concerned". So, to reflect the implication that "it takes two to tango", this sentence should be translated as, "As far as I am concerned, yes, I once indeed could chop it", or something similar.

### II. 雖然，臣之質死久矣！

Unlike in Modern Chinese, 雖然 is not a compound in Classical Chinese. 雖 alone means "though", while 然 means "to be like that". Thus, together they form the subordinate clause "though it is so". 臣之質死, a clause by itself, is the subject of the main clause, and 久矣 is its predicate. So the sentence can be rendered as: "Though it is so (that I once could do it), it has been a long time since my partner died!"

# 十四.《荀子・勸學》(節)[1]

## 📖 課文 (Text)

　　君子曰：學不可以已。青，取之於藍，而青於藍；[2] 冰，水為之，而寒於水。[3] 木直中繩，[4] 輮以為輪，[5] 其曲中規，[6] 雖有槁暴，[7] 不復挺者，[8] 輮使之然也。故木受繩則直，[9] 金就礪則利，[10] 君子博學而日參省乎己，[11] 則知明而行無過矣。[12] 故不登高山，[13] 不知天之高也；不臨深谿，[14] 不知地之厚也；不聞先王之遺言，[15] 不知學問之大也。[16] 干、越、夷、貉之子，[17] 生而同聲，長而異俗，[18] 教使之然也。…

　　積土成山，[19] 風雨興焉；[20] 積水成淵，[21] 蛟龍生焉；[22] 積善成德，而神明自得，[23] 聖心備焉。[24] 故不積蹞步，[25] 無以至千里；不積小流，無以成江海。騏驥一躍，[26] 不能十步；駑馬十駕，[27] 功在不舍。鍥而舍之，[28] 朽木不折；鍥而不舍，金石可鏤。[29] 螾無爪牙之利，[30] 筋骨之強，[31] 上食埃土，[32] 下飲黃泉，[33] 用心一也。蟹六跪而二螯，[34] 非蛇蟺之穴無可寄託者，[35] 用心躁也。[36] 是故無冥冥之志者，無昭昭之明；[37] 無惛惛之事者，[38] 無赫赫之功。[39]

## 📝 註釋 (Annotations)

1. 荀子    Xúnzǐ    a book written by Xún Kuàng 荀況 and his disciples. Xun Kuang, or Xunzi, was a philosopher of the Confucian School who lived in the later part of the Warring States period.

   勸學    Quàn xué    to encourage learning; here it is the title of a chapter.

2. 青    qīng    indigo. (A noun.)
dark blue. (An adjective.)

   藍    lán    the indigo plant. (Note that, to express the notion "blue", pre-Qin Chinese only employed 青, not 藍.)

3. 寒    hán    cold.

4. 木    mù    timber.

   直    zhí    straight.

   中    zhòng    to match with.

   繩    shéng    rope; carpenter's rule.

5. 輮    róu    to bake and bend. (A substitute for 煣.)

6. 曲    qū    curve.

   規    guī    compass.

7. 槁暴    gǎo pù    exposed to wind and rain; damaged by the natural elements.

8. 復    fù    again.

   挺    tǐng    to straighten.

9. 受    shòu    to receive.

10. 金    jīn    metal.

| | | |
|---|---|---|
| 就 | jiù | to go to; to meet. |
| 礪 | lì | whetstone. |
| 利 | lì | sharp. |
| 11. 博 | bó | extensively. |
| 參 | cān | to inspect. |
| 省 | xǐng | to examine. |
| 乎 | hū | same as 於, when it comes before a nominal. (A preposition.) |
| 12. 知 | zhì | wisdom. (Written as 智 in later times.) |
| 明 | míng | bright. |
| 行 | xíng | conduct; behavior. |
| 過 | guò | fault; excess. |
| 13. 登 | dēng | to ascend. |
| 14. 臨 | lín | to stand above and look down. |
| 谿 | xī | valley. |
| 15. 先王 | xiān wáng | the sage kings of the ancient times. |
| 遺 | yí | to hand down. |
| 16. 學問 | xué wèn | learning; knowledge. |
| 17. 干越夷貉 | gān yuè yí mò | names of four tribes. |
| 子 | zǐ | baby; child. |
| 18. 異 | yì | to be different. |
| 俗 | sú | folk customs; customary practices. |
| 19. 積 | jī | to accumulate. |

| | | |
|---|---|---|
| 20. 興 | xīng | to rise. |
| 21. 淵 | yuān | deep and large body of water. |
| 22. 蛟 | jiāo | the kind of dragon capable of creating storms and floods. |
| 23. 神明 | shén míng | wisdom. |
| 自得 | zì dé | to be obtained (comes) of itself. |
| 24. 聖心 | shèng xīn | the sagely mind. |
| 備 | bèi | to be ready or prepared (before the time of need). |
| 25. 蹞 | kuǐ | a half step. Also written as 跬. |
| 步 | bù | a step. |
| 26. 騏驥 | qí jì | a fine steed. |
| 躍 | yuè | leap. |
| 27. 駑馬 | nú mǎ | an inferior horse. |
| 駕 | jià | ride; a day's trip. |
| 28. 鍥 | qiè | to carve. |
| 29. 鏤 | lòu | to carve; here, to be carved. |
| 30. 螾 | yǐn | earthworm. (A variant form of 蚓.) |
| 31. 筋 | jīn | tendon. |
| 32. 食 | shí | to eat. |
| 埃 | āi | dust. |
| 33. 飲 | yǐn | to drink. |
| 黃泉 | Huángquán | the Yellow Springs, i.e., underground water. |
| 34. 蟹 | xiè | crab. |

|       | 螯    | áo          | pincers.                                      |
|-------|------|-------------|-----------------------------------------------|
| 35.   | 鱓    | shàn        | eel. (A variant form of 鱔.)                   |
|       | 穴    | xué         | hole; den.                                     |
|       | 寄託  | jì tuō      | to entrust (oneself) to; to rely on.           |
| 36.   | 躁    | zào         | rash; hot-tempered.                             |
| 37.   | 冥冥  | míng míng   | dark; hidden.                                   |
|       | 志    | zhì         | intention; here, concentration on learning.    |
|       | 昭昭  | zhāo zhāo   | bright; shining.                               |
| 38.   | 惛惛  | hūn hūn     | silent; of calm determination.                 |
| 39.   | 赫赫  | hè hè       | illustrious; grand and glorious.               |

## ☀ 文法闡釋 (Grammar Notes)

### I. 青，取之於藍，而青於藍。

This is a topic-comment type of sentence with 青 "indigo" as topic and the two clauses connected by the conjunction 而 as comment. The 之 in the first clause 取之於藍 refers to "indigo". Since the clause has no subject, it may be taken in the passive sense. The 青 in the second clause 青於藍 is an adjective meaning "dark blue". Since it is followed by 於 + N, it may be taken in the comparative sense. So the sentence can be translated as, "Indigo, taken from the indigo plant, is bluer than the indigo plant". This saying in modified form (青出於藍而勝於藍) has become a common expression meaning something like "that student is better than his teacher".

### II. 不復挺者，輮使之然也。

This is structurally an equational sentence. 不復挺者 is the subject, and 輮使之然也 is the predicate. The nominalizer 者 is abstract here, turning 不復挺 into a nominal "that (it) no longer straightens out". 輮 "bending (wood into wheels)" is the subject of the predicative clause. So the sentence can be translated as, "The reason why it no longer straightens is that bending makes it so". (The sentence 長而異俗，教使之然也 at the end of this paragraph, though without 者, shares the same structure. )

## III. 鍥而舍之，朽木不折。

In a conditional sentence, the conjunction 則 normally appears between its two clauses, but sometimes it is omitted, as it is in the present sentence. The first clause 鍥而舍之 itself contains two clauses connected by the conjunction 而, and should thus be syntactically rendered as: "If (we) give it up after (we started) chopping". The main clause 朽木不折 means simply "(even) a piece of rotten wood won't break".

## IV. 用心一也

This is an equational sentence with a clause as its predicate. The implied subject is the long narrative before it. In the clause, 用心 "using (or applying) the mind" is the subject and 一 "one (or undivided)" is the predicate. As an explanation for the narrative before it, this sentence can be rendered as: "That is because it is single-minded". (用心躁也 in the following sentence shares the same structure.)

## V. 蟹六跪而二螯

Syntactically, this sentence may puzzle some non-Chinese speakers. But, as far as Chinese grammar is concerned, nominal expressions serving as predicates in a descriptive sense are quite common and normal (e.g., 他三頭六臂 "he is three-headed and six-armed" in Modern Chinese). So, 六跪 and 二螯 in the present sentence are both predicates which are connected by the conjunction 而. The sentence, therefore, can be rendered as: "Crabs, in addition to having six legs, are armed with two pincers".

# 十五.《韓非子·說林上》：
## 巧詐不如拙誠[1]

## 📖 課文 (Text)

　　樂羊為魏將而攻中山，²其子在中山，中山之君烹
其子而遺之羹，³樂羊坐於幕下而啜之，⁴盡一杯，⁵文
侯謂堵師贊曰：⁶「樂羊以我故而食其子之肉。⁷」答曰：
「其子而食之，且誰不食？」樂羊罷中山，⁸文侯賞其功
而疑其心。⁹

## 📑 註釋 (Annotations)

| | | | |
|---|---|---|---|
| 1. | 韓非子 | Hán Fēizǐ | a book written by Hán Fēi 韓非, the most famous thinker of the so-called Fǎ Jiā 法家, or Legalist School, during the Warring States period. |
| | 說林 | Shuōlín | literally, "forest of sayings"; here, a chapter title. |
| | 巧 | qiǎo | cunning; clever. |
| | 詐 | zhà | trickery. |
| | 拙 | zhuó | clumsy. |
| | 誠 | chéng | honesty. |
| | 巧詐不如拙誠 | qiǎo zhà bù rú zhuó chéng | cunning trickery is not as good as clumsy honesty. |
| 2. | 樂羊 | Yuè Yáng | name of a person. |
| | 將 | jiàng | a general; a commander. |
| | 中山 | Zhōngshān | a small state of the Warring States period. |
| 3. | 烹 | pēng | to boil. |

|  | 遺 | wèi | to present. (Note that when it means "to present", 遺 should be pronounced wèi, otherwise, yí.) |
|  | 羹 | gēng | broth with meat. |
| 4. | 幕 | mù | top of tent; canopy. |
|  | 啜 | chuò | to drink; to sip. |
| 5. | 盡 | jìn | to finish. |
| 6. | 文侯 | Wénhóu | Marquis Wen, ruler of the state of Wei. |
|  | 堵師贊 | Dǔ Shīzàn | name of a person. |
| 7. | 故 | gù | reason; sake. (A noun.) |
| 8. | 罷 | bà | to end; to terminate. |
|  | 罷中山 | bà Zhōngshān | ended and returned from the Zhongshan campaign. |
| 9. | 賞 | shǎng | to reward. |
|  | 功 | gōng | achievement; accomplishment. |
|  | 疑 | yí | to suspect. |

## ☀ 文法闡釋 (Grammar Note)

### 其子而食之，且誰不食？

The conjunction 而 reveals that 其子 must be the predicate of a clause ["(it is) his son"] and 食之 is the predicate of another clause ["(someone) ate him"]. Together they form the conditional portion of this conditional sentence. So this portion can be translated as: "If he ate it even when it was his own son ('s flesh)". Since the main clause 且誰不食 includes the adverb 且 "further" it becomes even more natural to omit the conjunction 則. Note that 誰 is the object of the verb 食. It precedes the verb, because it is an interrogative. So the clause means: "then whom would he not eat?"

## 📖 課文—續 (Text — Continued)

　　孟孫獵得麑，[10] 使秦西巴持之歸，[11] 其母隨之而啼，[12] 秦西巴弗忍而與之，[13] 孟孫歸，至而求麑，答曰：「余弗忍而與其母。」大怒，[14] 逐之，[15] 居三月，復召以為其子傅，[16] 其御曰：[17]「曩將罪之，[18] 今召以為子傅，何也？[19]」孟孫曰：「夫不忍麑，又且忍吾子乎？」

　　故曰：「巧詐不如拙誠。」樂羊以有功見疑，[20] 秦西巴以有罪益信。[21]

## 📑 註 釋 (Annotations)

| | | | |
|---|---|---|---|
| 10. | 孟孫 | Mèngsūn | a lord of the Lu state. |
| | 獵 | liè | to hunt. |
| | 麑 | ní | fawn. |
| 11. | 秦西巴 | Qín Xībā | name of a person. |
| 12. | 啼 | tí | to cry. |
| 13. | 忍 | rěn | to bear; to endure. |
| | 與 | yǔ | to give; to bestow. |
| 14. | 怒 | nù | to be angry. |
| 15. | 逐 | zhú | to expel; to chase away. |
| 16. | 傅 | fù | tutor. |
| 17. | 御 | yù | driver. |

| 18. | 曩 | nǎng | in the past; formerly. |
| | 罪 | zuì | to punish. |
| 19. | 何也 | hé yě | what is the reason; why? |
| 20. | 見疑 | jiàn yí | to be suspected. (See 文法闡釋 III in Lesson 12.) |
| 21. | 信 | xìn | to trust; to be trusted. |

## ☀ 文法闡釋 (Grammar Note)

### 夫不忍麑，又且忍吾子乎？

As an initial modal particle to sentences, 夫 can perhaps be rendered as "Now (you listen)!" The verb 忍 means "to bear (something hard or terrible)". After both its occurrences in this sentence, another verb ("to hurt") is implied, and the negative form 不忍 also acquires the new sense of "cannot bear". So the sentence can be translated as: "Now, if he cannot even bear to hurt a fawn, can he then bear to hurt my son?" 又 is an adverb of intensification, implying something more than just hurting a fawn (i.e., "hurting my son"). As in the clause 且誰不食 discussed earlier on, the force of the adverb 且 can be shown in an English translation by the inclusion of "even" in the conditional clause. These two adverbs make the overt inclusion of the conjunction 則 unnecessary.

# 十六.《左傳・莊公十年》：
## 曹劌論戰[1]

## 📖 課文 (Text)

　　十年春，² 齊師伐我。³ 公將戰，曹劌請見。⁴ 其鄉人曰：⁵「肉食者謀之，⁶ 又何間焉？」⁷ 劌曰：「肉食者鄙，⁸ 未能遠謀。」⁹ 乃入見。問何以戰？公曰：「衣食所安，弗敢專也，¹⁰ 必以分人。」¹¹ 對曰：「小惠未徧，¹² 民弗從也。」公曰：「犧牲玉帛，¹³ 弗敢加也，¹⁴ 必以信。」¹⁵ 對曰：「小信未孚，¹⁶ 神弗福也。」¹⁷ 公曰：「小大之獄，¹⁸ 雖不能察，¹⁹ 必以情。」²⁰ 對曰：「忠之屬也，²¹ 可以一戰，²² 戰則請從。」公與之乘，²³ 戰于長勺，²⁴ 公將鼓之。²⁵ 劌曰：「未可。」²⁶ 齊人三鼓，劌曰：「可矣。」齊師敗績，²⁷ 公將馳之，²⁸ 劌曰：「未可。」下視其轍，²⁹ 登軾而望之，³⁰ 曰：「可矣。」遂逐齊師。³¹

　　既克，公問其故。對曰：「夫戰，勇氣也。³² 一鼓作氣，³³ 再而衰，³⁴ 三而竭。³⁵ 彼竭我盈，³⁶ 故克之。夫大國，難測也。³⁷ 懼有伏焉。³⁸ 吾視其轍亂，望其旗靡，³⁹ 故逐之。」

## 📑 註釋 (Annotations)

1. 左傳　　　　Zuǒzhuàn　　　*Zuo Commentary.* The original title of the book was *Chūnqiū Zuǒshì zhuàn*《春秋左氏傳》purporting to be a commentary on the *Chūnqiū* 《春秋》(*The Spring and Autumn Annals*) which is a succinct year-by-year record of events

significant for the state of Lu. The author of the *Zuozhuan* was assumed to be Zuǒ Qiūmíng 左丘明, but this is a controversial issue.

| 莊公十年 | Zhuānggōng shí nián | the tenth year of Duke Zhuang of Lu's reign; events listed in the *Spring and Autumn Annals* and narrated in fuller detail in the *Zuo Commentary* are arranged according to the chronology of the Lu state during the Spring and Autumn period. |
| 曹劌 | Cáo Guì | name of a person. |
| 論 | lùn | to discourse on (a subject). |
| 戰 | zhàn | battle. |
| 2. 十年春 | shí nián chūn | the spring of the tenth year (of Duke Zhuang of Lu)—684 B.C. |
| 3. 我 | wǒ | us; here referring to the state of Lu. |
| 4. 請 | qǐng | to request. |
| 5. 鄉人 | xiāng rén | the people who live in the same 鄉 (an administrative unit corresponding to a district in the Zhou Dynasty). |
| 6. 肉食者 | ròu shí zhě | meat eaters, i.e., the elite, who are allowed the privilege of participating in sacrifices. |
| 7. 間 | jiàn | to intervene. |
| 8. 鄙 | bǐ | shortsighted. (Note that the meaning of 鄙 in pre-Qin times is different from its Modern Chinese meaning of "despicable".) |
| 9. 遠謀 | yuǎn móu | to make a farsighted plan. |
| 10. 專 | zhuān | to monopolize. |
| 11. 分 | fēn | to share. |

| | | |
|---|---|---|
| 12. 惠 | huì | kindness; favor. |
| 偏 | biàn | universal. (A variant form of 遍.) |
| 13. 犧牲 | xī shēng | sacrificial animal. |
| 帛 | bó | silk. |
| 14. 加 | jiā | to overstate; here, to make a false report to the deities (about the quantities of sacrificial animals, jades, and silk). |
| 15. 信 | xìn | true; trustworthy. |
| 16. 孚 | fú | to trust. |
| 17. 福 | fú | to bless. (A verb.) |
| 18. 獄 | yù | lawsuit. (Note that the meaning of 獄 in pre-Qin times is different from its Modern Chinese meaning of "prison".) |
| 19. 察 | chá | to be discerning. |
| 20. 情 | qíng | fact; here, it refers to the facts of the case. |
| 21. 忠 | zhōng | devotion. |
| 屬 | shǔ | category. (A noun.) |
| 22. 可 | kě | may. |
| 以 | yǐ | with. (A preposition.) (The object 之, referring to 忠, is omitted.) |
| 23. 與 | yǔ | with. (A preposition.) |
| 乘 | chéng | to mount. |
| 24. 于 | yú | mostly equivalent to 於, but is often used before a place word. (A preposition.) |
| 長勺 | Chángsháo | name of a place. |

| 25. | 鼓 | gǔ | to drum. (A verb.) |
| | 鼓之 | gǔ zhī | to drum in order to order the soldiers forward. 之 refers to Lu's army. |
| 26. | 未可 | wèi kě | not yet. (Literally, it means "not yet possible".) |
| 27. | 敗績 | bài jī | utterly defeated. (The original meaning is "collapse of a chariot"; here, its derivative meaning is "collapse of an army".) |
| 28. | 馳 | chí | to gallop. |
| | 馳之 | chí zhī | galloping and pursuing them. 之 refers to Qi's army. |
| 29. | 轍 | zhé | track of a wheel. |
| 30. | 望 | wàng | to gaze into the distance. |
| 31. | 逐 | zhú | to pursue. |
| 32. | 勇氣 | yǒng qì | courageous spirit. |
| 33. | 作 | zuò | to rouse. |
| 34. | 衰 | shuāi | to flag. |
| 35. | 竭 | jié | to be exhausted. |
| 36. | 盈 | yíng | full. |
| 37. | 難測 | nán cè | difficult to fathom. |
| 38. | 懼 | jù | to fear. |
| | 伏 | fú | ambush. |
| 39. | 靡 | mǐ | to droop. |

## 文法闡釋 (Grammar Notes)

### I. 肉食者謀之，又何間焉？

The adverb 又 means "in addition to that", referring to what is just said, so it can simply be implied by "then" in translation. The verb 間 means literally "get between (certain things or people)", hence, "to get involved; to intervene". So the whole sentence means: "Since the meat-eaters are worrying about it, then why do you have to get involved in that?"

### II. 忠之屬也，可以一戰

Two separate but related sentences are given here. The first one is an equational sentence, with 忠之屬 as its predicate, so the sentence means "(That) is a type of devotion thing". The second sentence does not have an overt subject either, but the verb 可 generally means "it is possible". 以 is here a co-verb ("with") with "devotion" as its understood object. The phrase 以一戰 then functions as a complement to the verb 可. This sentence means, therefore, "It is possible therewith to fight a war".

# 十七.《左傳·僖公四年》： 齊桓公伐楚[1]

📖 **課文 (Text)**

　　四年春，齊侯以諸侯之師侵蔡。[2] 蔡潰，[3] 遂伐楚。楚子使與師言曰：[4]「君處北海，[5] 寡人處南海，唯是風馬牛不相及也。[6] 不虞君之涉吾地也，[7] 何故？」管仲對曰：[8]「昔召康公命我先君大公曰：[9] 五侯九伯，[10] 女實征之，[11] 以夾輔周室。[12] 賜我先君履：[13] 東至于海，西至于河，[14] 南至于穆陵，[15] 北至于無棣。[16] 爾貢包茅不入，[17] 王祭不共，[18] 無以縮酒，[19] 寡人是徵；[20] 昭王南征而不復，[21] 寡人是問。[22]」對曰：「貢之不入，寡君之罪也，[23] 敢不共給？[24] 昭王之不復，君其問諸水濱！[25]」師進，[26] 次于陘。[27]

　　夏，楚子使屈完如師。[28] 師退，[29] 次于召陵。[30] 齊侯陳諸侯之師，[31] 與屈完乘而觀之。齊侯曰：「豈不穀是為？[32] 先君之好是繼！[33] 與不穀同好，[34] 如何？」對曰：「君惠徼福於敝邑之社稷，[35] 辱收寡君，[36] 寡君之願也。[37]」齊侯曰：「以此眾戰，[38] 誰能禦之？以此攻城，何城不克？[39]」對曰：「君若以德綏諸侯，[40] 誰敢不服。[41] 君若以力，楚國方城以為城，[42] 漢水以為池，[43] 雖眾，無所用之！」屈完及諸侯盟。

## 📋 註釋 (Annotations)

1. 僖公四年　Xī gōng sì nián　the fourth year of Duke Xi of Lu—656 B.C.

   齊桓公　Qí Huángōng　Duke Huan of Qi, a sovereign of the Qi state, the first of the five most influential feudal lords of the Spring and Autumn period.

2. 齊侯　Qí Hóu　the Marquis of Qi. (See 文法闡釋 I.)

   諸侯　zhū hóu　a general reference to the sovereigns of states who were vassals of the King of Zhou.

   侵　qīn　to invade without declaration of war.

   蔡　Cài　a small state located between Chu and other states in central China.

3. 潰　kuì　to collapse.

4. 楚子　Chǔ Zǐ　the Viscount of Chu. (Here it refers to the King Chéng of Chu 楚成王. The King of Zhou designated the ruler of Chu as a "viscount", but the ruler of Chu called himself "king".)

   使　shǐ　through a messenger; by means of a representative. (An adverb.)

   言　yán　to speak. (A verb.)

5. 君　jūn　the honorific form for the second-person pronoun, here it refers to 齊桓公.

   處　chǔ　to live (in or by). (A verb.)

6. 風馬牛不相及　fēng mǎ niú bù xiāng jí　As a horse and a cow are at the time of mating, they do not reach out to each other. (This is a very early metaphor, meaning, "You and I [or any two entities] have absolutely nothing to do with each other".)

7. 不虞      bù yú      do not expect.

     涉      shè      to wade through or into (water), here, to enter.

8. 管仲      Guǎn Zhòng      prime minister of Qi under 桓公.

9. 召康公      Shào Kānggōng      Duke Kang of Shao, a high minister of King Chéng of Zhou 周成王.

     先君      xiān jūn      the late lord. (A term referring to one's ancestor.)

     大公      Tàigōng      King Wu's prime minister who assisted him in founding the Zhou Dynasty and was enfeoffed as the first Marquis of Qi.

10. 伯      bó      chief.

     五侯九伯      wǔ hóu jiǔ bó      all the sovereigns who are vassals to the king.

11. 女      rǔ      you. (Written as 汝 in later times.)

     實      shí      expressing the imperative mood. (A particle.)

     征      zhēng      to make a punitive attack (when necessary).

12. 夾      jiā      to buttress. (夾 is equivalent to 輔.)

     輔      fǔ      to assist (a ruler).

     周室      Zhōu shì      the royal house of Zhou.

13. 履      lǚ      to step on; to set foot on. Here used as a noun meaning "footwear".

14. 河      Hé      the Yellow River. (See Lesson 12, p. 104.)

15. 穆陵      Mùlíng      a place (in southern Shandong province).

16. 無棣      Wúdì      a place (now in northern Shandong province).

17. 爾貢      ěr gòng      the tribute for which you are responsible.

     包茅      bāo máo      bundled rush.

| | 入 | rù | to enter; to be entered; to be presented. |
| 18. | 祭 | jì | sacrifice. |
| | 共 | gōng | to supply. (Written as 供 in later times.) |
| 19. | 縮酒 | suō jiǔ | to pour the wine through the bundled rush. (This is the sacrificial rite which symbolizes the deities drinking the wine.) |
| 20. | 徵 | zhēng | to ask for; to demand an explanation for. |
| 21. | 昭王 | Zhāowáng | King Zhao, a tyrannical king of the Zhou Dynasty. (When he went on an inspection tour and had to cross the Han River, the local people provided him with a fancy boat assembled with glue. Consequently, the boat disintegrated and he drowned.) |
| | 復 | fù | to return; to come back. |
| 22. | 問 | wèn | to ask about; to demand an explanation for. |
| 23. | 寡君 | guǎ jūn | a term used for referring to one's own ruler when speaking to the ruler of another state. |
| | 罪 | zuì | fault; offense. |
| 24. | 敢不 | gǎn bù | how dare I not … ? (See 文法闡釋 III.) |
| 25. | 濱 | bīn | shore; waterfront. |
| 26. | 進 | jìn | to go forward; to advance. |
| 27. | 次 | cì | (army) to be temporarily stationed; to encamp. |
| | 陘 | Xíng | a mountain (in Henan province). |
| 28. | 屈完 | Qū Wán | a minister of Chu. |
| | 如 | rú | to go to. |
| 29. | 退 | tuì | to retreat; to pull back. |

| 30. | 召陵 | Shàolíng | a place (in Henan province). |
|---|---|---|---|
| 31. | 陳 | chén | to display; to line up in formation. |
| 32. | 不穀 | bù gǔ | humble reference to oneself used by a king or prince. (Literally, it means "this no good person".) |
|  | 為 | wèi | to be for; to work for. |
| 33. | 好 | hǎo | good relationship; friendship. |
|  | 繼 | jì | to resume. |
| 34. | 同好 | tóng hǎo | to enjoy good relations with each other; to share the same intention. |
| 35. | 惠 | huì | kindly (a term often used in polite speech to show appreciation). (An adverb.) |
|  | 徼福 | jiǎo fú | to ask for blessings. |
|  | 敝 | bì | humble form for "my" or "our". |
|  | 邑 | yì | state. |
| 36. | 辱 | rǔ | by disgracing yourself. (An adverb.) |
|  | 收 | shōu | to accept. |
| 37. | 願 | yuàn | wish. |
| 38. | 眾 | zhòng | multitude; here it means "the multitude of soldiers". |
| 39. | 克 | kè | to conquer; to subdue. |
| 40. | 綏 | suí | to placate. |
| 41. | 服 | fú | to obey; to be submissive. |
| 42. | 方城 | Fāngchéng | a mountain range between Chu and central China. |
|  | 城 | chéng | fortress; fortification. |

43. 漢水　　　Hànshuǐ　　　the Han River.

池　　　　chí　　　　moat.

## ☀ 文法闡釋 (Grammar Notes)

### I. 齊侯 versus 齊桓公

These two titles refer to the same person in the present selection, but there is a technical difference. In both the 《春秋》 and the 《左傳》, when general reference to the ruler of a state was made, the formula is: state-name plus its feudal rank, for example, 齊侯 "The Marquis of Qi", 楚子 "The Viscount of Chu", and 周公 "The Duke of Zhou", etc. But when a particular ruler was mentioned, the formula is: state-name plus the ruler's name plus "gong", regardless of the particular feudal rank of the state, for example, 齊桓公, 晉文公, and 魯哀公. The term 公 used in this way means "lord", rather than "duke". But in translation, 公 is usually rendered as "duke".

### II. 楚子使與師言

The noun 使 "envoy" functions in this sentence as an adverb, meaning "through an envoy". Therefore, the words carried by the envoy represent direct speech from the boss, as it is here in this and the following examples. So this sentence should be translated as, "The Viscount of Chu said to the (Qi) army through an envoy".

### III. 敢不共給

The formula 敢不 + VP represents a rhetorical question of courtesy, with the speaker as the understood subject. Therefore, the sentence means: "How would I dare not to supply?"

### IV. 君其問諸水濱

其 is a modal marker for non-assertiveness, hence, courtesy. 諸 is here the phonetic fusion of the pronoun 之 and the particle 於. In Classical Chinese, "river" is simply 水 (江 and 河 are proper nouns, meaning the Yangtze and Yellow Rivers respectively). So this sentence means: "Your Highness should perhaps ask about that by the bank of the river".

## V. 豈不穀是為？先君之好是繼！

These two sentences share the same understood subject ("what we are doing" or "this campaign"), and form a pair as question and answer. The question is rhetorical because of the adverb 豈 "How could it be that … ?" 不穀 is the object of the verb 為, and the pronoun 是 refers back to 不穀 for emphasis. The structure of 先君之好是繼 is the same. So these two sentences can be translated as: "How could it be that this is just for me? It is actually to resume the good relations between our forefathers!"

## VI. 君惠徼福於敝邑之社稷，辱收寡君，寡君之願也。

Syntactically, this is an equational sentence with a complex subject. Its predicate is simply 寡君之願也, but its subject consists of two clauses which are closely related semantically, that is, the first clause 君惠徼福於敝邑之社稷 implies the second 辱收寡君. Note that the two words 惠 and 辱 both function here as adverbs. So this sentence can be literally translated as: "That Your Highness kindly comes to seek blessings at the national shrine of our humble state, and (by that gesture), at the risk of disgracing yourself, accept our humble ruler (as an associate of yours), is exactly the wish of our humble ruler".

# 十八.《左傳‧襄公三十一年》：
## 子產論治[1]

## 📖 課文 (Text)

　　子皮欲使尹何為邑，²子產曰：「少，³未知可否。」⁴
子皮曰：「愿，⁵吾愛之，不吾叛也。⁶使夫往而學焉，⁷
夫亦愈知治矣。」子產曰：「不可。人之愛人，求利之
也。今吾子愛人則以政，猶未能操刀而使割也，⁸其傷
實多。⁹子之愛人，傷之而已。其誰敢求愛於子，¹⁰子
於鄭國，棟也。¹¹棟折榱崩，¹²僑將厭焉，¹³敢不盡言。
子有美錦，不使人學製焉。¹⁴大官大邑，¹⁵身之所庇
也，¹⁶而使學者製焉。¹⁷其為美錦不亦多乎？¹⁸僑聞學
而後入政，未聞以政學者也。若果行此，¹⁹必有所害。
譬如田獵，²⁰射御貫則能獲禽，²¹若未嘗登車射御，²²
則敗績厭覆是懼，²³何暇思獲？」²⁴子皮曰：「善哉！虎
不敏，²⁵吾聞君子務知大者遠者，²⁶小人務知小者近
者。我小人也。衣服附在吾身，²⁷我知而慎之。²⁸大官
大邑所以庇身也，我遠而慢之。²⁹微子之言，³⁰吾不知
也⋯。」

## 📑 註釋 (Annotations)

1. 襄公　　　Xiānggōng　the thirty-first year of Duke Xiang of Lu—542 B.C.
　三十一年　sān shí yī nián

　子產　　　Zǐchǎn　　name of a person. A famous statesman in the
　　　　　　　　　　　Spring and Autumn period.

| | | |
|---|---|---|
| 治 | zhì | to govern; here, how to govern. |
| 2. 子皮 | Zǐpí | name of a person. A minister of the state of Zhèng 鄭. |
| 尹何 | Yǐn Hé | name of a person. |
| 為 | wéi | to do; to manage. (A verb.) |
| 邑 | yì | town; district. |
| 為邑 | wéi yì | to be the administrator of a town. |
| 3. 少 | shào | young. (It means Yin He is too young.) |
| 4. 否 | fǒu | or not. |
| 5. 愿 | yuàn | honest. (It means Yin He is honest.) |
| 6. 叛 | pàn | to betray. |
| 7. 夫 | fú | here it means "he". (A demonstrative pronoun.) |
| 8. 操 | cāo | to hold; to handle. |
| 9. 實 | shí | definitely. (An adverb.) |
| 10. 其 | qí | (A modal particle.) if I may ask, …. (An adverb suggesting non-assertion, hence, courtesy.) |
| 11. 於 | yú | for. (A preposition.) |
| 棟 | dòng | ridgepole. |
| 12. 榱 | cuī | rafter. |
| 崩 | bēng | to collapse. |
| 13. 僑 | Qiáo | formal name of 子產. |
| 厭 | yā | to press down on. (Written as 壓 in later times.) |
| 14. 製 | zhì | to make (clothing). |
| 15. 官 | guān | office. (See Lesson 5, p. 65–66.) |

| 16. 庇 | bì | to shelter; to protect. |
|---|---|---|
| 17. 學者 | xué zhě | learner; student. |
| 18. 為 | wéi | used here as 於, expressing comparison. |
| 19. 果 | guǒ | indeed; really. (An adverb.) |
| 行 | xíng | to put into practice; to carry out. |
| 20. 田 | tián | to hunt. (A verb.) |
| 21. 射 | shè | to shoot. |
| 御 | yù | to drive. |
| 貫 | guàn | to be accustomed. (Written as 慣 in later times.) |
| 獲 | huò | to catch. |
| 禽 | qín | to catch. (Written as 擒 in later times.) |
| 22. 未嘗 | wèi cháng | never. |
| 車 | chē | chariot; carriage. The old reading for 車 is jū. |
| 23. 敗績 | bài jī | overturning of the chariot. (This is the original meaning of the word.) |
| 覆 | fù | to turn over. |
| 24. 暇 | xiá | leisure. |
| 思 | sī | to think of. |
| 25. 虎 | Hǔ | formal name of 子皮. |
| 26. 務 | wù | to make an effort towards; to seek. |
| 27. 附 | fù | to adhere; here, to be next to. |
| 28. 慎 | shèn | careful. |
| 29. 遠 | yuàn | to distance from; to regard (it) as being far away from oneself. (Used as a putative verb.) |
| 慢 | màn | to slight; to ignore. (A verb.) |
| 30. 微 | wēi | but for. |

## ☀ 文法闡釋 (Grammar Notes)

### I. 人之愛人，求利之也。今吾子愛人則以政。

We have here two sentences which contrast with each other. The contrastive force comes from the conjunction 則 which may seem a bit unusual, because it does not seem to help form a conditional sentence as it usually does, though it comes between the two verb phrases 愛人 and 以政. Actually, the use of 則 is triggered by analogy with the first sentence which implies 人愛人, 則求利之, and thus acquires a contrastive sense which can better be expressed by "but" in English. So the two sentences can be translated as: "When other people love someone, (they) seek to benefit him; but now when you love someone, (you) assign a government office (to him, which will probably hurt him)".

### II. 大官大邑，身之所庇也。

The predicate of this equational sentence should actually be 身之所以庇也, that is, with the co-verb 以 after the nominalizer 所. This can be seen from 大官大邑所以庇身也, a slightly different version of the sentence that comes later in the text. The difference between the two versions is that the object (here, 身) of the main verb (here, 庇) may be moved to the position before 所 and serves as a possessive noun. When this happens, "omission" of co-verbs like 以 and 於 after 所 is a common practice in standard Classical Chinese, though later imitations normally include them. Thus, this sentence is translated as, "High office and large towns are what protect the person".

### III. 若果行此，必有所害。

Note that 若 and 果 are separate words in Classical Chinese (not a compound as in Modern Chinese). Alone, the first is a conjunction meaning "if", while the second is an adverb meaning "truly; really". The sentence means, therefore, "If (you) really do this, there will definitely be someone/something that gets hurt."

# 十九.《國語‧越語上》：
## 句踐治越[1]

## 📖 課文 (Text)

　　句踐之地，南至於句無，<sup>2</sup> 北至於禦兒，<sup>3</sup> 東至於
鄞，<sup>4</sup> 西至於姑蔑，<sup>5</sup> 廣運百里。<sup>6</sup> 乃致其父母昆弟而誓
之曰：<sup>7</sup>「寡人聞，古之賢君，四方之民歸之，<sup>8</sup> 若水之
歸下也。今寡人不能，<sup>9</sup> 將帥二三子夫婦以蕃。<sup>10</sup>」令壯
者無取老婦，<sup>11</sup> 令老者無取壯妻。女子十七不嫁，其父
母有罪；丈夫二十不取，其父母有罪。將免者以告，<sup>12</sup>
公令醫守之。<sup>13</sup> 生丈夫，<sup>14</sup> 二壺酒，一犬；生女子，二
壺酒，一豚。<sup>15</sup> 生三人，公與之母；<sup>16</sup> 生二人，公與之
餼。<sup>17</sup> 當室者死，<sup>18</sup> 三年釋其政；<sup>19</sup> 支子死，<sup>20</sup> 三月釋
其政。必哭泣葬埋之，如其子。<sup>21</sup> 令孤子、寡婦、疾
疹、貧病者，納宦其子。<sup>22</sup> 其達士，絜其居，<sup>23</sup> 美其
服，飽其食，而摩厲之於義。<sup>24</sup> 四方之士來者，必廟禮
之。<sup>25</sup> 句踐載稻與脂於舟以行，<sup>26</sup> 國之孺子之遊者，<sup>27</sup> 無
不餔也，<sup>28</sup> 無不歠也，<sup>29</sup> 必問其名。非其身之所種則不
食，<sup>30</sup> 非其夫人之所織則不衣，<sup>31</sup> 十年不收於國，<sup>32</sup> 民
俱有三年之食。<sup>33</sup>

## 📋 註釋 (Annotations)

1. 國語　　　　　Guóyǔ　　　　*Conversations from the States*. A semi-historical
　　　　　　　　　　　　　　　　record of events and dialogues from the Spring
　　　　　　　　　　　　　　　　and Autumn period organized by state.

| | | | |
|---|---|---|---|
| | 越語 | Yuè yǔ | "Conversations from Yue." A section from the *Guoyu*. Yue was a state in the southeastern part of China. |
| | 句踐 | Gōu Jiàn | a king of the state of Yue. He was earlier defeated by the state of Wú 吳. This text relates how he built up his strength and prepared to seek revenge against Wu. (句 is also written as 勾.) |
| 2. | 句無 | Gōuwú | name of a place. |
| 3. | 禦兒 | Yù' ér | name of a place. |
| 4. | 鄞 | Yín | name of a place. |
| 5. | 姑蔑 | Gūmiè | name of a place. |
| 6. | 廣 | guǎng | length from east to west. |
| | 運 | yùn | length from north to south. |
| | 廣運百里 | guǎng yùn bǎi lǐ | an area of 100,000 (100 × 100) square *li*. (1 *li* is about a third of a mile.) |
| 7. | 致 | zhì | to call together. |
| | 昆 | kūn | elder brother. |
| | 誓 | shì | to swear. |
| 8. | 四方 | sì fāng | four directions; places in all four directions. |
| 9. | 不能 | bù néng | incapable. |
| 10. | 帥 | shuài | to lead. (Usually written as 率.) |
| | 二三子 | èr sān zǐ | a polite term for "you gentlemen". (See Lesson 5, p. 62–63.) |
| | 蕃 | fán | to multiply; to increase a population. |
| 11. | 無 | wú | do not. (A substitute for 毋 wú.) |

| 取 | qǔ | (of a man) to get married. (Written as 娶 in later times.) |
| 婦 | fù | wife. |
| 12. 免 | miǎn | to give birth to a child. (Written as 娩 in later times.) |
| 13. 公 | gōng | official. |
| 醫 | yī | doctor. (A variant form of 醫.) |
| 14. 丈夫 | zhàng fū | a man; a male. |
| 15. 豚 | tún | pig. |
| 16. 生三人 | shēng sān rén | here, to give birth to triplets. |
| 母 | mǔ | here, a wet nurse. |
| 17. 餼 | xì | grain (presented to others). |
| 18. 當室者 | dāng shì zhě | here, the eldest son. |
| 19. 釋 | shì | to release. |
| 政 | zhèng | government affairs; here it refers to corvée. |
| 20. 支子 | zhī zǐ | a son by a concubine. |
| 21. 葬埋 | zàng mái | to bury. |
| 其子 | qí zǐ | his son; here it refers to "his eldest son" (referring to the 當室者, thus the funeral rites resemble those for the eldest son). |
| 22. 孤子 | gū zǐ | orphan (a boy) whose father is dead. |
| 寡婦 | guǎ fù | widow. |
| 疾 | jí | illness. |
| 疹 | zhěn | disease. |

| 納 | nà | to let somebody enter. |
| 宦 | huàn | to study in a school run by officials. (A verb.) |
| 納宦其子 | nà huàn qí zǐ | to let their sons enter a school run by officials (so that the officials will supply food for their sons). |
| 23. 達士 | dá shì | a learned scholar. |
| 絜 | jié | clean. (Same as 潔, here used as a causative verb. The ensuing 美 and 飽 are used in a similar fashion. Note that the causative 美 is different from the putative 美.) (See Lesson 10, p. 95–96.) |
| 居 | jū | residence. (A noun.) |
| 24. 摩 | mó | to grind. (This character borrows its meaning from 磨.) |
| 厲 | lì | to grind. |
| 摩厲 | mó lì | here, it means "to cultivate". |
| 25. 廟 | miào | ancestral temple. |
| 禮 | lǐ | ritual; here used as a verb, meaning "to greet according to ritual". |
| 26. 脂 | zhī | fat; here it means meat. |
| 27. 孺子 | rú zǐ | children; here it means the young. |
| 遊 | yóu | to travel; here it means "to travel to study in a place far away from one's hometown". |
| 28. 無 | wú | no one. (A pronoun.) |
| 餔 | bū | to feed. |
| 29. 歠 | chuò | to drink; here it is a causative, thus, to make somebody drink. |
| 30. 種 | zhòng | to plant. |

31.  夫人    fū rén    wife (of the king).

     織      zhī       to weave.

     衣      yī        to wear. (A verb.)

32.  收      shōu      to collect; here it refers to collecting taxes.

33.  俱      jù        all. (An adverb.)

     食      shí       food; here it refers to grains.

## ☀ 文法闡釋 (Grammar Notes)

## I. 女子十七不嫁，其父母有罪。

This is a conditional sentence, though it does not include the conjunction 則 between its two clauses. (The next eight sentences are of the same kind.) 有罪 means literally "to have a crime", but in actual terms, "to be punished". So the sentence should be translated as: "If/When a girl, turning seventeen, does not marry, her parents will be punished".

## II. 其達士，絜其居，美其服，飽其食⋯。

This is also a conditional sentence. 其達士 is a noun phrase but stands as the conditional clause "If/When it comes to (or As for) the learned figures of the state". The verb phrases that follow represent the main clause with "he (the king)" as the understood subject. 絜, 美, and 飽 are all causative verbs. So the main clause means "he made their residence clean, their clothes beautiful, and their food abundant".

# 二十.《戰國策·齊策一》：
## 靖郭君將城薛[1]

## 📖 課文 (Text)

靖郭君將城薛，客多以諫。² 靖郭君謂謁者，³ 无
為客通。⁴ 齊人有請者曰：⁵ 「臣請三言而已矣！⁶ 益一
言，⁷ 臣請烹。」靖郭君因見之。⁸ 客趨而進曰：⁹ 「海大
魚。」因反走。君曰：「客，有於此。」¹⁰ 客曰：「鄙臣不
敢以死為戲。」¹¹ 君曰：「亡，¹² 更言之。」¹³ 對曰：「君不
聞大魚乎？網不能止，¹⁴ 鉤不能牽，蕩而失水，¹⁵ 則螻
蟻得意焉。¹⁶ 今夫齊亦君之水也。君長有齊，奚以薛
為？¹⁷ 夫齊，雖隆薛之城到於天，¹⁸ 猶之無益也。」君
曰：「善。」乃輟城薛。¹⁹

## 📒 註釋 (Annotations)

| | | | |
|---|---|---|---|
| 1. | 戰國策 | Zhànguó cè | *The Intrigues of the Warring States*, a book purportedly containing the historical events, the speeches, and the actions of the strategists in the Warring States period. |
| | 齊策一 | Qí cè yī | "Intrigues of Qi: Part One", title of a section from the *Zhanguo ce*. |
| | 靖郭君 | Jìngguō jūn | a lord of the state of Qi. 靖郭 is his title. |
| | 城 | chéng | city wall; here used as a verb meaning "to build a city wall". |
| | 薛 | Xuē | name of a place. 靖郭君's fief. |
| 2. | 客 | kè | a retainer in a lord's household. |

| 諫 | jiàn | (for one in a lower position) to advise (one of a higher status). |
| 3. 謁 | yè | to have an audience. |
| 謁者 | yè zhě | person in charge of receiving guests and visitors. |
| 4. 无 | wú | more commonly written as 无, it is the same as 無. |
| 通 | tōng | to announce a visitor. |
| 5. 請 | qǐng | to request; here it means "to request an audience". |
| 6. 言 | yán | word. |
| 三言 | sān yán | here, to say three words. |
| 7. 益 | yì | to add to. |
| 8. 因 | yīn | therefore. (An adverb.) |
| 9. 進 | jìn | to go forward. (Note that in pre-Qin Chinese 進 does not mean "to enter".) |
| 10. 客，有於此 | kè, yǒu yú cǐ | sir, remain in this place, i.e., sir, please stay. |
| 11. 鄙臣 | bǐ chén | your humble servant. |
| 以死為戲 | yǐ sǐ wéi xì | to treat death as a joke. |
| 12. 亡 | wú | nothing; here it means "forget it". |
| 13. 更 | gèng | further. (An adverb.) |
| 14. 網 | wǎng | net; here it means a fishnet. |
| 止 | zhǐ | to stop. |
| 15. 蕩 | dàng | to wash up. |
| 蕩而失水 | dàng ér shī shuǐ | to be out of the water after being washed ashore. |

16. 螻          lóu          mole cricket.

    蟻          yǐ           ant.

    得意        dé yì        to get one's wish.

17. 奚          xī           why?

18. 隆          lóng         high; here used as a causative verb meaning "to
                             make something high".

19. 輟          chuò         to stop.

---

### ☼ 文法闡釋 (Grammar Note)

## 君長有齊，奚以薛為？

This is a conditional sentence, though the conjunction 則 is not included. In the
conditional clause, 長 is an adverb ("always; permanently"), so the clause can be
translated as: "If Your Highness always has Qi", or idiomatically, "As long as you
keep Qi". The main clause is a rhetorical question where 奚 (same as 何) means
"why", so the clause can be rendered as: "why do you have to do (anything) with
Xue?"

# 二十一.《戰國策·齊策四》:
## 馮諼客孟嘗君[1]

📖 **課文 (Text)**

　　齊人有馮諼者，貧乏不能自存，²使人屬孟嘗君，³願寄食門下。⁴孟嘗君曰：「客何好？⁵」曰：「客無好也。」曰：「客何能？」曰：「客無能也。」孟嘗君笑而受之曰：⁶「諾。⁷」

　　左右以君賤之也，⁸食以草具。⁹居有頃，¹⁰倚柱彈其劍，¹¹歌曰：¹²「長鋏歸來乎，¹³食無魚！」左右以告。孟嘗君曰：「食之，比門下之客。¹⁴」居有頃，復彈其鋏，歌曰：「長鋏歸來乎，出無車！」左右皆笑之，以告。孟嘗君曰：「為之駕，¹⁵比門下之車客。¹⁶」於是乘其車，揭其劍，¹⁷過其友曰：¹⁸「孟嘗君客我。¹⁹」後有頃，復彈其劍鋏，歌曰：「長鋏歸來乎，無以為家！」²⁰左右皆惡之，²¹以為貪而不知足。²²孟嘗君問：「馮公有親乎？²³」對曰：「有老母。」孟嘗君使人給其食用，²⁴無使乏。²⁵於是馮諼不復歌。

　　後孟嘗君出記，²⁶問門下諸客：「誰習計會，²⁷能為文收責於薛者乎？²⁸」馮諼署曰：²⁹「能。」孟嘗君怪之，³⁰曰：「此誰也？」左右曰：「乃歌夫長鋏歸來者也。³¹」孟嘗君笑曰：「客果有能也，吾負之，³²未嘗見也。³³」請而見之，謝曰：³⁴「文倦於事，³⁵憒於憂，³⁶而性懧愚，³⁷

沉於國家之事，[38] 開罪於先生。[39] 先生不羞，[40] 乃有意欲為收責於薛乎？[41]」馮諼曰：「願之。[42]」於是約車治裝，[43] 載券契而行，[44] 辭曰：[45]「責畢收，[46] 以何市而反？[47]」孟嘗君曰：「視吾家所寡有者。[48]」

　　驅而之薛，[49] 使吏召諸民當償者，悉來合券。[50] 券遍合，起，[51] 矯命以責賜諸民，[52] 因燒其券，[53] 民稱萬歲。[54]

　　長驅到齊，[55] 晨而求見。[56] 孟嘗君怪其疾也，[57] 衣冠而見之，[58] 曰：「責畢收乎？來何疾也！」曰：「收畢矣。」「以何市而反？」馮諼曰：「君云『視吾家所寡有者』。臣竊計君宮中積珍寶，[59] 狗馬實外廄，[60] 美人充下陳。[61] 君家所寡有者以義耳！[62] 竊以為君市義。[63]」孟嘗君曰：「市義奈何？[64]」曰：「今君有區區之薛，[65] 不拊愛子其民，[66] 因而賈利之。[67] 臣竊矯君命，以責賜諸民，因燒其券，民稱萬歲。乃臣所以為君市義也。[68]」孟嘗君不說，[69] 曰：「諾，先生休矣！[70]」

　　後期年，[71] 齊王謂孟嘗君曰：[72]「寡人不敢以先王之臣為臣。[73]」孟嘗君就國於薛，[74] 未至百里，[75] 民扶老攜幼，[76] 迎君道中。[77] 孟嘗君顧謂馮諼：「先生所為文市義者，乃今日見之。」

## 📝 註釋 (Annotations)

1. 馮諼      Féng Xuān      name of a person.

     客      kè      to be a guest. (A verb.) Here, to be a retainer to (someone).

     孟嘗君      Mèngcháng jūn      Lord Mengchang, a prince of the state of Qi, known for his patronage of numerous 客, or retainers.

     N. B. In the original, the title for this story is "齊人有馮諼者"—the first sentence from the main text.

2. 乏      fá      lack.

     自存      zì cún      to keep oneself alive.

3. 使      shǐ      to let.

     屬      zhǔ      to entrust.

4. 寄食      jì shí      to depend on others for one's food.

     門下      mén xià      in someone's house.

     願寄食門下      yuàn jì shí mén xià      to wish to be a retainer in someone's, here Lord Mengchang's, house.

5. 好      hào      to like.

6. 受      shòu      to accept.

7. 諾      nuò      corresponding to "yes" in English.

8. 左右      zuǒ yòu      attendants; close aides.

     君      jūn      the lord, i.e., Lord Mengchang.

     賤      jiàn      lowly; humble. Here, used as a putative verb meaning "to look down on (someone)".

9. 食      sì      to feed. (A verb.)

| 草具 | cǎo jù | coarse food. Some interpret this as "coarse food container". |
| 10. 有頃 | yǒu qǐng | after a little while. |
| 11. 倚 | yǐ | to lean on. |
| 彈 | tán | to tap. |
| 劍 | jiàn | sword. |
| 12. 歌 | gē | to sing; to chant. (A verb.) |
| 13. 鋏 | jiá | sword hilt; here, the sword. |
| 來 | lái | similar to 了 in Modern Chinese. (A particle.) |
| 14. 比 | bǐ | on par with. |
| 15. 駕 | jià | chariot and horses. |
| 16. 車客 | chē kè | a retainer equipped with a carriage. |
| 17. 揭 | jiē | to hold up in the air. (Note that in Classical Chinese 揭 does not mean "to tear off" or "to uncover" as it does in Modern Chinese.) |
| 18. 過 | guò | to visit. |
| 19. 客我 | kè wǒ | to accept me as a retainer. |
| 20. 無以為家 | wú yǐ wéi jiā | to have nothing with which to maintain one's family. |
| 21. 惡 | wù | to dislike. |
| 22. 貪 | tān | greedy. |
| 知足 | zhī zú | content. (Literally, knowing what is enough.) |
| 23. 公 | gōng | honorific term for addressing a person, corresponding to "Mister" in English. |

| 親 | qīn | parents. (Note that in Classical Chinese 親 always means "parents", not "relatives".) |
| 24. 用 | yòng | daily necessities. (A noun.) |
| 25. 無 | wú | don't. (A substitute for 毋.) |
| 26. 後 | hòu | later. |
| 出 | chū | to take out. |
| 記 | jì | account book. |
| 27. 習 | xí | to be learned in. |
| 計會 | jì kuài | accounting. |
| 28. 責 | zhài | debt. (Written as 債 in later times.) |
| 薛 | Xuē | Lord Mengchang's fief. |
| 29. 署 | shǔ | to write and sign one's name. |
| 30. 怪 | guài | strange; here used as a putative verb meaning "to find it strange". |
| 31. 夫 | fú | that. (A demonstrative pronoun.) |
| 32. 負 | fù | to be unfair to. |
| 33. 見 | jiàn | to give an audience. |
| 34. 謝 | xiè | to apologize. |
| 35. 倦 | juàn | weary; tired. |
| 於 | yú | due to. |
| 事 | shì | affairs. |
| 36. 憒 | kuì | to be muddled. |
| 37. 性 | xìng | nature. |
| 懧 | nuò | weak. (This normally is written as 懦.) |

| | | |
|---|---|---|
| 愚 | yú | foolish. |
| 38. 沉 | chén | to be immersed or overwhelmed. |
| 國家 | guó jiā | state. |
| 39. 開罪 | kāi zuì | to offend. |
| 先生 | xiān shēng | honorific form of address, corresponding to "sir" in English. |
| 40. 羞 | xiū | shame; here used as putative verb meaning "to think it is shameful". |
| 41. 乃 | nǎi | a modal particle implying unexpectedness or surprise. (A adverb.) |
| 為 | wèi | for. (Its object, Lord Mengchang, is omitted.) |
| 42. 之 | zhī | refers to collecting the debts. (A pronoun.) |
| 43. 約 | yuē | to tie together. |
| 約車 | yuē chē | to harness a horse to a carriage. |
| 治裝 | zhì zhuāng | to pack. |
| 44. 券契 | quàn qì | these two words both mean "tally". |
| 行 | xíng | to leave; to go. |
| 45. 辭 | cí | to take leave of. |
| 46. 畢 | bì | completely. |
| 47. 市 | shì | to buy. |
| 反 | fǎn | to return. (Written as 返 in later times.) |
| 48. 視 | shì | to see. |
| 49. 驅 | qū | to drive. |
| 之 | zhī | to go to. (A verb.) |

| 50. | 吏 | lì | minor officer. |
| | 召 | zhào | to summon. |
| | 諸 | zhū | all. |
| | 當 | dāng | should; ought to. |
| | 償 | cháng | to repay. |
| | 悉 | xī | all; entirely. |
| | 合 | hé | to put together; to match. |
| 51. | 起 | qǐ | to stand up. |
| 52. | 矯 | jiǎo | to falsify. |
| | 矯命 | jiǎo mìng | to falsify orders. |
| | 以責賜諸民 | yǐ zhài cì zhū mín | grant the people their debts, i.e., forgive the people their debts. (See 文法闡釋 III.) |
| 53. | 因 | yīn | thereupon. (An adverb.) |
| 54. | 稱 | chēng | to call; here, to shout. |
| | 萬歲 | wàn suì | an expression of praise, corresponding to "hurray" in English. |
| 55. | 長驅 | cháng qū | to drive without stopping. |
| | 到 | dào | to arrive. |
| 56. | 求 | qiú | to ask for; to beg. |
| 57. | 疾 | jí | fast. |
| 58. | 衣 | yì | to put on clothes; to wear clothes. (A verb.) |
| | 冠 | guàn | to put on a cap; to wear a cap. (A verb.) |
| 59. | 竊 | qiè | in my humble opinion. (A self-deprecatory adverb.) |

| | | |
|---|---|---|
| 計 | jì | to consider. |
| 宮 | gōng | house. (Note that in Classical Chinese 宮 means "house", not "palace".) |
| 積 | jī | to accumulate. |
| 珍 | zhēn | treasure. |
| 60. 實 | shí | to fill. |
| 廄 | jiù | stables. |
| 外廄 | wài jiù | in contrast to 內室, the stables are called 外廄. |
| 61. 美人 | měi rén | beauties. |
| 充 | chōng | to fill. |
| 下陳 | xià chén | the road in front of the hall. |
| 62. 以 | yǐ | only. (A substitute for 已.) |
| 義 | yì | justice; loyalty. |
| 63. 以 | yǐ | with. (A preposition.) (The object "money" is omitted.) |
| 64. 奈何 | nài hé | how; what do you mean? (An idiomatic form.) |
| 市義奈何 | shì yì nài hé | how do you buy loyalty? |
| 65. 區區 | qū qū | very small. |
| 66. 拊 | fǔ | to caress; to nurture. |
| 子 | zǐ | to treat as a son. (A verb.) (Note that the three verbs 拊, 愛, and 子 are used together with the object 其民.) |
| 67. 因 | yīn | because of. (A preposition.) (The object 有薛 is omitted.) |

| | 賈 | gǔ | merchant; here used as an adverb, meaning "as a merchant". |
|---|---|---|---|
| | 利 | lì | to seek profit. (A verb.) |
| 68. | 乃臣所以為君市義也 | nǎi chén suǒ yǐ wèi jūn shì yì yě | this is exactly how I bought loyalty for you! |
| 69. | 說 | yuè | pleased; delighted. (Written as 悅 in later times. See Lesson 1, p. 10.) |
| 70. | 休 | xiū | to rest. |
| 71. | 期 | jī | an entire (day, month, or year). |
| | 期年 | jī nián | a full year. |
| 72. | 齊王 | Qí Wáng | here referring to King Mǐn of Qi 齊湣王. |
| 73. | 先王 | xiān wáng | the late king, i.e., King Xuān of Qi 齊宣王. (Note that Lord Mengchang had been a minister of King Xuan. This is King Min's excuse to dismiss Lord Mengchang from his post.) |
| 74. | 就 | jiù | to go to. (A verb.) |
| | 就國 | jiù guó | to go back to one's fief. (An idiomatic phrase.) |
| 75. | 未至百里 | wèi zhì bǎi lǐ | still a hundred *li* away. |
| 76. | 扶 | fú | to support with the hand. |
| | 老 | lǎo | the old. (A noun.) |
| | 攜 | xié | to bring along. |
| | 幼 | yòu | the young. (A noun.) |
| 77. | 迎君道中 | yíng jūn dào zhōng | to welcome their lord on the way (in the middle of his journey). |

## 🔆 文法闡釋 (Grammar Notes)

### I. 左右以君賤之也，食以草具。

The first 以 is a co-verb with 君賤之 (a clause) as its object. As such, it means "because of; due to". The second 以 is, however, the main verb of the sentence, with 草具 as its object, and it means "to use". The verb 食 "to feed" represents here a subordinate clause with an adverbial role. So the sentence can be translated as: "Because the lord had a low opinion of him, the aides used coarse utensils when they brought food to him", implying that he was given low-quality food.

### II. 食無魚

This sentence has two clauses 食 and 無魚, meaning "When I eat, there is no fish". It expresses an ongoing situation, not a single event.

### III. 左右以告

The omitted object of the co-verb 以 is "what Feng did", while the omitted object of the verb 告 is "the lord". So the sentence means "The attendants reported it to Lord Mengchang." Note that verbs like 告 "to tell" and 贈 "to give" in Classical Chinese always have people as their object, while the thing transmitted is often introduced with the co-verb (preposition) 以.

### IV. 為之駕

為之駕 means "to make ready a chariot for him." 為 is here a verb. 之 and 駕 are double objects. This construction is similar to 為之足. (See 文法闡釋 V in Lesson 1, p. 21.)

### V. 孟嘗君客我 (馮諼) versus 馮諼客孟嘗君

The two sentences in this pair have switched subject and object. Thus, one would expect that they have different meanings, but actually they mean the same thing. This is because, when 客 functions as a verb, it may be either transitive or intransitive. In the first sentence, it is a causative verb (hence, transitive), meaning "to make or treat (someone) as a guest". In the second sentence, it is an intransitive verb, meaning "to be or live as a guest". In this case, we normally would expect to see the word 於 before its object, but that word is often skipped in Classical Chinese (e.g., 客美 means "to live as a visitor in the United States"). Therefore, the two sentences above should be translated as "Lord Mengchang makes me a guest of his" and "Feng Xuan lives as a guest of Lord Mengchang" respectively.

## VI. 竊以為君市義

The subject of this sentence is the speaker ("I"), with 市 "to trade" as the main verb and 義 "loyalty" as its object. 竊 is here an adverb ("stealthily") which people of lower positions often use as an apology when speaking to their superior, in the sense of "without proper authorization" or "presumptuously". 以 and 為 are unrelated co-verbs (they do not form a compound). So the sentence means, word by word, "(I), without asking for your authorization, with (the money I was supposed to have collected), for the sake of Your Lordship, purchased loyalty". (Note the word order in this sentence. In English, we would normally say, "I purchased justice for you with the money".)

# 二十二.《戰國策‧燕策一》：
## 燕昭王收破燕後即位[1]

## 📖 課文 (Text)

　　燕昭王收破燕後即位，卑身厚幣以招賢者，<sup>2</sup> 欲將以報讎。<sup>3</sup> 故往見郭隗先生曰：<sup>4</sup>「齊因孤國之亂而襲破燕。<sup>5</sup> 孤極知燕小力少不足以報。<sup>6</sup> 然得賢士與共國，以雪先王之恥，<sup>7</sup> 孤之願也。敢問以國報讎者奈何？<sup>8</sup>」

　　郭隗先生對曰：「…王誠博選國中之賢者而朝其門下，<sup>9</sup> 天下聞王朝其賢臣，天下之士必趨於燕矣。」

　　昭王曰：「寡人將誰朝而可？」郭隗先生曰：「臣聞古之君人，有以千金求千里馬者，三年不能得。涓人言於君曰：<sup>10</sup>『請求之。』君遣之。<sup>11</sup> 三月得千里馬，馬已死，買其首五百金，<sup>12</sup> 反以報君。<sup>13</sup> 君大怒曰：『所求者生馬，安事死馬而捐五百金？<sup>14</sup>』涓人對曰：『死馬且買之五百金，<sup>15</sup> 況生馬乎？<sup>16</sup> 天下必以王為能市馬，馬今至矣。<sup>17</sup>』於是不能期年，<sup>18</sup> 千里之馬至者三。今王誠欲致士，先從隗始；隗且見事，<sup>19</sup> 況賢於隗者乎？豈遠千里哉？」於是昭王為隗築宮而師之。<sup>20</sup> 樂毅自魏往，<sup>21</sup> 鄒衍自齊往，<sup>22</sup> 劇辛自趙往，<sup>23</sup> 士爭湊燕…。<sup>24</sup>

## 📑 註釋 (Annotations)

1. 燕策一　　　Yān cè yī　　　"Intrigues of Yan: Part One", title of a section from the *Zhanguo ce*.

| 燕昭王 | Yān Zhāowáng | King Zhao of Yan. Yan was located in what is now the Beijing area. |
|---|---|---|
| 收 | shōu | to collect; here, it means "to clear up (the mess)". |
| 破 | pò | to break or destroy; here, broken or destroyed. |
| 即位 | jí wèi | to ascend the throne. |
| 2. 卑 | bēi | humble; here used as a verb, to be humble. |
| 厚 | hòu | generous; handsome. |
| 幣 | bì | gift. (The original meaning is "a present of silk".) |
| 招 | zhāo | to invite. |
| 3. 報讎 | bào chóu | to take revenge. |
| 4. 郭隗 | Guō Wěi | name of a person. |
| 5. 孤 | gū | humble term used by a king to refer to himself. |
| 襲 | xí | to make a surprise attack on. |
| 齊因孤國之亂而襲破燕 | Qí yīn gū guó zhī luàn ér xí pò Yān | During the reign of King Kuài of Yan 燕噲王, King Zhao's father, Qi took advantage of some disorder in Yan, invaded, and subjugated the latter. |
| 6. 極 | jí | extremely. (An adverb.) |
| 報 | bào | to avenge. |
| 7. 雪 | xuě | to wipe out. |
| 恥 | chǐ | humiliation; shame. |
| 8. 奈何 | nài hé | how (to do). |
| 9. 誠 | chéng | indeed; really. |
| 選 | xuǎn | to select. |

|         | 朝           | cháo         | to have an audience with; to respectfully visit (someone for advice). |
|---------|-------------|--------------|--------------------------------|
| 10.     | 涓人         | juān rén     | a person whose job is to clean the palace. |
| 11.     | 遣           | qiǎn         | to send.                       |
| 12.     | 首           | shǒu         | head.                          |
| 13.     | 報           | bào          | to report.                     |
| 14.     | 事           | shì          | to do. (A verb.)               |
|         | 安事死馬      | ān shì sǐ mǎ | why are you searching for a dead horse? |
|         | 捐           | juān         | to discard; here, it means "to lose". |
| 15.     | 且           | qiě          | even. (A conjunction.)         |
| 16.     | 況           | kuàng        | let alone. (A conjunction.)    |
| 17.     | 今           | jīn          | now; in the context of this story, "immediately". |
| 18.     | 期年         | jī nián      | a full year.                   |
| 19.     | 事           | shì          | to serve; to wait on.          |
| 20.     | 築           | zhù          | to build.                      |
|         | 師           | shī          | instructor; here used as a verb meaning "to treat as an instructor". |
| 21.     | 樂毅         | Yuè Yì       | name of a person.              |
| 22.     | 鄒衍         | Zōu Yǎn      | name of a person.              |
| 23.     | 劇辛         | Jù Xīn       | name of a person.              |
| 24.     | 湊           | còu          | to go toward; to rush to.      |

## ☀ 文法闡釋 (Grammar Notes)

### I. 死馬且買之五百金，況生馬乎？

且 serves here as a conjunction that comes between two clauses. It may be called a conjunction of concession, because it implies "even A, how much more so B". So 死馬且買之五百金 can be translated as: "Even when it was a dead horse, (we) bought it with five hundred pieces of gold". 況 is also a conjunction that, together with 乎, forms a question in the form of a retort which cannot be translated word for word, but means something like "is there any doubt that … ?" 況生馬乎 can thus be translated as "is there any doubt that (we will pay more) if it is a living horse?" This kind of question frequently appears after a sentence with the conjunction 且 or 猶. For example, 子猶不能, 況吾乎? "Even you cannot do it, how much more so if it were me?"

### II. 千里之馬至者三

千里之馬至者 is the subject, meaning, literally, "of the horses that can run a thousand *li*, those that arrived". The construction of 千里之馬至者 is similar to 國之孺子之遊者. (See Lesson 19.) 三 is the predicate. In Classical Chinese, numerals can function as predicates on their own. So the sentence can be translated more idiomatically as: "Three of the horses that could run a thousand *li* a day came".

# 二十三.《史記‧項羽本紀》(節)[1]

📖 **課文 (Text)**

項王軍壁垓下，兵少食盡，[2] 漢軍及諸侯兵圍之數重。[3] 夜聞漢軍四面皆楚歌，[4] 項王乃大驚曰：「漢皆已得楚乎？是何楚人之多也！」項王則夜起，[5] 飲帳中。[6] 有美人名虞，[7] 常幸從；[8] 駿馬名騅，[9] 常騎之。於是項王乃悲歌忼慨，[10] 自為詩曰：「力拔山兮氣蓋世，[11] 時不利兮騅不逝。[12] 騅不逝兮可奈何，[13] 虞兮虞兮奈若何！[14]」歌數闋，[15] 美人和之。[16] 項王泣數行下，[17] 左右皆泣，[18] 莫能仰視。[19]

於是項王乃上馬騎，麾下壯士騎從者八百餘人，[20] 直夜潰圍南出，馳走。[21] 平明，[22] 漢軍乃覺之，令騎將灌嬰以五千騎追之。[23] 項王渡淮，[24] 騎能屬者百餘人耳。[25] 項王至陰陵，[26] 迷失道，[27] 問一田父，[28] 田父紿曰：[29]「左。[30]」左，乃陷大澤中。[31] 以故漢追及之。

項王乃復引兵而東，[32] 至東城，[33] 乃有二十八騎。漢騎追者數千人。項王自度不得脫，[34] 謂其騎曰：「吾起兵至今八歲矣，身七十餘戰，所當者破，[35] 所擊者服，[36] 未嘗敗北，[37] 遂霸有天下；[38] 然今卒困於此，[39] 此天之亡我，非戰之罪也。今日固決死，[40] 願為諸君快戰，[41] 必三勝之，為諸君潰圍，斬將，刈旗，[42] 令諸君知天亡我，非戰之罪也。」乃分其騎以為四隊，四嚮。[43] 漢軍圍之數重。項王謂其騎曰：「吾為公取彼一將。」令四面騎馳下，期山東為三處。[44]

於是項王大呼馳下，漢軍皆披靡，[45] 遂斬漢一將。是時，赤泉侯為騎將，[46] 追項王，項王瞋目而叱之，[47] 赤泉侯人馬俱驚，辟易數里。[48] 與其騎會為三處。[49] 漢軍不知項王所在，乃分軍為三，復圍之。項王乃馳，復斬漢一都尉，[50] 殺數十百人，復聚其騎，亡其兩騎耳。乃謂其騎曰：「何如？[51]」騎皆伏曰：[52]「如大王言。[53]」

是項王乃欲東渡烏江。[54] 烏江亭長檥船待，[55] 謂項王曰：「江東雖小，[56] 地方千里，[57] 眾數十萬人，[58] 亦足王也。[59] 願大王急渡。今獨臣有船，漢軍至，無以渡。」項王笑曰：「天之亡我，我何渡為！且籍與江東子弟八千人渡江而西，[60] 今無一人還，縱江東父兄憐而王我，[61] 我何面目見之？[62] 縱彼不言，籍獨不愧於心乎？[63]」乃謂亭長曰：「吾知公長者。[64] 吾騎此馬五歲，所當無敵，嘗一日行千里，不忍殺之，以賜公！」乃令騎皆下馬步行，持短兵接戰。[65] 獨籍所殺漢軍數百人。項王身亦被十餘創。[66] 顧見漢騎司馬呂馬童，[67] 曰：「若非吾故人乎？[68]」馬童面之，[69] 指王翳曰：[70]「此項王也！」項王乃曰：「吾聞漢購我頭千金，<sup>71</sup> 邑萬户，<sup>72</sup> 吾為若德。<sup>73</sup>」
乃自刎而死。<sup>74</sup>

## 🗒 註 釋 (Annotations)

| | | | |
|---|---|---|---|
| 1. | 史記 | Shǐjì | *Records of the Historian* by Sīmǎ Qiān 司馬遷 (c.145–86 B.C.), the first general history of China, presented through a series of biographies and treatises. |
| | 項羽 | Xiàng Yǔ | One of the military leaders who overthrew the Qín 秦 (221–207 B.C.) empire. After the fall of the Qin empire, he established himself as Xī Chǔ Bà Wáng 西楚霸王 (Overlord of Western Chu) in 207 B.C. and enfeoffed the other leaders as kings. |
| | 本紀 | Běn jì | "Basic Annals". A section in the *Shiji*. |
| 2. | 項王 | Xiàng Wáng | King Xiang, i.e., Xiang Yu 項羽. |
| | 壁 | bì | earthworks; here used as a verb, meaning "to build the earthworks (fortifications)". |
| | 垓下 | Gāixià | name of a place. |
| | 兵 | bīng | army; soldiers. |
| 3. | 漢軍 | Hàn jūn | the Han army. Liú Bāng 劉邦 was the leader of another army involved in overthrowing the Qin empire. He had been enfeoffed as Hàn Wáng 漢王 (King of Han), so his army was called the Han army. After the Qin empire was overthrown, Liu Bang fought with Xiang Yu for the throne. Finally he defeated Xiang Yu and became the first emperor of the Han 漢 Dynasty (206 B.C.–220 A.D.). He was later called Hàn Gāozǔ 漢高祖. |

| | | |
|---|---|---|
| 諸侯兵 | zhū hóu bīng | the armies of other leaders who followed Liu Bang to fight against Xiang Yu. |
| 圍 | wéi | to surround. |
| 重 | chóng | layers. |
| 4. 楚歌 | Chǔ gē | songs of Chu. |
| 5. 則 | zé | used like 即, corresponding to 就 in Modern Chinese. (An adverb.) |
| 6. 帳 | zhàng | tent. |
| 7. 虞 | Yú | name of a person. Xiang Yu's concubine. |
| 8. 幸 | xìng | to enjoy the favor of. |
| 9. 駿馬 | jùn mǎ | fine steed. |
| 騅 | zhuī | a dark blue and white horse; here, the name of a horse. |
| 10. 忼慨 | kāng kǎi | used to describe passionate sorrow. (A sound-correlated disyllabic word.) |
| 11. 拔 | bá | to pluck; to pull up. |
| 兮 | xī | exclamatory particle. |
| 氣 | qì | spirit. |
| 蓋 | gài | to surpass. |
| 12. 逝 | shì | to go by; to go away. Here it means "to run away". |
| 13. 奈何 | nài hé | what can one do about it? 奈若何 in the next sentence means "what can I do about you?" (An idiomatic form.) |
| 14. 若 | ruò | you. (A pronoun.) |

| 15. 闋 | què | one round or one complete performance of a song is called a 闋. |
| 16. 和 | hè | to sing in response; to accompany. |
| 17. 泣 | qì | tears. 泣 in the next sentence is a verb meaning "to weep". |
| 行 | háng | line. |
| 18. 左右 | zuǒ yòu | the people around (someone). (Not only referring to attendants.) |
| 19. 仰 | yǎng | to raise one's head. |
| 20. 麾下 | huī xià | under one's command. |
| 騎 | jì | a man and the horse he rides. |
| 21. 直 | zhí | at, corresponding to 當著 in Modern Chinese. |
| 潰圍 | kuì wéi | to break out of an encirclement. |
| 馳 | chí | to gallop. |
| 22. 平明 | píng míng | at dawn. |
| 23. 騎將 | jì jiàng | cavalry general. |
| 灌嬰 | Guàn Yīng | name of a person. |
| 24. 渡 | dù | to cross (a river). |
| 淮 | Huái | the Huai River. |
| 25. 屬 | zhǔ | to follow. |
| 26. 陰陵 | Yīnlíng | name of a place. |
| 27. 迷 | mí | confused. |
| 迷失道 | mí shī dào | to lose one's way. |
| 28. 田父 | tián fǔ | old farmer. |

| | | |
|---|---|---|
| 29. 紿 | dài | to deceive. |
| 30. 左 | zuǒ | left; here used as a verb meaning "to go left". The next 左 works in the same way. |
| 31. 陷 | xiàn | to fall into (something). |
| 澤 | zé | marsh. |
| 32. 引 | yǐn | to lead. |
| 東 | dōng | east; here used as a verb meaning "to go east". |
| 33. 東城 | Dōngchéng | name of a place. |
| 34. 度 | duò | to reckon; to figure. |
| 脫 | tuō | to escape. |
| 35. 當 | dāng | to face. |
| 破 | pò | to destroy; here functioning in the passive voice, meaning "to be destroyed". |
| 36. 擊 | jī | to attack. |
| 服 | fú | to submit. |
| 37. 敗 | bài | to be defeated. |
| 北 | běi | to run away after being defeated. |
| 38. 霸 | bà | hegemony; here used as a verb meaning "to have hegemony over". |
| 39. 卒 | zú | at last. |
| 困 | kùn | to fall into dire straits. |
| 40. 決死 | jué sǐ | to resolve to die. |
| 41. 快戰 | kuài zhàn | to fight a satisfying battle. |
| 42. 斬 | zhǎn | to behead; to cut off. |

|  | 刈 | yì | to sever; to cut down. |
|---|---|---|---|
| 43. | 分 | fēn | to divide. |
|  | 嚮 | xiàng | to face. |
|  | 四嚮 | sì xiàng | to face in four directions. |
| 44. | 期 | qī | to make an appointment. |
|  | 期山東為三處 | qī shān dōng wéi sān chù | to make an arrangement to meet in three places east of the hill. |
| 45. | 披靡 | pī mí | to scatter. (A sound-correlated disyllabic word.) |
| 46. | 赤泉侯 | Chìquánhóu | the Marquis of Chiquan. |
| 47. | 瞋 | chēn | to stare angrily. |
|  | 叱 | chì | to shout at. |
| 48. | 辟易 | bì yì | to move back; to shy away from in fear. (A sound-correlated disyllabic word.) |
| 49. | 會 | huì | to meet; here, to join forces. |
| 50. | 都尉 | dū wèi | regional military commander. |
| 51. | 何如 | hé rú | what do you think of that? (An idiomatic form.) |
| 52. | 伏 | fú | to prostrate oneself. |
| 53. | 如大王言 | rú dài wáng yán | just like what you said. |
| 54. | 烏江 | Wūjiāng | name of a place, a town on the west side of the Yangtze River. |
|  | 東渡烏江 | dōng dù Wūjiāng | to cross the Yangtze River from Wujiang to go east. |
| 55. | 亭 | tíng | an administrative unit in the Qin-Han period roughly corresponding to a village. |

| 檥 | yǐ | to moor. |
| 待 | dài | to wait for. |
| 56. 江東 | jiāng dōng | the area on the southeast side of the Yangtze River. |
| 57. 方千里 | fāng qiān lǐ | a square with each side measuring one thousand *li*. Note that 方千里 does not mean "one thousand square li". |
| 58. 眾 | zhòng | the masses. |
| 59. 王 | wàng | to rule as king. |
| 60. 籍 | Jí | the formal name of Xiang Yu. |
| 子弟 | zǐ dì | sons and younger brothers, i.e., the young men. |
| 61. 縱 | zòng | even if. (A conjunction.) |
| 62. 面目 | miàn mù | face. (An idiomatic form.) |
| 63. 獨 | dú | how can …?, corresponding to 難道 in Modern Chinese. (An adverb.) |
| 愧 | kuì | ashamed. |
| 64. 長者 | zhǎng zhě | senior; worthy man. |
| 65. 短兵 | duǎn bīng | short weapon (knife or sword). |
| 接戰 | jiē zhàn | to engage in hand-to-hand fighting. |
| 66. 被 | bèi | to receive; here it means "to suffer". |
| 創 | chuāng | wounds. |
| 67. 司馬 | sī mǎ | a low ranking military officer (at that time and later). |
| 呂馬童 | Lǚ Mǎtóng | name of a person. |
| 68. 故人 | gù rén | old acquaintance. |

| 69. | 面 | miàn | to face. |
|---|---|---|---|
| 70. | 王翳 | Wáng Yì | name of a person, a Han general. |
| 71. | 購 | gòu | to offer a reward to get something. (Note that this meaning is different from the Modern Chinese meaning of "to buy".) |
| 72. | 邑 | yì | fief. |
|  | 萬戶 | wàn hù | ten thousand households. |
| 73. | 德 | dé | favor. |
| 74. | 刎 | wěn | to cut one's throat. |

## 文法闡釋 (Grammar Notes)

### I. 項王軍壁垓下

Omission of such grammatical particles as 於 and 以 was not uncommon in earlier standard Classical Chinese, but became even more common in later works such as the 史記. So this must be kept in mind when we read such works. The above sentence should obviously have 於 before 垓下, and it means, therefore, "King Xiang's army walled itself up in Gaixia". Other examples in this selection are 乃陷 (於) 大澤中; 期 (於) 山東; and 漢購我頭 (以) 千金. More examples can be found in the following two selections.

### II. 地方千里，眾數十萬人。

These two sentences describe the region known as 江東. 地 is the subject and 方千里 is the predicate of the first sentence (note that 地方 is not a compound in Classical Chinese). Similarly, 眾 is the subject and 數十萬人 is the predicate of the second sentence. They should, therefore, be rendered as: "Its territory, as a square, extends a thousand *li* (on each side), and its population is as large as several hundreds of thousands".

## III. 天之亡我，我何渡為！

之 helps to indicate that 天亡我 is a subordinate clause, and means, therefore, "if/since heaven wants me to lose". 我何 + VP + 為 is an idiomatic way in Classical Chinese to say emphatically that taking a certain action is meaningless. It is probably a transformation of 我 + VP + 何為 (compare this with the Modern Chinese way of saying 我 (還) 做那個幹什麼？). So the main clause 我何渡為 (wéi) means: "why should I cross the river, after all?"

## IV. 吾為若德

為 is a co-verb here with 若 "you" as its object. 德 is here the main verb meaning "to do a good deed". So the sentence means, "I do a good deed for you", or idiomatically, "Let me do you a favor".

# 二十四.《史記·留侯世家》(節)

## 📖 課文 (Text)

留侯張良者，其先韓人也。² 大父開地，³ 相韓昭侯、宣惠王、襄哀王；⁴ 父平，相釐王、悼惠王。⁵ 悼惠王二十三年，平卒。卒二十歲，秦滅韓。良年少，未宦事韓。⁶ 韓破，良家僮三百人，⁷ 弟死不葬，悉以家財求客刺秦王，⁸ 為韓報仇，以大父、父五世相韓故。⁹

良嘗學禮淮陽，¹⁰ 東見倉海君，¹¹ 得力士，¹² 為鐵椎重百二十斤。¹³ 秦皇帝東游，¹⁴ 良與客狙擊秦皇帝博浪沙中，¹⁵ 誤中副車。¹⁶ 秦皇帝大怒，大索天下，¹⁷ 求賊急甚，為張良故也。良乃更名姓，¹⁸ 亡匿下邳。¹⁹

良嘗閒從容步游下邳圯上，²⁰ 有一老父，衣褐，至良所，²¹ 直墮其履圯下，²² 顧謂良曰：「孺子下取履！」良鄂然，²³ 欲毆之。²⁴ 為其老，彊忍，下取履。父曰：「履我！」²⁵ 良業為取履，²⁶ 因長跪履之。²⁷ 父以足受，²⁸ 笑而去。良殊大驚，²⁹ 隨目之。³⁰ 父去里所，³¹ 復還，曰：「孺子可教矣！後五日平明，與我會此。」良因怪之，跪曰：「諾。」

五日平明，良往。父已先在，怒曰：「與老人期，後，³² 何也？」去，曰：「後五日早會！」五日雞鳴，良往，父又先在，復怒曰：「後，何也？」去，曰：「後五

日復早來！」五日，良夜未半往。<sup>33</sup> 有頃，父亦來，喜
曰：「當如是。」出一編書，<sup>34</sup> 曰：「讀此則為王者師
矣！後十年，興。<sup>35</sup> 十三年，<sup>36</sup> 孺子見我，濟北穀城山
下黃石，<sup>37</sup> 即我矣。」遂去，無他言，不復見。

旦日視其書，<sup>38</sup> 乃太公兵法也。<sup>39</sup> 良因異之，<sup>40</sup> 常
習誦讀之。<sup>41</sup>

## 註 釋 (Annotations)

1. 留侯　　　Liúhóu　　　the Marquis of Liu, the title conferred on Zhāng
　　　　　　　　　　　　Liáng 張良. Zhang Liang was the descendant of
　　　　　　　　　　　　a lord of the state of Hán 韓. He later became the
　　　　　　　　　　　　main advisor to Liu Bang, and was granted the
　　　　　　　　　　　　title of Marquis of Liu after the establishment of
　　　　　　　　　　　　the Hàn 漢 empire.

　　世家　　　Shì jiā　　　"Hereditary Houses". A section in the *Shiji*.

2. 先　　　　xiān　　　　ancestor.

　　韓　　　　Hán　　　　a state during the Warring States period.

3. 大父　　　dà fù　　　　grandfather.

　　開地　　　Kāidì　　　　name of a person.

4. 相　　　　xiàng　　　　to serve as prime minister of.

　　韓昭侯　　Hán Zhāohóu　Marquis Zhao, a ruler of the state of Han.

　　宣惠王　　Xuānhuìwáng　King Xuanhui, a ruler of the Han state, who was
　　　　　　　　　　　　the son of Marquis Zhao. From this ruler on, the
　　　　　　　　　　　　rulers of Han styled themselves as kings.

襄哀王　　　Xiāng'āiwáng　King Xiang'ai, a ruler of the Han state who was the son of King Xuanhui.

5. 平　　　　Píng　　　　name of a person.

釐王　　　　Xīwáng　　　King Xi, a ruler of the Han state. The son of King Xiang'ai. 釐 is the same as 僖 xī when used as a name.

悼惠王　　　Dàohuìwáng　King Daohui, a ruler of the Han state who was the son of King Xi.

6. 宦　　　　huàn　　　　official; here used as an adverb.

宦事韓　　　huàn shì Hán　to serve Han as an official.

7. 僮　　　　tóng　　　　(male) servant.

8. 刺　　　　cì　　　　　to assassinate, literally, to stab.

9. 世　　　　shì　　　　　generation.

五世　　　　wǔ shì　　　the five successive Kings of Han.

10. 淮陽　　　Huáiyáng　　name of a place.

11. 倉海君　　Cānghǎijūn　name of a person.

12. 力士　　　lì shì　　　a man of great strength.

13. 椎　　　　chuí　　　　hammer.

14. 秦皇帝　　Qín Huángdì　the emperor of Qin; here it refers to Qín Shǐhuáng 秦始皇, the first emperor of the Qin Dynasty.

15. 狙擊　　　jū jī　　　to target covertly.

博浪沙　　　Bólàngshā　name of a place.

16. 中　　　　zhòng　　　to hit.

| 副車 | fù chē | auxiliary chariot. When Qin Shihuang traveled, he always prepared several chariots with the same appearance. One was the chariot in which he himself rode. Others were the chariots in which his attendants rode. The latter were called 副車. |
|---|---|---|
| 17. 索 | suǒ | to search for. |
| 18. 更 | gēng | to change. |
| 19. 匿 | nì | to hide. |
| 下邳 | Xiàpéi | name of a place. |
| 20. 閒 | xián | leisure. (An adjective.) |
| 從容 | cōng róng | leisurely. (A sound-correlated disyllabic word.) |
| 圯 | yí | bridge. |
| 21. 所 | suǒ | place. |
| 22. 直 | zhí | intentionally. (In this context, the character normally should be 持.) |
| 墮 | duò | to fall; here used as a causative verb, to make (something) fall. |
| 履 | lǚ | shoe. |
| 23. 鄂然 | è rán | to be astonished. |
| 24. 毆 | ōu | to hit. |
| 25. 履 | lǚ | here used as a verb, to put shoes on. |
| 26. 業 | yè | already. (Same as 已). |
| 27. 長跪 | cháng guì | to kneel with back straight and buttocks on the heels. (Kneeling with the buttocks close to the heels is called 跪.) |

| | | |
|---|---|---|
| 28. 以足受 | yǐ zú shòu | to receive with the foot, i.e., to stretch out his foot and let Zhang Liang put the shoe on for him. |
| 29. 殊 | shū | particularly; unusually. |
| 30. 隨目之 | suí mù zhī | keeping his eyes on him all the way. |
| 31. 所 | suǒ | appended to a measure word to express an approximate amount. (A quantity word.) |
| 32. 後 | hòu | to come late. |
| 33. 夜未半 | yè wèi bàn | before the night is half-through, i.e., before midnight. |
| 34. 編 | biān | the original meaning is "to weave; to thread". In ancient China, books were made of bamboo strips threaded together with a rope, so 編 was used as a measure word for books. (A measure word.) |
| 35. 興 | xīng | to rise; to succeed. |
| 36. 十三年 | shí sān nián | here, it means "after thirteen years". |
| 37. 濟 | Jǐ | name of a river. |
| 穀城山 | Gǔchéngshān | name of a mountain. |
| 38. 旦日 | dàn rì | the next day. |
| 39. 太公兵法 | Tàigōng bīngfǎ | *Taigong's Art of War.* 太公 refers to Jiāng Tàigōng 姜太公, the main advisor to King Wu of Zhou and a famous strategist. |
| 40. 異 | yì | unusual; here used as a putative verb, meaning "to think it unusual". |
| 41. 誦 | sòng | to recite. |

## 文法闡釋 (Grammar Note)

### 良業為取履

Because of sound changes over the course of time, or certain variations in different dialects, a grammatical word in Classical Chinese may be represented by a different graph in later texts. 業 in this sentence is an example as such. It is the same as 已 "already". (Another example is 若 in the last selection, Lesson 23, where it is read as 女 or 汝 "you".) So this sentence means, "Liang already picked up his sandals for him".

📖 **課文 (Text)**

魏有隱士曰侯嬴，年七十，家貧，為大梁夷門監者。[2] 公子聞之，往請，欲厚遺之。[3] 不肯受。公子於是乃置酒大會賓客。坐定，公子從車騎，虛左，[4] 自迎夷門侯生。侯生攝敝衣冠，[5] 直上載公子上坐，[6] 不讓，欲以觀公子。公子執轡愈恭。[7] 侯生又謂公子曰：「臣有客在市屠中，[8] 願枉車騎過之。[9]」公子引車入市，侯生下見其客朱亥，俾倪故久立，[10] 與其客語，微察公子。公子顏色愈和。當是時，魏將相宗室賓客滿堂，待公子舉酒，市人皆觀公子執轡。從騎皆竊罵侯生。侯生視公子色終不變，乃謝客就車。至家，公子引侯生坐上坐，遍贊賓客，[11] 賓客皆驚⋯。侯生遂為上客⋯。

魏安釐王二十年，秦昭王已破趙長平軍，⋯圍邯鄲。[12] 公子姊為趙惠文王弟平原君夫人，[13] 數遺魏王及公子書，請救於魏。魏王使將軍晉鄙將十萬眾救趙。留軍壁鄴，[14] 名為救趙，實持兩端以觀望。[15] 平原君使者冠蓋相屬於魏，[16] ⋯公子患之，數請魏王，及賓客辯士說王萬端。[17] 魏王畏秦，終不聽⋯。公子⋯乃請賓客，約車騎百餘乘，欲赴秦軍，與趙俱死。

行過夷門，見侯生，⋯侯生曰：「公子勉之矣，老臣不能從。」公子行數里，⋯復引車還，問侯生。侯生笑曰：「臣固知公子之還也。」⋯乃屏人間語曰：[18]「嬴聞晉鄙之兵符常在王臥內，[19]而如姬最幸，[20]出入王臥內，力能竊之。嬴聞如姬父為人所殺，⋯如姬為公子泣，公子使客斬其仇頭，敬進如姬。如姬之欲為公子死，無所辭⋯。公子誠一開口請如姬，如姬必許諾⋯。」公子從其計，請如姬。如姬果盜晉鄙兵符與公子。

　　公子行，侯生曰：「⋯晉鄙不授公子兵而復請之，事必危矣。臣客屠者朱亥可與俱，此人力士。晉鄙聽，大善；不聽，可使擊之。」⋯於是公子請朱亥。⋯朱亥遂與公子俱。公子過謝侯生。侯生曰：「臣宜從，老不能。請數公子行日，以至晉鄙軍之日，北鄉自剄以送公子。」公子遂行。至鄴，矯魏王令代晉鄙。[21]晉鄙合符，疑之，⋯欲無聽。朱亥袖四十斤鐵椎，椎殺晉鄙，公子遂將晉鄙軍⋯秦軍解去⋯。公子與侯生決，至軍，侯生果北鄉自剄。

## 📝 註釋 (Annotations)

1. 魏公子　　Wèi gōng zǐ　　Prince of Xinling (信陵君 Xìnlíngjūn) of Wei. His name was Wújì 無忌 and his title was derived from his fief located at Xinling.

　　列傳　　liè zhuàn　　"Biographies". A section in the *Shiji*.

2. 夷門    Yímén    the eastern gate of Dàliáng 大梁, capital of Wei, so named for the hill Yíshān 夷山 nearby.

    監    jiān    gate keeper.

3. 遺    wèi    to send gifts or money.

4. 虛左    xū zuǒ    leaving empty the left seat. (In ancient China, the left side was considered the position of honor, reserved for superiors or guests of honor.)

5. 攝敝衣冠    shè bì yī guān    to lift up one's ragged clothes and hat.

6. 載    zài    to get aboard.

7. 轡    pèi    reins; bridle.

8. 市屠    shì tú    butchers in a market.

9. 枉    wǎng    to trouble somebody to (do something).

10. 俾倪    bì nì    to look in askance at. (Same as 睥睨.)

11. 遍贊    biàn zàn    introduce to everyone. 贊, to announce; to introduce.

12. 邯鄲    Hán Dān    capital of the Zhào 趙 state, in what is now Héběi 河北 province.

13. 平原君    Píngyuánjūn    Lord of Pingyuan, another prince famous for his generosity, whose name was Shèng 勝. He served as the prime minister of Zhao at that time. He and the Lord of Xinling were brothers-in-law.

14. 壁    bì    to encamp the troops within fortifications. 壁, meaning wall, is used here as a verb.

15. 持兩端    chí liǎng duān    holding both ends, i.e., to be indecisive or fence-sitting; to wait-and-see.

16. 相屬    xiāng zhǔ    (wagons and messengers) each hard on the heels of another.

| 17. | 萬端 | wàn duān | all kinds of reasons. |
|---|---|---|---|
| 18. | 屏 | bǐn | to order (servants, etc.) to go away; to keep others away. |
|  | 閒語 | jiàn yǔ | private conversation. |
| 19. | 兵符 | bīng fú | a kind of tally with special designs on it that can be split into two pieces, used in traditional China as a credential between a king and his general. Each would hold one half and if the two halves matched when a message was sent, it would mean the message was authentic. |
| 20. | 最幸 | zuì xìng | the most favored. |
| 21. | 矯 | jiǎo | to alter without authority; to falsify. |

## ☀ 文法闡釋 (Grammar Note)

晉鄙聽，大善；不聽，可使擊之。

We have here two conditional sentences, both with the conditional conjunction 則 omitted (which is very common in Classical Chinese grammar). Since 則 always connects two clauses which do not have to share the same subject, the two sentences here mean: "If Jin Bi listens, that will be wonderful; if he doesn't listen, you may (or it will be okay) to order (him, 朱亥) to hit him (晉鄙)".

## 📖 參考篇章 (Reference Text)

### 《夷門歌》　王維 (701–761)

七雄雄雌猶未分，[1] 攻城殺將何紛紛？[2]

秦兵益圍邯鄲急，魏王不救平原君。

公子為嬴停駟馬，執轡愈恭意愈下。

亥為屠肆鼓刀人，嬴乃夷門抱關者。

非但慷慨獻奇謀，[3] 意氣兼將身命酬。[4]

向風刎頸送公子，[5] 七十老翁何所求？

## 📋 註 釋 (Annotations)

| | | | |
|---|---|---|---|
| 1. | 七雄 | qī xióng | the seven males, i.e., the seven strongest states of the Warring States period. |
| 2. | 紛紛 | fēn fēn | numerous and disorderly. |
| 3. | 慷慨 | kāng kǎi | ardent; generous; unselfish. |
| 4. | 意氣 | yì qì | heroic spirit of devotion or commitment. |
| 5. | 刎頸 | wěn jǐng | to commit suicide (by slashing one's own neck). |

# 二十六.《史記・李將軍列傳》(節)[1]

## 📖 課文 (Text)

　　匈奴大入上郡，天子使中貴人從廣勒習兵擊匈奴。² 中貴人將騎數十縱，³ 見匈奴三人，與戰；三人還射，傷中貴人，殺其騎且盡。中貴人走廣。⁴ 廣曰：「是必射雕者也。⁵」廣乃遂從百騎往馳三人。⁶ 三人亡馬步行，行數十里。廣令其騎張左右翼，⁷ 而廣身自射彼三人者，殺其二人，生得一人，果匈奴射雕者也。已縛之上馬，⁸ 望匈奴有數千騎。見廣，以為誘騎，⁹ 皆驚，上山陳。¹⁰ 廣之百騎皆大恐，欲馳還走。廣曰：「吾去大軍數十里；今如此以百騎走，匈奴追射我立盡。今我留，匈奴必以我為大軍誘之，必不敢擊我。」廣令諸騎曰：「前！¹¹」前未到匈奴陳二里所，止。令曰：「皆下馬解鞍！¹²」其騎曰：「虜多且近，¹³ 即有急，¹⁴ 奈何？」廣曰：「彼虜以我為走；今皆解鞍以示不走，¹⁵ 用堅其意。¹⁶」於是胡騎遂不敢擊。¹⁷

　　有白馬將出護其兵，¹⁸ 李廣上馬與十餘騎奔射殺胡白馬將，而復還至其騎中，¹⁹ 解鞍，令士皆縱馬臥。²⁰ 是時會暮，²¹ 胡兵終怪之，不敢擊。夜半時，胡兵亦以為漢有伏軍於旁欲夜取之，胡皆引兵而去。²² 平旦，²³ 李廣乃歸其大軍。

## 📖 註釋 (Annotations)

1. 李將軍　Lǐ jiāng jūn　General Lǐ Guǎng 李廣, a famous general of the Han Dynasty. He is referred to as 廣 in the text.

2. 匈奴　Xiōngnú　an ancient nomadic group active on the northern borders of China.

    上郡　Shàng jùn　a northern border prefecture in the Han Dynasty.

    中貴人　zhōng guì rén　a favorite eunuch.

    勒　lè　to command; to control.

3. 縱　zòng　to let loose; here, to let his horse gallop.

4. 走　zǒu　to run; here, to run towards.

5. 雕　diāo　eagle.

    射雕者　shè diāo zhě　eagle shooter; a Xiongnu archer of excellence.

6. 從　cóng　to make somebody follow.

7. 張　zhāng　to stretch out.

    翼　yì　flank.

    廣令其騎張左右翼　Guǎng lìng qí jì zhāng zuǒ yòu yì　Li Guang ordered his cavalrymen to divide into left and right flanks (in order to protect him).

8. 縛　fù　to tie up.

9. 誘　yòu　to lure.

    誘騎　yòu jì　cavalrymen for luring the enemy.

10. 陳　zhèn　to line up in battle formation. (Written as 陣 in later times.) The next 陳 in the text is a noun, meaning "ranks".

11. 前　qián　to go forward.

| | | |
|---|---|---|
| 12. 解 | jiě | to untie; here, to remove (a saddle). |
| 鞍 | ān | saddle. |
| 13. 虜 | lǔ | its original meaning is "slave", but it is also a pejorative term for an enemy (especially one from a non-Han Chinese group). |
| 14. 即 | jí | immediately; right away. (An adverb.) |
| 15. 示 | shì | to show. |
| 16. 用 | yòng | in order to; so as to. (A preposition.) |
| 堅 | jiān | firm; here used as a causative verb. (An adjective.) |
| 堅其意 | jiān qí yì | to bolster their belief. |
| 17. 胡 | Hú | a broad term referring to the northern nomadic tribes in ancient China. |
| 18. 白馬將 | bái mǎ jiàng | a general riding a white horse. |
| 護 | hù | to protect; here, to supervise. |
| 19. 其騎中 | qí jì zhōng | among his own cavalrymen. |
| 20. 士 | shì | soldier. |
| 縱馬 | zòng mǎ | to let their horses loose, i.e., not to tie them up. |
| 臥 | wò | to lie down. |
| 21. 會 | huì | to happen to be. |
| 暮 | mù | dusk. |
| 22. 引 | yǐn | to retreat. |
| 23. 平旦 | píng dàn | at dawn. |

## 文法闡釋 (Grammar Note)

### 匈奴必以我為大軍誘之

Though the pattern 以 A 為 B normally means "to regard A as B", it is not so in this sentence. Instead, 以 here is the main verb with the clause 我為大軍誘之 as its object. So the sentence should be rendered as, "The Xiongnu will definitely think that we are trying to draw them out for our main force". 為 is here a co-verb, meaning "for".

# 二十七.《漢書‧循吏傳》：
## 龔遂傳(節)<sup>1</sup>

📖 課文 **(Text)**

渤海左右郡歲飢，[2] 盜賊並起，[3] 二千石不能禽制。[4] 上選能治者，[5] 丞相御史舉遂可用，[6] 上以為渤海太守。[7] 時遂年七十餘，召見，形貌短小。[8] 宣帝望見，[9] 不副所聞，[10] 心內輕焉，謂遂曰：「渤海廢亂，[11] 朕甚憂之。[12] 君欲何以息其盜賊，[13] 以稱朕意？[14]」遂對曰：「海瀕遐遠，[15] 不霑聖化，[16] 其民困於飢寒而吏不恤，[17] 故使陛下赤子盜弄陛下之兵於潢池中耳。[18] 今欲使臣勝之邪？[19] 將安之也？」上聞遂對，[20] 甚說，答曰：「選用賢良，固欲安之也。」遂曰：「臣聞治亂民猶治亂繩，不可急也；唯緩之，然後可治。[21] 臣願丞相御史且無拘臣以文法，[22] 得一切便宜從事。[23]」

上許焉，加賜黃金，贈遣乘傳。[24] 至渤海界，[25] 郡聞新太守至，發兵以迎，遂皆遣還。移書敕屬縣：[26]「悉罷逐捕盜賊吏，[27] 諸持鉏鉤田器者皆為良民，[28] 吏無得問，[29] 持兵者乃為盜賊。[30]」遂單車獨行至府，[31] 郡中翕然，[32] 盜賊亦皆罷。渤海又多劫掠相隨，[33] 聞遂教令，[34] 即時解散，[35] 棄其兵弩而持鉤鉏。[36] 盜賊於是悉平，[37] 民安土樂業。[38]

## 📋 註 釋 (Annotations)

1. 漢書    Hànshū    *History of the Former Han Dynasty* by Bān Gù 班固 (32–92 A.D.).

   循吏傳    Xún lì zhuàn    "Biographies of Law-Abiding Officials". The biography of 龔遂 forms part of this chapter from the *Hanshu*.

   龔遂    Gōng Suì    name of a Former (or Western) Han official. He is referred to as 遂 in the text.

2. 渤海    Bóhǎi    name of a place, a prefecture in the Western Han Dynasty.

   歲    suì    the year's harvest.

   飢    jī    famine; hunger. (Also written as 饑.)

   歲飢    suì jī    a year of famine.

3. 盜賊    dào zéi    robber. Here, 盜 and 賊 are synonymous.

   並    bìng    together; simultaneously. (An adverb.)

4. 二千石    èr qiān dàn    referring to the magistrate of a prefecture, the 太守 [see (7)], whose salary is about two thousand *dan* of grain a year. (An idiomatic form.) 石 is a large measure unit for grain.

   禽    qín    to capture; to catch. (Also written as 擒 in later times.)

   制    zhì    to control.

5. 上    shàng    the Emperor.

6. 丞相    chéng xiàng    prime minister.

   御史    yù shǐ    censor, an official title. Here, the 御史大夫, the vice prime minister in the Western Han Dynasty.

   舉    jǔ    to nominate somebody for office.

7. 太守 | tài shǒu | magistrate of a prefecture.

8. 形貌 | xíng mào | stature and appearance; here, referring to stature only.

9. 宣帝 | Xuāndì | Emperor Xuan of the Western Han Dynasty.

10. 副 | fù | to correspond to; to match.

11. 廢 | fèi | (of law) to cease to be binding.

12. 朕 | zhèn | first person pronoun, used only by emperors from the Qin Dynasty onwards.

13. 息 | xī | to subside; here used as a causative verb.

14. 稱 | chèng | to suit.

稱朕意 | chèng zhèn yì | to meet my wish; to gratify me.

15. 瀕 | bīn | water's edge. (Also written as 濱.)

遐 | xiá | far.

16. 霑 | zhān | to wet; here it means "to benefit from" or "to receive".

聖化 | shèng huà | the teaching and influence of the emperor.

17. 恤 | xù | to sympathize with; to take care of.

18. 陛下 | bì xià | an honorific address to the emperor.

赤子 | chì zǐ | baby; here, "the innocent people".

盜 | dào | to steal; to rob. (Note that in Classical Chinese, 盜 more often means "to steal".)

弄 | nòng | to play; to tease.

潢 | huáng | pond. (Note that 龔遂 used such expressions as 赤子, 盜弄, and 潢池 to imply that these robbers are not a serious problem.)

| 19. | 勝之 | shèng zhī | to overcome them; to crack down forcefully on them. |
| 20. | 對 | duì | an answer; a reply; the way one responds to a question. (A noun.) |
| 21. | 緩 | huǎn | slow; unhurried; here used as a verb meaning "to do something unhurriedly". |
| 22. | 拘 | jū | to restrict. |
| | 文法 | wén fǎ | law; regulations. |
| 23. | 一切 | yī qiè | for the time being; under the circumstances. (An adverb.) (Note that this term means literally "one cut" in Classical Chinese. As an adverb, it means "with one cut" or "with a quick fix", i.e., temporarily ignoring the rules. ) |
| | 便宜 | biàn yí | flexibly. |
| | 從事 | cóng shì | to handle. |
| | 便宜從事 | biàn yí cóng shì | to handle the affairs of this prefecture flexibly, not asking the emperor for approval in advance. |
| 24. | 遣 | qiǎn | to send off. |
| | 傳 | zhuàn | a kind of official chariot. |
| 25. | 界 | jiè | boundary. |
| 26. | 移 | yí | to deliver. |
| | 敕 | chì | to order. (Note that 敕 later refers only to the orders of an emperor, though until the Six Dynasties period it was used with reference to the orders of a superior to an inferior.) |
| | 屬縣 | shǔ xiàn | subordinate counties. |
| 27. | 罷 | bà | to stop; here, it means "to withdraw". |

| 28. | 鉏 | chú | hoe. (A variant form of 鋤.) |
|  | 鉤 | gōu | here it means "sickle". |
|  | 田器 | tián qì | farming tools. |
| 29. | 問 | wèn | here it means "to interrogate". |
| 30. | 持兵者 | chí bīng zhě | those who carry weapons. |
| 31. | 府 | fǔ | government office. |
| 32. | 翕然 | xì rán | calm. |
| 33. | 劫掠 | jié lüè | to plunder. (劫 and 掠 are synonyms.) |
|  | 相隨 | xiāng suí | one after another. |
| 34. | 教令 | jiào lìng | instructions and orders. |
| 35. | 即時 | jí shí | immediately. |
| 36. | 弩 | nǔ | crossbow. |
| 37. | 平 | píng | to subside. |
| 38. | 業 | yè | work; job; occupation. |
|  | 安土樂業 | ān tǔ lè yè | to be attached to one's native land and take delight in one's work. |

## ☀ 文法闡釋 (Grammar Note)

### 唯緩之，然後可治。

Unlike in Modern Chinese, the phrase 然後 is not a compound in standard Classical Chinese. It means "being so, then …". But it became a compound quite early in the history of the Chinese language, meaning simply "then", as it does in this sentence. (In standard Classical Chinese, this sentence probably would appear as 唯緩之，而後可治。) So this sentence can be simply rendered as: "Only when it is handled slowly (i.e., not hastily) will it then be possible to govern".

# 二十八.《後漢書・酷吏列傳》：
# 董宣傳(節)[1]

## 📖 課文 (Text)

宣特徵為洛陽令。²時湖陽公主蒼頭白日殺人，³因
匿主家，⁴吏不能得。及主出行，而以奴驂乘，⁵宣於
夏門亭候之，⁶乃駐車叩馬，⁷以刀畫地，⁸大言數主之
失，⁹叱奴下車，因格殺之。¹⁰主即還宮訴帝，¹¹帝
大怒，召宣，欲箠殺之。¹²宣叩頭曰：¹³「願乞一言而
死。¹⁴」帝曰：「欲何言？」宣曰：「陛下聖德中興，¹⁵而
縱奴殺良人，¹⁶將何以理天下乎？¹⁷臣不須箠，¹⁸請得
自殺。」即以頭擊楹，¹⁹流血被面。²⁰帝令小黃門持之，²¹
使宣叩頭謝主。²²宣不從，²³彊使頓之，²⁴宣兩手據地，²⁵
終不肯俯。²⁶主曰：「文叔為白衣時，²⁷臧亡匿死，²⁸吏
不敢至門。今為天子，²⁹威不能行一令乎？³⁰」帝笑曰：
「天子不與白衣同。」因敕彊項令出，³¹賜錢三十萬，宣
悉以班諸吏。³²由是搏擊豪彊，³³莫不震慄。³⁴京師號
為「臥虎」，³⁵歌之曰：「枹鼓不鳴董少平。³⁶」

## 📑 註釋 (Annotations)

1. 後漢書　　　Hòuhànshū　　*History of the Later Han Dynasty* by Fàn Yè 范曄
(398–445 A.D.).

   酷吏列傳　Kù lì liè zhuàn　"Biographies of Harsh Officials". The biography
of 董宣 forms part of this chapter from the
*Houhanshu*.

|  | 董宣 | Dǒng Xuān | name of a Later (or Eastern) Han official. He is referred to as 宣 in the text. |
| 2. | 徵 | zhēng | to summon or recruit and appoint somebody as an official. |
|  | 洛陽 | Luòyáng | capital of the Later Han empire. |
|  | 令 | lìng | magistrate of a city or local district. |
| 3. | 時 | shí | at that time (In Modern Chinese, 當時). |
|  | 湖陽公主 | Húyáng Gōngzhǔ | Princess Huyang, the elder sister of Emperor Guāngwǔ 光武. |
|  | 蒼頭 | cāng tóu | a slave. |
| 4. | 因 | yīn | subsequently. |
|  | 主 | zhǔ | princess, i.e., 公主. |
| 5. | 奴 | nú | slave. |
|  | 驂乘 | cān shèng | guard of a chariot; here used as a verb, meaning "to serve as a guard of a chariot". |
| 6. | 夏門亭 | Xiàméntíng | name of a place. |
|  | 候 | hòu | to wait. |
| 7. | 駐 | zhù | to halt. |
|  | 叩 | kòu | to rein in (a horse). |
| 8. | 畫 | huà | to draw (a line). |
| 9. | 大言 | dà yán | with loud voice. |
|  | 數 | shǔ | to enumerate. |
|  | 失 | shī | faults; mistakes. |
| 10. | 格 | gé | to hit. |

11. 訴      sù          to pour out one's woes. (Note that in Classical Chinese, 訴 does not mean "to tell", but "to pour out one's woes or troubles".)

    帝      dì          the emperor; here, Emperor Guangwu.

12. 箠      chuí        whip. (A noun.)
                        to flog; to whip. (A verb.)

13. 叩頭    kòu tóu     to kowtow.

14. 乞      qǐ          to beg for.

    願乞一言  yuàn qǐ yī   I beg you to allow me to say one word before I
    而死      yán ér sǐ    die.

15. 中興    zhōng xīng  to resurrect; here it means "to resurrect the Han empire". The Han empire (Former Han) was ended by Wáng Mǎng 王莽. Emperor Guangwu restored the Han empire, which is known to posterity as the Later or Eastern Han.

16. 縱      zòng        to indulge.

    良人    liáng rén   innocent people.

17. 理      lǐ          to regulate; to govern; to rule.

18. 不須    bù xū       there is no need to.

19. 楹      yíng        column; pillar.

20. 被      bèi         to cover.

21. 黃門    huáng mén   eunuch.

    持      chí         to hold; here it means "to grip".

22. 謝      xiè         to apologize to.

23. 從      cóng        to obey.

24. 彊      qiǎng       an ancient form of 強, meaning "to force".

    頓      dùn         to kowtow.

25. 據　　　jù　　　　to prop; to press against.

26. 俯　　　fǔ　　　　to bow one's head.

27. 文叔　　Wénshū　　courtesy name of Emperor Guangwu.

　　白衣　　bái yī　　equivalent to 布衣 bù yī, meaning "common people".

28. 臧　　　cáng　　　this character is used in place of 藏, meaning "to hide".

　　亡　　　wáng　　　to flee; here used as a noun meaning "the people who fled from home; the fugitives".

　　匿　　　nì　　　　to hide.

　　死　　　sǐ　　　　to die; here used as a noun meaning "the people who committed capital offences".

　　臧亡匿死　cáng wáng nì sǐ　to let fugitives and those who committed capital offences hide in one's home.

29. 天子　　tiān zǐ　　emperor. (In ancient China, emperors claimed that they were the sons of Heaven.)

30. 威　　　wēi　　　might.

　　行　　　xíng　　　to carry out; to prevail over.

　　令　　　lìng　　　a magistrate; here referring to 董宣, the 洛陽令.

31. 彊　　　jiàng　　unbending. (Written as 強 in later times.)

　　項　　　xiàng　　neck.

32. 班　　　bān　　　to distribute.

33. 由是　　yóu shì　　from then on.

　　搏　　　bó　　　　to pounce.

　　豪彊　　háo qiáng　the rich and powerful local magnates.

| | | |
|---|---|---|
| 34. 震 | zhèn | to be shocked. |
| 慄 | lì | to tremble (with fear). |
| 35. 京師 | jīng shī | capital; here, referring to the people of the capital. |
| 號 | hào | appellation; here used as a verb, meaning "to give someone an appellation". |
| 臥虎 | wò hǔ | crouching tiger. |
| 36. 枹 | fú | drumstick. |
| 鳴 | míng | to sound. |
| 枹鼓不鳴 | fú gǔ bù míng | In ancient China, people who wanted to complain about an injustice would beat the drum in front of the government offices. So 枹鼓不鳴 (no one is beating the drum) means that there was no injustice. |
| 董少平 | Dǒng Shàopíng | 少平 is 董宣's courtesy name. |

## ☼ 文法闡釋 (Grammar Notes)

### I. 威不能行一令乎？

Grammatically, the only crucial point is the omission of 於 between 行 and 一令, a feature increasingly common in later writings. So this sentence means simply, "(Your awe-inspiring) power can't (even) prevail over a single magistrate, oh?" (Note that 令 here refers to Dong Xuan, the 洛陽令. Though the word 令 can also mean "order", that is not the case here. So this sentence should not be translated as, "Can't your power carry out even a single order?")

### II. 因敕彊項令出

The word 敕 as a noun means "imperial order", but it can also function as a verb (as it does in this sentence) meaning "to order; to designate" (when the action is done by someone in authority). 彊項 as a compound means "a stiff neck", and 令 as a verb means "to order". The implied subject of the sentence is the emperor. So the sentence may be translated as: "Subsequently (the emperor) designated (i.e., called) him a stiff-neck and ordered him to go out". (An alternative reading of this sentence is to regard 彊項令 as a title meaning "the stiff-necked magistrate". There are, however, two problems with that interpretation. First, 董宣 was not known to have such a title or nickname. Second, 敕 and 令 often come in tandem as verbs.)

# 二十九.《後漢書·南匈奴傳》：
## 昭君(節)[1]

## 📖 課文 (Text)

　　昭君字嬙，南郡人也。² 初，元帝時以良家子選入
掖庭。³ 時呼韓邪來朝，⁴ 帝敕以宮女五人賜之。⁵ 昭君
入宮數歲不得見御，積悲怨，乃請掖庭令求行。⁶ 呼韓
邪臨辭大會，帝召五女以示之。昭君豐容靚飾，⁷ 光明
漢宮，顧景裴回，⁸ 竦動左右。⁹ 帝見大驚，意欲留之，
而難於失信，遂與匈奴。生二子。及呼韓邪死，其前閼
氏子代立，¹⁰ 欲妻之，昭君上書求歸，成帝敕令從胡
俗，遂復為後單于閼氏焉。¹¹

## 📝 註釋 (Annotations)

| | | | |
|---|---|---|---|
| 1. | 匈奴 | Xiōngnú | a nomadic people living to the north of China. |
| | 昭君 | Zhāojūn | Wáng Zhāojūn 王昭君, a famous Han court lady sent as a bride to appease the king of the Xiongnu. |
| 2. | 嬙 | Qiáng | another name for Wang Zhaojun. |
| | 南郡 | Nánjùn | a place name, also known as Jīngzhōu 荊州, in today's Hubei province. |
| 3. | 元帝 | Yuándì | Emperor Yuan of the Former Han, who reigned from 48 to 38 B.C. |
| | 良家子 | liáng jiā zǐ | a child of good parentage. |
| | 掖庭 | yì tíng | secondary housing in the palace complex. |
| 4. | 呼韓邪 | Hū Hán Yé | name of a chieftain of a branch of the Xiongnu. |

5. 敕　　　chì　　　an imperial order; here used as an adverb.

6. 御　　　yù　　　the emperor.

   令　　　lìng　　　the official in charge.

7. 豐容靚飾　fēng róng jìng shì　beautiful looks and elegant adornment.

8. 光　　　guāng　　brightness; brilliance.

   明　　　míng　　to brighten.

   顧景裴回　gù yǐng péi huí　looking at her own shadow, she moved slowly back and forth, i.e., reluctant to leave. (裴回, also written as 徘徊 pái huái; 景, same as 影.)

9. 竦動　　sǒng dòng　to startle.

10. 閼氏　　yān zhī　wife of the chieftain of the Xiongnu.

11. 令　　　lìng　　command; order.

    單于　　chán yú　a title off a leader of the Xiongnu.

## 📖 參考篇章一 (Reference Text I)

《明妃曲》[1]　王安石 (1021–1086) [2]

明妃初出漢宮時，淚溼春風鬢腳垂。[3]

低佪顧影無顏色，[4] 尚得君王不自持。

歸來卻怪丹青手，[5] 入眼平生幾曾有？

意態由來畫不成，[6] 當時枉殺毛延壽。[7]

一去心知更不歸，可憐著盡漢宮衣。

寄聲欲問塞南事，[8] 只有年年鴻雁飛。

家人萬里傳消息，好在氈城莫相憶。<sup>9</sup>

君不見咫尺長門閉阿嬌，<sup>10</sup> 人生失意無南北！

## 📋 註 釋 (Annotations)

| | | | |
|---|---|---|---|
| 1. | 明妃 | Míngfēi | Wang Zhaojun. |
| | 曲 | qǔ | a song. |
| 2. | 王安石 | Wáng Ānshí | a high official and writer of the Sòng 宋 Dynasty whose courtesy name is Jièfǔ 介甫. |
| 3. | 春風 | chūn fēng | spring breeze; used here in reference to the face, because the term is often used to describe a beautiful face. |
| 4. | 低佪 | dī huí | moving slowly with the head bending down, i.e., reluctant to go. |
| | 顧影 | gù yǐng | to look at one's own shadow, i.e., feeling self-pity. |
| 5. | 丹青 | dān qīng | painting. (丹 "red" and 青 "blue" are colors used in painting.) |
| 6. | 由來 | yóu lái | since the beginning; up to now; so far. |
| 7. | 枉殺 | wǎng shā | to kill wrongly. |
| | 毛延壽 | Máo Yánshòu | a Han painter who allegedly often distorted the appearance of a palace girl in his paintings if she refused to bribe him. |
| 8. | 塞南 | sài nán | the area of the Great Wall. |
| 9. | 氈城 | zhān chéng | city of felt (tents), i.e., yurts, referring to where the Xiongnu lived. |
| 10. | 咫尺 | zhǐ chǐ | a distance of inches and feet, i.e., very close. |

| 長門 | Chángmén | 長門宮, name of a palace where a queen of Emperor Wǔ of the Han 漢武帝 lived after she fell into disfavor. |
| 阿嬌 | Ā jiāo | name of the said queen for whom Emperor Wu once promised to build a house of gold. |

## 參考篇章二 (Reference Text II)

《明妃曲和王介甫作》[1]　歐陽修 (1007–1072)[2]

　　胡人以鞍馬為家，射獵為俗。泉甘草美無常處，鳥驚獸駭爭馳逐。誰將漢女嫁胡兒？風沙無情貌如玉。身行不遇中國人，馬上自作思歸曲。[3] 推手為琵卻手琶，胡人共聽亦咨嗟。[4] 玉顏流落死天涯，[5] 琵琶卻傳來漢家。漢宮爭按新聲譜，遺恨已深聲更苦。纖纖女手生洞房，[6] 學得琵琶不下堂。[7] 不識黃雲出塞路，[8] 豈知此聲能斷腸？

## 註釋 (Annotations)

1. 和　　　hè　　　to write a poem in reply.

   王介甫　Wáng Jièfǔ　Wang Anshi.

2. 歐陽修　Ōuyáng Xiū　a famous Song official and writer whose courtesy name is Yǒngshū 永叔.

3. 思歸曲　sī guī qǔ　song of homesickness.

4. 咨嗟　zī jiē　to sigh and lament.

5. 天涯　tiān yá　the edge of the world, i.e., a faraway, distant place.

6.  纖纖    xiān xiān    slender; delicate; fine.

7.  下堂    xià táng    to step down from the hall; to leave the house.

8.  黃雲    huáng yún    yellow clouds, i.e., the dusty clouds often seen in the desert.

# 三十.《桃花源記》[1]

## 陶淵明 (365–427) [2]

## 📖 課文 (Text)

晉太元中，³武陵人，捕魚為業。⁴緣溪行，⁵忘路之遠近。忽逢桃花林，⁶夾岸數百步，⁷中無雜樹，⁸芳草鮮美，⁹落英繽紛；¹⁰漁人甚異之。¹¹復前行，欲窮其林。林盡水源，便得一山。¹²山有小口，彷彿若有光，¹³便舍船，從口入。

初極狹，¹⁴纔通人；復行數十步，豁然開朗。¹⁵土地平曠，¹⁶屋舍儼然。¹⁷有良田、美池、桑、竹之屬。¹⁸阡陌交通，¹⁹雞犬相聞。其中往來種作，男女衣著，²⁰悉如外人，黃髮垂髫，²¹並怡然自樂。²²

見漁人，乃大驚，問所從來；具答之。²³便要還家，²⁴設酒、殺雞、作食。²⁵村中聞有此人，咸來問訊。²⁶自云：「先世避秦時亂，率妻子邑人來此絕境，²⁷不復出焉；遂與外人間隔。²⁸」問：「今是何世？」乃不知有漢，無論魏、晉！²⁹此人一一為具言所聞，皆歎惋。³⁰餘人各復延至其家，³¹皆出酒食。停數日，³²辭去。³³此中人語云：「不足為外人道也。³⁴」

既出，得其船，便扶向路，³⁵處處誌之。³⁶及郡下，詣太守，³⁷說如此。太守即遣人隨其往，尋向所誌，³⁸遂迷不復得路。

南陽劉子驥，<sup>39</sup> 高尚士也，<sup>40</sup> 聞之，欣然規往。<sup>41</sup>
未果，<sup>42</sup> 尋病終。<sup>43</sup> 後遂無問津者。<sup>44</sup>

## 📝 註釋 (Annotations)

1. 桃花　　　táo huā　　　peach blossom(s).

   源　　　　yuán　　　　source of a river.

   記　　　　jì　　　　　account; anecdote.

   桃花源記　táo huā yuán jì　The Story of the Peach Blossom Stream.

2. 陶淵明　　Táo Yuānmíng　a major poet of the Jìn 晉 Dynasty, whose formal name is Qián 潛; also known by another courtesy name, Yuánliàng 元亮.

3. 晉　　　　Jìn　　　　　name of a dynasty.

   太元　　　Tàiyuán　　　name of the period (376–397) under the reign of Emperor Xiàowǔ 孝武 of Jin.

4. 武陵　　　Wǔlíng　　　name of a place, in present-day Húnán 湖南 province.

5. 緣　　　　yuán　　　　along.

   溪　　　　xī　　　　　stream.

6. 忽　　　　hū　　　　　suddenly.

   逢　　　　féng　　　　to meet; to come upon.

7. 夾　　　　jiá　　　　　to be on both sides of.

8. 雜　　　　zá　　　　　mixed; here, other (types).

9. 芳　　　　fāng　　　　fragrant.

   鮮　　　　xiān　　　　fresh.

| | | |
|---|---|---|
| 10. 英 | yīng | flowers. |
| 繽紛 | bīn fēn | in riotous profusion. (A sound-related disyllabic word.) |
| 11. 異 | yì | to find (it) strange; to be surprised by. (A putative verb.) |
| 12. 便 | biàn | just then. (Similar to 就 in Modern Chinese.) |
| 13. 彷彿 | fǎng fú | to seem. |
| 14. 狹 | xiá | narrow. |
| 15. 豁然 | huò rán | unexpectedly opening up to a broad vista. (An adverb.) |
| 開朗 | kāi lǎng | open and clear. |
| 16. 曠 | kuàng | vast. |
| 17. 儼然 | yǎn rán | in neat order. |
| 18. 桑 | sāng | mulberry. |
| 屬 | shǔ | kind; here it means "such (things) like". |
| 19. 阡 | qiān | a footpath between fields running from north to south. |
| 陌 | mò | a footpath between fields running from east to west. |
| 交 | jiāo | to cross; to intersect. |
| 通 | tōng | to lead to; to connect with. |
| 20. 衣著 | yī zhuó | clothes. |
| 21. 黃髮 | huáng fà | very old men. (It is said that as old men get even older, their white hair will turn yellow.) |
| 髫 | tiáo | a child's hairstyle, with hair hanging loose. |

| | | |
|---|---|---|
| 垂髫 | chuí tiáo | children. |
| 22. 並 | bìng | both. |
| 怡然 | yí rán | cheerfully. |
| 23. 具 | jù | all; completely. (An adverb.) |
| 24. 要 | yāo | to invite. (Same as 邀.) |
| 25. 設 | shè | to place; to set up. |
| 26. 咸 | xián | all. (An adverb.) (Similar to 都 in Modern Chinese.) |
| 訊 | xùn | to inquire about. |
| 27. 率 | shuài | to lead. |
| 邑人 | yì rén | fellow villagers. |
| 絕 | jué | to cut off. |
| 境 | jìng | place; area. |
| 絕境 | jué jìng | an isolated place. |
| 28. 間隔 | jiàn gé | to be cut off from; to be separated from. |
| 29. 世 | shì | age. |
| 無論 | wú lùn | let alone. |
| 魏 | Wèi | a dynasty falling between the Han and Jin Dynasties. |
| 30. 惋 | wǎn | to feel sad. |
| 31. 延 | yán | to invite. |
| 32. 停 | tíng | to stay. |
| 33. 辭 | cí | to take leave of. |
| 34. 不足 | bù zú | not to be worth. |

| 35. | 扶 | fú | to follow. |
| | 向 | xiàng | former; previous. (The next 向 in the text is the same.) |
| 36. | 誌 | zhì | to mark. |
| 37. | 郡下 | jùn xià | the capital of a prefecture. (Equivalent to 郡中 jùn zhōng.) |
| | 詣 | yì | to go (to see somebody). |
| 38. | 尋 | xún | to seek; to look for. |
| 39. | 南陽 | Nányáng | name of a place. |
| | 劉子驥 | Liú Zǐjì | name of a person. |
| 40. | 高尚 | gāo shàng | noble; distinguished. |
| 41. | 欣然 | xīn rán | joyfully. |
| | 規 | guī | to plan. |
| 42. | 未果 | wèi guǒ | not to realize (an aim). |
| 43. | 尋 | xún | soon. |
| | 終 | zhōng | to die. |
| 44. | 津 | jīn | ferry crossing. |
| | 問津 | wèn jīn | to inquire about the ferry crossing; here, to ask about the way to the village. |

## ☀ 文法闡釋 (Grammar Note)

(其中) 往來種作，男女衣著，悉如外人。

There is a tendency among readers of Classical Chinese prose to mark off words in a sentence in groups of four. So most anthologies which include the present essay punctuate the above sentence as 往來種作，男女衣著，悉如外人。But actually it would be better to punctuate the sentence as 往來種作男女，衣著悉如外人。(Remember, Classical Chinese texts were not originally punctuated.) This would better reveal that 往來種作 modifies 男女 as the subject of the sentence, while 衣著悉如外人 is a clause serving as the predicate. So this sentence can be translated as: "As to the men and women either walking back and forth or working in the field, their clothes are all just like (those of) the people outside".

## 參考篇章 (Reference Text)

《桃源行》[1] 王維 (701–761) [2]

漁舟逐水愛山春，兩岸桃花夾去津。

坐看紅樹不知遠，行盡青溪不見人。

山口潛行始隈隩，[3] 山開曠望旋平陸。

遙看一處攢雲樹，[4] 近入千家散花竹。

樵客初傳漢姓名，[5] 居人未改秦衣服。

居人共住武陵源，還從物外起田園。[6]

月明松下房櫳靜，[7] 日出雲中雞犬喧。

驚聞俗客爭來集，競引還家問都邑。

平明閭巷掃花開，[8] 薄暮漁樵乘水入。[9]

初因避地去人間，及至成仙遂不還。

峽裡誰知有人事，[10] 世中遙望空雲山。

不疑靈境難聞見，[11] 塵心未盡思鄉縣。[12]

出洞無論隔山水，辭家終擬長游衍。[13]

自謂經過舊不迷，安知峰壑今來變。[14]

當時知記入山深，青溪幾曲到雲林。

春來遍是桃花水，不辯仙源何處尋。[15]

## 📑 註 釋 (Annotations)

1. 行　　　　xíng　　　　　song; ballad.

2. 王維　　　Wáng Wéi　　a major Tang poet.

3. 隈隩　　　wēi ào　　　　sharply curved and winding (referring to a river).

4. 攢　　　　zān　　　　　cluster.

5. 樵客　　　qiáo kè　　　　a wood cutter. (In the Chinese tradition, wood cutters and fishermen are often taken to be people who live in harmony with nature, or "out of this world", as hermits.)

6. 物外　　　wù wài　　　　another world.

7. 櫳　　　　lóng　　　　　window.

8. 平明　　　píng míng　　　dawn.

　　閭巷　　lǚ xiàng　　　　alley and lane.

9. 薄暮　　　bó mù　　　　　dusk.

10. 人事　　　rén shì　　　　worldly affairs.

11. 靈境　　　líng jìng　　　　divine or marvelous place.

12. 塵心　　　chén xīn　　　　(vulgar) human aspirations.

13. 游衍　　　yóu yǎn　　　　to travel for pleasure.

14. 峰壑　　　fēng huò　　　　peaks and valleys.

15. 仙源　　　xiān yuán　　　fairy land; place where celestial beings live.

# 三十一.《蘭亭集序》[1]

王羲之 (c. 303–361)[2]

## 📖 課文 (Text)

　　永和九年，歲在癸丑，³ 暮春之初，會于會稽山陰之蘭亭，⁴ 修禊事也。⁵ 群賢畢至，少長咸集。⁶ 此地有崇山峻嶺，⁷ 茂林修竹，⁸ 又有清流激湍，⁹ 映帶左右，¹⁰ 引以為流觴曲水，¹¹ 列坐其次。雖無絲竹管絃之盛，¹² 一觴一詠，¹³ 亦足以暢敘幽情。¹⁴ 是日也，天朗氣清，¹⁵ 惠風和暢，¹⁶ 仰觀宇宙之大，¹⁷ 俯察品類之盛，¹⁸ 所以游目騁懷，¹⁹ 足以極視聽之娛，信可樂也。²⁰

　　夫人之相與，²¹ 俯仰一世，²² 或取諸懷抱，²³ 晤言一室之內，²⁴ 或因寄所託，放浪形骸之外。²⁵ 雖趣舍萬殊，²⁶ 靜躁不同，²⁷ 當其欣於所遇，暫得於己，快然自足，不知老之將至。及其所之既倦，²⁸ 情隨事遷，感慨係之矣。²⁹ 向之所欣，³⁰ 俛仰之間，³¹ 已為陳跡，³² 猶不能不以之興懷；況修短隨化，³³ 終期於盡。古人云：「死生亦大矣。」豈不痛哉！

　　每覽昔人興感之由，若合一契，³⁴ 未嘗不臨文嗟悼，³⁵ 不能喻之於懷。³⁶ 固知一死生為虛誕，³⁷ 齊彭殤為妄作，³⁸ 後之視今，亦猶今之視昔，悲夫！故列敘時人，³⁹ 錄其所述，雖世殊事異，所以興懷，⁴⁰ 其致一也。⁴¹ 後之覽者，亦將有感於斯文。

## 📑 註釋 (Annotations)

1. 蘭亭    Lántíng    Orchid Pavilion.

   集    jí    collection (of compositions).

   序    xù    preface.

2. 王羲之    Wáng Xīzhī    a Jin Dynasty scholar noted for his calligraphy. His dates have also been given as 321–379 and 307–365.

3. 永和    Yǒnghé    name of one of the reign periods of Emperor Mù 穆 (345–361) of the Jin Dynasty.

   歲    suì    the planet Jupiter (太歲 tài suì); here, the calendar or year.

   癸丑    guǐ chǒu    the year of 癸丑. 癸 is the tenth of the ten so-called Heavenly Stems and 丑 is the second of the twelve so-called Earthly Branches (地支 dì zhī). The stems and branches are combined to form a sixty-year cycle. The year 癸丑 corresponds to the fiftieth stem-branch combination.

4. 暮春    mù chūn    late spring; the third month of the spring season.

   會稽山陰    Kuàijī Shānyīn    Kuaiji and Shanyin are both place names, in today's Shàoxīng 紹興 of Zhèjiāng 浙江 province.

5. 修禊事    xiū xì shì    An ancient ritual held on the third day of the third month in the lunar calendar, usually at a scenic spot near a river, to exorcize the evil spirits; later the occasion was often used for a party. 禊, rite of purification.

6. 群賢畢至    qún xián bì zhì    the many worthies have all arrived. 畢 is an adverb, meaning "all".

   少長咸集    shào zhǎng xián jí    young and old have all gathered together. 咸, is an adverb, meaning "all".

7.  崇山峻嶺　　chóng shān jùn lǐng　　lofty mountains and precipitous peaks.

8.  茂林修竹　　mào lín xiū zhú　　exuberant growth of trees and bamboos. 茂, flourishing; 修, slender; long.

9.  清流激湍　　qīng liú jī tuān　　clear streams and rushing rapids.

10. 映帶左右　　yìng dài zuǒ yòu　　the reflected light of the stream flickers around the pavilion. 映, the reflection of the light; 帶, to encircle like a belt.

11. 流觴曲水　　liú shāng qū shuǐ　　a winding course of water along which a wine cup could float. When the cup is stopped near someone, he has to pick it up and drink from it, and compose a poem. 觴, wine cup.

12. 絲竹管絃　　sī zhú guǎn xián　　(silk) strings and (bamboo) tubes, i.e., stringed and woodwind instruments—musical instruments.

13. 一觴一詠　　yī shāng yī yǒng　　to drink a cup of wine, and then chant a poem or sing a song.

14. 暢敘幽情　　chàng xù yōu qíng　　to fully express one's deep feelings.

15. 天朗氣清　　tiān lǎng qì qīng　　the sky is bright and the air is clear.

16. 惠風　　huì fēng　　tender breeze.

    和暢　　hé chàng　　smooth and comforting.

17. 宇宙　　yǔ zhòu　　the universe; the cosmos.

18. 品類之盛　　pǐn lèi zhī shèng　　the multitudes of all kinds of things and animals. 品類, categories; 盛, flourishing.

19. 游目騁懷　　yóu mù chěng huái　　to let the eyes roam and set the mind free. 騁, to gallop.

| 20. | 信 | xìn | really; truly. |
|---|---|---|---|
| 21. | 相與 | xiāng yǔ | to associate with one another, i.e., to be friends. |
| 22. | 俯仰一世 | fǔ yǎng yī shì | for all one's life. 俯, to lower one's head; 仰, to raise one's head. |
| 23. | 取諸懷抱 | qǔ zhū huái bào | to take it from one's bosom, i.e., privately. (諸 is the same as 之於.) |
| 24. | 晤言 | wù yán | to talk with one another; face to face. |
| 25. | 放浪形骸 | fàng làng xíng hái | to let one's body roam unbridled; here, in the natural world. 形骸, the human body. |
| 26. | 趣舍萬殊 | qū shě wàn shū | differences in people's aims and means. 趣 is the same as 趨, to hasten somewhere; 舍, to discard or to abandon. |
| 27. | 靜躁 | jìng zào | being quiet or being impatient, meaning that each has his or her own temperament. |
| 28. | 所之 | suǒ zhī | what one pursues. 之 here is a verb, meaning "to go; to pursue". |
| 29. | 係之 | xì zhī | go along with or follow it. |
| 30. | 向之所欣 | xiàng zhī suǒ xīn | that which one enjoyed in the past. 向, the past. |
| 31. | 俛仰之間 | fǔ yǎng zhī jiān | in between a bending and lifting of the head—a very short instance of time. |
| 32. | 陳跡 | chén jī | past traces; historical remains. |
| 33. | 修短隨化 | xiū duǎn suí huà | the length of human life has to accord with natural or cosmic law. 修, long. |
| 34. | 若合一契 | ruò hé yī qì | to appear in complete agreement. 契, a tally split into two halves, with each half held by one party and if the two halves match, legal authority is established. Hence 合一契. |

35. 臨文嗟悼    lín wén jiē dào    to feel sad or woeful when reading their essays.

36. 喻之於懷    yù zhī yú huái    to understand in one's own mind. 喻, to understand.

37. 一死生    yī sǐ shēng    to regard death and life as one and the same thing, and to make no distinction between them. (This notion comes from Zhuangzi.)

     虛誕    xū dàn    虛, empty; untrue. 誕, absurd; grotesque.

38. 齊彭殤    qí Péng shāng    to make no distinction between a man who lived a long life and one who died young. 彭 is the same as 彭祖 Péng Zǔ, a legendary figure who was said to have lived eight hundred and eighty years. 殤, those who die young.

     妄作    wàng zuò    words with no basis; fantastic talk.

39. 列敘時人    liè xù shí rén    to mention one by one all those who participated in this gathering. 敘, to narrate; to describe.

40. 興懷    xīng huái    to raise one's spirits; to cheer up.

41. 其致一也    qí zhì yī yě    the mood and feeling are the same. 致 is the same as 情致, feeling; emotion; mood.

# 三十二.《雜説四》[1]

韓愈 (768-824)[2]

## 📖 課文 (Text)

世有伯樂，³ 然後有千里馬。⁴ 千里馬常有，⁵ 而伯
樂不常有。故雖有名馬，⁶ 祇辱於奴隸人之手，⁷ 駢死
於槽櫪之間，⁸ 不以千里稱也。馬之千里者，一食或盡
粟一石。⁹ 食馬者，¹⁰ 不知其能千里而食也。是馬也，
雖有千里之能，食不飽，力不足，才美不外見，¹¹ 且欲
與常馬等不可得，¹² 安求其能千里也。¹³ 策之不以其
道，¹⁴ 食之不能盡其材，鳴之而不能通其意，¹⁵ 執策而
臨之曰：¹⁶「天下無馬。」嗚呼！其真無馬邪？¹⁷ 其真不
知馬也！

## 📑 註釋 (Annotations)

| | | | |
|---|---|---|---|
| 1. | 雜説 | zá shuō | miscellaneous essays. (There are four miscellaneous essays by Han Yu. This is the fourth one.) |
| 2. | 韓愈 | Hán Yù | the most famous prose writer of the Táng 唐 Dynasty, whose courtesy name is Tuìzhī 退之. |
| 3. | 伯樂 | Bó Lè | a man of the Qin Dynasty who was known as the best judge of horses. |
| 4. | 千里馬 | qiān lǐ mǎ | horses that can travel a thousand *li* a day. |
| 5. | 常 | cháng | often. |
| 6. | 名 | míng | famous. |
| 7. | 祇 | zhǐ | an ancient form of 只, meaning "only". |

| | | |
|---|---|---|
| 辱 | rǔ | to humiliate; here, to be humiliated. |
| 奴隸人 | nú lì rén | servant. |
| 8. 駢 | pián | (of two horses) standing or harnessed together side by side. |
| 槽櫪 | cáo lì | manger. 槽 and 櫪 are synonyms. |
| 9. 或 | huò | sometimes. |
| 盡 | jìn | to exhaust; here it means "to eat (all of)". |
| 10. 食 | sì | to feed. (The 食 in 食馬 and 食之 are the same.) |
| 11. 見 | xiàn | to appear. |
| 12. 常馬 | cháng mǎ | ordinary horse. |
| 等 | děng | to be equal to; to be well-matched. |
| 13. 求 | qiú | to demand; to expect. |
| 14. 策 | cè | whip; here used as a verb, meaning "to whip a horse on". |
| 15. 鳴 | míng | to neigh. |
| 之 | zhī | this character serves only a rhythmical function. |
| 通 | tōng | to understand. |
| 鳴之而不能通其意 | míng zhī ér bù néng tōng qí yì | when the horse neighs, (one) cannot understand its wish. |
| 16. 執 | zhí | to hold. |
| 臨 | lín | to face. |
| 17. 其 | qí | modal particle expressing uncertainty and non-assertion, hence implying courtesy. (An adverb.) (The next 其 works in the same way.) |

## ☀ 文法闡釋 (Grammar Note)

### 安求其能千里也

安, normally meaning "where", functions here as an adverb and can thus be better represented by "how". The verb 求 "request; demand" often implies "expect". 其能千里, the object of 求, means literally "its being able (to run) a thousand *li* (in one day)", but can also be rendered as a dependent clause, "that it can run a thousand *li* in one day", in translation. Since the sentence has no subject, its implied subject can be assumed to be "anyone" ("how can anyone expect that …"), or it can be translated in the passive voice ("how can it be expected that …").

# 三十三.《師說》[1]

韓愈 (768–824)

## 📖 課文 (Text)

古之學者必有師。師者，所以傳道、受業、解惑也。[2] 人非生而知之者，孰能無惑？惑而不從師，其為惑也，終不解矣。

生乎吾前，其聞道也，固先乎吾，吾從而師之。[3] 生乎吾後，其聞道也，亦先乎吾，吾從而師之。吾師道也，夫庸知其年之先後生於吾乎？[4] 是故無貴無賤，無長無少，[5] 道之所存，[6] 師之所存也。

嗟乎！[7] 師道之不傳也久矣！欲人之無惑也難矣！古之聖人，其出人也遠矣，[8] 猶且從師而問焉。[9] 今之眾人，[10] 其下聖人也亦遠矣，而恥學於師。[11] 是故聖益聖，[12] 愚益愚，聖人之所以為聖，愚人之所以為愚，其皆出於此乎？[13]

愛其子，擇師而教之，[14] 於其身也，則恥師焉，[15] 惑矣！[16] 彼童子之師，[17] 授之書而習其句讀者，[18] 非吾所謂傳其道、解其惑者也。句讀之不知，惑之不解，或師焉，或不焉，[19] 小學而大遺，[20] 吾未見其明也。

巫、醫、樂師、百工之人，不恥相師；[21] 士大夫之族，[22] 曰師、曰弟子云者，[23] 則群聚而笑之。[24] 問之，[25] 則曰：「彼與彼年相若也，[26] 道相似也。」位卑則足羞，[27] 官盛則近諛。[28] 嗚呼！[29] 師道之不復可知矣。[30]

巫、醫、樂師、百工之人，君子不齒，<sup>31</sup> 今其智乃反不能及，其可怪也歟？！

## 📝 註釋 (Annotations)

1. 師説　　shī shuō　　an essay about teachers.

2. 傳　　　chuán　　　to pass on; to hand down.

   受　　　shòu　　　 to hand over; to teach. (A substitute for 授.)

   業　　　yè　　　　 learning; profession; trade.

   解　　　jiě　　　　to solve.

   惑　　　huò　　　　puzzlement; confusion.

3. 師　　　shī　　　　to treat somebody as one's teacher; to learn from.

4. 庸　　　yōng　　　equivalent to 豈 or 哪裡 in Modern Chinese. 庸知, how am I to know? (See 文法闡釋 I).

   先後生　xiān hòu　　to be born earlier or later than I.
   於吾　　shēng yú wú

5. 無　　　wú　　　　it doesn't matter whether … or … (Similar to the Modern Chinese 無論.)

   無貴無賤　wú guì wú jiàn　whether noble or ordinary.

6. 存　　　cún　　　　to exist.

7. 嗟乎　　jiē hū　　　exclamation, like "alas!" in English.

8. 出　　　chū　　　　to surpass.

9. 猶且　　yóu qiě　　　even … still.

   猶且從師　yóu qiě cóng　Even (the sages) still had teachers and learned
   而問焉　　shī ér wèn　 from them.
   　　　　　yān

| | | |
|---|---|---|
| 10. 眾人 | zhòng rén | the common multitude. |
| 11. 恥 | chǐ | to feel ashamed (to do something). |
| 12. 聖益聖 | shèng yì shèng | the sages became more sagely. The first 聖 is a noun, the second 聖 is an adjective. (The next sentence is similar. 益 is an adverb indicating intensification.) |
| 13. 出於 | chū yú | to proceed from; to come out of. |
| 14. 擇 | zé | to select. |
| 15. 其身 | qí shēn | himself. |
| 16. 惑 | huò | to be confused. |
| 17. 童子 | tóng zǐ | child. |
| 18. 習 | xí | to practice. |
| 句讀 | jù dòu | Classical Chinese texts were not punctuated. Readers had to punctuate as they read, putting a ◦ at the end of a sentence or clause, and a 、 at a pause in a sentence. ◦ was called 句 and 、 was called 讀. So 句讀 means "punctuation". |
| 習其句讀 | xí qí jù dòu | to make the children practice their punctuation. |
| 19. 不 | fǒu | to not do (something). |
| 20. 遺 | yí | to leave out. |
| 小學而大遺 | xiǎo xué ér dà yí | to learn the minor matters (referring to 句讀) but leave out the important matters (referring to 解惑). |
| 21. 巫 | wū | witch doctor. |
| 樂師 | yuè shī | musician. |
| 百工 | bǎi gōng | all kinds of craftsmen. |

| 22. | 士大夫 | shì dà fū | literati and officials. The old reading for 大 here is dài. |
| | 族 | zú | group. |
| 23. | 云 | yún | used to introduce a quotation, indicating that it is an indirect and approximate quotation. (A particle). |
| 24. | 群聚 | qún jù | to gather in groups. |
| 25. | 問之 | wèn zhī | to ask them. |
| 26. | 彼與彼 | bǐ yǔ bǐ | referring to the person who was called the teacher and the person who called himself the disciple. |
| | 年 | nián | age. |
| | 相若 | xiāng ruò | similar; close. (相似 in the next sentence has the same meaning.) |
| 27. | 位 | wèi | position. |
| | 卑 | bēi | humble. |
| | 足羞 | zú xiū | very shameful. |
| 28. | 盛 | shèng | great; high. |
| | 諛 | yú | to flatter. |
| 29. | 嗚呼 | wū hū | exclamation, similar to "alas" in English. |
| 30. | 復 | fù | to revive. |
| 31. | 不齒 | bù chǐ | to despise; to look down on. |

## 📖 課文—續 (Text — Continued)

聖人無常師。[32] 孔子師郯子、萇弘、師襄、老聃。[33] 郯子之徒，[34] 其賢不及孔子。孔子曰：「三人行，必有

我師。<sup>35</sup>」是故弟子不必不如師，<sup>36</sup> 師不必賢於弟子，聞
道有先後，術業有專攻，<sup>37</sup> 如是而已。

李氏子蟠，<sup>38</sup> 年十七，好古文，<sup>39</sup> 六藝經傳皆通習
之。<sup>40</sup> 不拘於時，<sup>41</sup> 學於余，余嘉其能行古道，<sup>42</sup> 作師
說以貽之。<sup>43</sup>

## 📝 註 釋 (Annotations)

| | | | |
|---|---|---|---|
| 32. | 常師 | cháng shī | permanent teacher; a single teacher. |
| 33. | 郯子 | Tán Zǐ | a ruler of the state of Tán 郯 during the Spring and Autumn period from whom Confucius was said to have learned about the names of officials. |
| | 萇弘 | Cháng Hóng | a minister of the Zhou Dynasty from whom Confucius was said to have learned about music. |
| | 師襄 | Shī Xiāng | a musician of the Lu state from whom Confucius was said to have learned how to play the 琴 qín. |
| | 老聃 | Lǎo Dān | namely Lǎozǐ 老子 from whom Confucius was said to have learned about rituals. |
| 34. | 徒 | tú | group or kind (of people). (Note that in Classical Chinese the common meaning of 徒 is not "disciple".) |
| 35. | 三人行，必有我師 | sān rén xíng, bì yǒu wǒ shī | In any group of people, there must be some whom I can call a teacher. |
| 36. | 不必 | bú bì | not necessarily. (This is different from 不必 in Modern Chinese meaning "need not".) |
| 37. | 術業 | shù yè | learning. |
| | 專 | zhuān | special. |

| | | |
|---|---|---|
| 攻 | gōng | to study diligently; to research. |
| 38. 李氏子蟠 | Lǐ shì zǐ Pán | the young man of the Li family named Pan. |
| 39. 古文 | gǔ wén | a style of prose which is contrasted to parallel prose (駢文 pián wén). |
| 40. 六藝 | Liùyì | the six Confucian Classics, i.e., *Yì*《易》, *Shū*《書》, *Shī*《詩》, *Lǐ*《禮》, *Yuè*《樂》, *Chūnqiū*《春秋》. |
| 經 | jīng | a classic. |
| 傳 | zhuàn | commentary to a classic. |
| 通 | tōng | thoroughly. |
| 41. 時 | shí | here it means "fad", the conventions of the time. (This refers to the practice of denying the need for a teacher.) |
| 42. 嘉 | jiā | to commend. |
| 43. 貽 | yí | to give; to present. |

## ☀ 文法闡釋 (Grammar Notes)

## I. 夫庸知其年之先後生於吾乎？

As an initial marker for argumentative sentences, 夫 means something like "Now, …". 庸知, which often appears as 庸詎知 in the *Zhuangzi*, often marks a rhetorical question in the sense of "how do I know" or "do I have to know". Strictly speaking, 其年之先後生於吾, the object of the verb 知, is illogical semantically. It is perhaps a loose combination of 其年之先後於吾 "his age's being older or younger than mine" and 其先後生於吾 "his being born earlier or later than I". The sentence can thus be translated as: "Do I have to know whether he is older or younger than I am?"

## II. 師道之不傳也久矣！

Literally, the subject of this sentence 師道之不傳也 means "the Dao of teachers' not being passed on", but it is better to translate it as a clause, "that the teachers' Dao was not passed on". 久矣 is the predicate, but it should be translated as: "It has been a long time since (the teachers' Dao was not passed on)". 難矣 and 遠矣 in the next two sentences working in similar ways.

## III. 句讀之不知，惑之不解，或師焉，或不焉。

This is a fairly complex sentence. It relates two contrasting cases: (a) when the punctuation (of books) is not known, (b) when confusion (about moral issues in life) is not resolved. It then comments that in the first case [i.e., case (a)], people look for a teacher, but in the second case [i.e., case (b)], they do not. So this sentence is followed by the author's lament that people look for teachers for minor things but neglect the big issues 小學而大遺.

## IV. 位卑則足羞，官盛則近諛。

Since these two sentences both have 則 in the middle, they are "conditional" in nature. They are somewhat confusing because in each case, the clause before 則 and the one after it refer to different subjects (fairly common in sentences of this type). The first clause is about the (potential) teacher and the second is about the (potential) student. So these two sentences should be rendered as: "If a teacher's position is low, one may feel it is quite shameful (to have him as a teacher); if a teacher's official rank is high, one may feel it is almost like toadying (to go to him as a disciple)". The implication is that the teacher-student relationship among the 士大夫之族 is difficult to establish.

# 三十四.《黔之驢》[1]

## 柳宗元 (773–819) [2]

## 📖 課文 (Text)

　　黔無驢，有好事者，船載以入；<sup>3</sup> 至則無可用，放之山下。虎見之，龐然大物也，<sup>4</sup> 以為神。蔽林間窺之，<sup>5</sup> 稍出近之，<sup>6</sup> 憖憖然莫相知。<sup>7</sup>

　　他日，<sup>8</sup> 驢一鳴，<sup>9</sup> 虎大駭，<sup>10</sup> 遠遁，<sup>11</sup> 以為且噬己也，<sup>12</sup> 甚恐！然往來視之，覺無異能者，<sup>13</sup> 益習其聲，<sup>14</sup> 又近出前後，終不敢搏。稍近益狎，<sup>15</sup> 蕩倚衝冒。<sup>16</sup> 驢不勝怒，<sup>17</sup> 蹄之。<sup>18</sup> 虎因喜，計之曰：<sup>19</sup>「技止此耳！<sup>20</sup>」因跳踉大㘚，<sup>21</sup> 斷其喉，盡其肉，乃去。

　　噫！<sup>22</sup> 形之龐也，類有德，<sup>23</sup> 聲之宏也，類有能。向不出其技，<sup>24</sup> 虎雖猛，疑畏卒不敢取，<sup>25</sup> 今若是焉，悲夫！<sup>26</sup>

## 📑 註釋 (Annotations)

| | | | |
|---|---|---|---|
| 1. | 黔 | Qián | a prefecture of the Tang Dynasty, in present-day Guìzhōu 貴州 province. |
| 2. | 柳宗元 | Liǔ Zōngyuán | the second most famous prose writer in the Tang Dynasty, whose courtesy name is Zǐhòu 子厚. |
| 3. | 好事者 | hào shì zhě | busybody. |
| | 載 | zài | to carry; to be loaded. |
| 4. | 龐然 | páng rán | large. |
| 5. | 蔽 | bì | to take cover. |

|     | 窺       | kuī        | to spy. |
| 6.  | 稍       | shāo       | slightly. |
| 7.  | 憖憖然   | yìn yìn rán | cautiously. |
|     | 莫       | mò         | in pre-Han Chinese, 莫 means "no one" or "nothing"; "not" is its later meaning. |
| 8.  | 他日     | tā rì      | another day. |
| 9.  | 鳴       | míng       | to call. |
| 10. | 駭       | hài        | to be astonished. |
| 11. | 遁       | dùn        | to flee. |
| 12. | 且       | qiě        | to be about to. |
|     | 噬       | shì        | to bite. |
| 13. | 異能     | yì néng    | unusual ability or skill. |
| 14. | 習       | xí         | to be accustomed to. |
| 15. | 狎       | xiá        | to be familiar with and not care about. |
| 16. | 蕩       | dàng       | to shake. |
|     | 倚       | yǐ         | to lean. |
|     | 衝       | chōng      | to rush. |
|     | 冒       | mào        | to dash out. |
| 17. | 不勝     | bù shēng   | cannot bear or overcome. |
| 18. | 蹄       | tí         | hoof; here used as a verb, to kick. |
| 19. | 計       | jì         | to figure; to calculate. |
| 20. | 技       | jì         | skill; ability. |
| 21. | 跳踉     | tiào liáng | to bound; to jump up and down. |

| | | |
|---|---|---|
| 闞 | hǎn | to roar. |
| 22. 噫 | yī | exclamation, corresponding to "ah" in English. |
| 23. 類 | lèi | to seem. |
| 24. 向 | xiàng | formerly; in past times. |
| 出 | chū | to bring out; to show. |
| 25. 疑 | yí | to doubt; to have misgivings. |
| 26. 夫 | fú | used at the end of a sentence as an exclamation. (A particle.) |

## ☀ 文法闡釋 (Grammar Notes)

## I. 覺無異能者，益習其聲。

Omission of some unnecessary elements, especially grammatical particles, when context permits, is not uncommon in early Classical Chinese texts, but the great masters of Classical Chinese prose in the Tang/Song period sometimes seemed to have carried that a bit too far. The present sentence may be such an example. On the surface, both 覺 and 習 are immediately followed by nominal expressions (無 異能者 and 其聲), which seems to make them transitive verbs. If so, the sentence would mean, "(he) awakened those without special ability, and (he) further imitated their voice". This, of course, is not true. We know from the context that the sentence means: "The tiger then sensed that the donkey was one without any special ability, and he became more used to his voice". This interpretation is possible only when we agree that the full form of the sentence should be 覺 (其為) 無異能者，益 習 (於) 其聲, that is, 覺 is followed by a clause as its object, while 習, followed by 於, is an intransitive verb.

## II. 形之龐也，類有德。

The noun 類 "kind; type" serves here as a transitive verb, in the sense of "to look like the kind of (things or people)". Its object 有德 is not a clause ("[he] has virtue"), but a simplified form of 有德者, meaning "those who have virtue". The first part of the sentence 形之龐也 gives the fact (i.e., "it is huge") as the basis for suggesting the conclusion 類有德. So the sentence can be rendered as: "Since its body is huge, it looks like the kind of things which have virtue". The sentence following this shares the same structure.

# 三十五.《小石城山記》[1]

## 柳宗元 (773–819)

## 📖 課文 (Text)

自西山道口徑北，²踰黃茅嶺而下，³有二道：其一西出，尋之無所得。⁴其一少北而東，不過四十丈，土斷而川分，⁵有積石橫當其垠。⁶其上為睥睨梁欐之形，⁷其旁出堡塢，⁸有若門焉，窺之正黑。⁹投以小石，洞然有水聲。¹⁰其響之激越，¹¹良久乃已。¹²環之可上，¹³望甚遠。

無土壤而生嘉樹美箭，¹⁴益奇而堅。其疏數偃仰，¹⁵類智者所施設也。¹⁶

噫！吾疑造物者之有無久矣。¹⁷及是愈以為誠有。¹⁸又怪其不為之中州，¹⁹而列是夷狄，²⁰更千百年不得一售其伎，²¹是固勞而無用，²²神者儻不宜如是，²³則其果無乎？

或曰：²⁴「以慰夫賢而辱於此者。²⁵」或曰：「其氣之靈，不為偉人，²⁶而獨為是物，故楚之南，少人而多石。²⁷」是二者，余未信之。²⁸

## 📝 註釋 (Annotations)

1. 小石城山　Xiǎoshíchéng shān　Stonecastle Hill, which was in Yǒngzhōu 永州.

2. 徑　jìng　straight.

   北　běi　here used as a verb, meaning "to go north".

3. 踰     yú     to cross over.

    黃茅嶺     Huángmáolǐng     Huangmao Hill.

4. 尋     xún     to seek; to try to find.

5. 川     chuān     stream; river.

6. 橫     héng     transversely.

    當     dāng     to block.

    垠     yín     margin; bank.

7. 睥睨     bì nì     battlements on a city wall.

    梁     liáng     beam.

    欐     lì     ridgepole.

8. 堡塢     bǎo wù     earthen fort.

9. 正黑     zhèng hēi     very dark.

10. 洞然     dòng rán     describing the sound of water. (An onomatopoeia.)

11. 響     xiǎng     echo. (Note that in Classical Chinese, 響 basically means "echo", not "sound".)

    激越     jī yuè     loud and clear.

12. 良久     liáng jiǔ     a good while.

13. 環     huán     to wind around; to walk around.

14. 土壤     tǔ rǎng     soil.

    嘉     jiā     good.

    箭     jiàn     bamboo.

15. 疏     shū     sparse; thin.

    數     cù     dense.

| | | |
|---|---|---|
| 偃 | yǎn | bending. |
| 仰 | yǎng | standing straight. |
| 16. 類 | lèi | to resemble. |
| 施設 | shī shè | to arrange. |
| 17. 疑 | yí | to doubt. |
| 造物者 | zào wù zhě | the divine force that created the universe; the Creator. |
| 18. 愈 | yù | more. |
| 誠 | chéng | indeed. |
| 19. 中州 | zhōng zhōu | central states, referring to China proper. |
| 20. 列 | liè | to line up; to place. |
| 夷狄 | yí dí | a shortened form for 夷狄之地 "barbarian land", i.e., Yongzhou, which the ancients considered a barbarian area. |
| 21. 更 | gēng | to pass. (Note that in Classical Chinese 更 does not mean "more".) |
| 售 | shòu | to sell. |
| 伎 | jì | skill. (This word is normally written as 技.) |
| 售其伎 | shòu qí jì | to sell his skill, i.e., to make people appreciate it. |
| 22. 勞 | láo | to work hard. |
| 23. 儻 | tǎng | perhaps. |
| 24. 或 | huò | somebody. |
| 25. 慰 | wèi | to comfort; to console. |
| 辱 | rǔ | to humiliate. (See Lesson 29.) Here, to be humiliated, i.e., being banished. |

26. 氣          qì          an invisible substance, once believed to be the
                            basic constituent of everything in the universe.

    靈          líng        spirit.

27. 楚          Chǔ         a name for Hubei and part of Hunan, which in the
                            Zhou Dynasty constituted the state of Chu.
                            Yongzhou was to the south of this region.

28. 余          yú          I; me.

## 文法闡釋 (Grammar Note)

其疏數偃仰，類智者所施設也。

The structure of this sentence is the same as that of the second example in the Grammar Notes section of Lesson 34. The first part seems to be different only because 其, instead of "N + 之", is used, but they play the same syntactic role. The nominalizer 所 in 智者（之）所施設 indicates that the phrase (the object of 類) is definitely a nominal ("that which some intelligent beings arranged"). The sentence can thus be rendered as: "They (the trees and bamboos) are either sparse or dense, either bending down or standing straight, and thus look like they were arranged by some intelligent beings".

# 三十六.《琵琶行》并序[1]

## 白居易（772–846）[2]

## 📖 課文 (Text)

序

　　元和十年，³予左遷九江郡司馬。⁴明年秋，送客
湓浦口。⁵聞船中夜彈琵琶者，聽其音錚錚然有京都
聲。⁶問其人，本長安倡女，⁷嘗學琵琶於穆曹二善才。⁸
年長色衰，委身為賈人婦。⁹遂命酒使快彈數曲。曲罷
憫然，¹⁰自敘少小時歡樂事；今漂淪憔悴，¹¹轉徙於江
湖間。¹²予出官二年，恬然自安，¹³感斯人言，是夕，
始覺有遷謫意，¹⁴因為長句，歌以贈之。凡六百一十六
言，命曰：¹⁵「琵琶行。」

## 📑 註釋 (Annotations)

| | | | |
|---|---|---|---|
| 1. | 琵琶 | pí pá | a stringed musical instrument; moon-guitar. |
| | 并 | bìng | to combine; here, it means "and; with". |
| 2. | 白居易 | Bó (Bái) Jūyì | a Tang poet. |
| 3. | 元和 | Yuánhé | the reign name (806–820) of Emperor Xiànzōng 憲宗 of the Tang Dynasty. |
| 4. | 左遷 | zuǒ qiān | to move to the left, i.e., to be demoted in an official position. The right side (右 yòu) is traditionally considered the position of honor. |
| | 九江 | Jiǔjiāng | a place name, in present-day Jiāngxī 江西 province. |
| | 司馬 | sī mǎ | an official title. |

| 5. | 湓浦口 | Pénpǔkǒu | a place name, in Jiujiang county. |
| 6. | 錚錚然 | zhēng zhēng rán | the clanging sounds of music. |
| | 京都 | jīng dū | the capital, i.e., Cháng'ān 長安. |
| 7. | 倡女 | chāng nǚ | a singing girl; a female entertainer. |
| 8. | 善才 | shàn cái | a pipa master; literally, a talented person. |
| 9. | 委身 | wěi shēn | to entrust oneself to; here, to get married to (someone). |
| | 賈人 | gǔ rén | merchant. |
| 10. | 憫然 | mǐn rán | subdued and pitiful. |
| 11. | 漂淪 | piāo lún | wandering and homeless. |
| 12. | 轉徙 | zhuǎn xǐ | frequently moving around. |
| 13. | 恬然 | tián rán | being at ease. |
| 14. | 遷謫 | qiān zhé | being demoted and banished from the capital. |
| 15. | 命 | mìng | to name or to title (it) as; here used as 名 míng. |

## 📖 課文—續 (Text — Continued)

《琵琶行》

　　尋陽江頭夜送客，<sup>16</sup>楓葉荻花秋瑟瑟。<sup>17</sup>主人下馬客在船，舉酒欲飲無管絃；<sup>18</sup>醉不成歡慘將別，別時茫茫江浸月。<sup>19</sup>忽聞水上琵琶聲，主人忘歸客不發。尋聲闇問彈者誰？<sup>20</sup>琵琶聲停欲語遲。移船相近邀相見，添酒回燈重開宴。<sup>21</sup>千呼萬喚始出來，<sup>22</sup>猶抱琵琶半遮面。轉軸撥絃三兩聲，[23] 未成曲調先有情；絃絃掩抑聲聲思，[24] 似訴平生不得意。低眉信手續續彈，[25] 說盡心中無限事，輕攏慢撚抹復挑，[26] 初為霓裳後六么。[27] 大絃嘈嘈如急雨，[28] 小絃切切如私語，[29] 嘈嘈切切錯雜彈，大珠小珠落玉盤。閒關鶯語花底滑，[30] 幽咽泉流水下灘；[31] 水泉冷澀絃凝絕，[32] 凝絕不通聲暫歇。別有幽愁闇恨生，此時無聲勝有聲。銀瓶乍破水漿迸，[33] 鐵騎突出刀鎗鳴。曲終收撥當心畫，四絃一聲如裂帛。[34] 東船西舫悄無言，[35] 唯見江心秋月白。沉吟放撥插絃中，[36] 整頓衣裳起斂容。[37] 自言：「本是京城女，家在蝦蟆陵下住，[38] 十三學得琵琶成，名屬教坊第一部。[39] 曲罷曾教善才服，妝成每被秋娘妒；[40] 武陵年少爭纏頭，[41] 一曲紅綃不知數；[42] 鈿頭銀篦擊節碎，[43] 血色羅裙翻酒污。[44] 今年歡笑復明年，秋月春風等閒度。[45] 弟走從軍阿姨死，暮去朝來顏色故。[46] 門前冷落車馬稀，老大嫁作商人婦！商人重利輕離別，前月浮梁買茶去；[47] 去來江口守空船，遶船月明江水寒。夜深忽夢少年事，夢啼妝淚紅闌干。[48]」我聞琵琶已歎息，又聞此語重唧唧！[49] 同是天涯淪落人，[50] 相逢何必曾相識！我從去年辭帝京，謫居臥病潯陽城；潯陽地僻無音樂，終歲不聞絲竹

聲。<sup>51</sup> 住近湓江地低溼，<sup>52</sup> 黃蘆苦竹繞宅生；其間旦暮
聞何物？杜鵑啼血猿哀鳴。<sup>53</sup> 春江花朝秋月夜，<sup>54</sup> 往往
取酒還獨傾。<sup>55</sup> 豈無山歌與村笛？嘔啞嘲哳難為聽。<sup>56</sup>
今夜聞君琵琶語，如聽仙樂耳暫明。莫辭更坐彈一曲，
為君翻作琵琶行。感我此言良久立，卻坐促絃絃轉
急；<sup>57</sup> 淒淒不似向前聲，<sup>58</sup> 滿座重聞皆掩泣。<sup>59</sup> 座中泣
下誰最多？江州司馬青衫溼。<sup>60</sup>

## 📝 註 釋 (Annotations)

| | | | |
|---|---|---|---|
| 16. | 潯陽 | Xúnyáng | another name for Jiujiang. |
| | 江頭 | jiāngtóu | the edge of the river. 江 here refers to the Yangtze River. |
| 17. | 楓葉荻花 | fēng yè dí huā | maple leaves and reed tassels (both symbols of autumn). |
| | 瑟瑟 | sè sè | the sound of wind blowing through maple leaves and reeds; usually referring to an atmosphere of desolation or loneliness. |
| 18. | 無管絃 | wú guǎn xián | having no music. 管, wind instrument; 絃, stringed instrument. |
| 19. | 茫茫 | máng máng | so vast and boundless that it seems empty. |
| 20. | 尋聲闇問 | xún shēng àn wèn | following the music and searching for the player in the dim light (in the sense of "quietly, without disturbing the player"). (闇 is now more commonly written as 暗.) |
| 21. | 回燈 | huí dēng | light up the lamp again. |

22. 千呼萬喚    qiān hū wàn    after a lot of requests.
                   huàn

23. 轉軸    zhuǎn zhóu    to adjust the strings for the right pitch.

24. 掩抑    yǎn yì    subdued and suppressed. 掩, to cover; 抑, to suppress.

25. 信手    xìn shǒu    at random; casually.

26. 輕攏慢撚 抹復挑    qīng lǒng màn niǎn mǒ fù tiāo    different finger movements on the strings when playing the pipa.

27. 霓裳    ní cháng    name of a famous song, also called 霓裳羽衣曲 ní cháng yǔ yī qǔ.

     六么    liù yāo    name of another tune.

28. 嘈嘈    cáo cáo    a multitude of sounds going together.

29. 切切    qiè qiè    low, gentle but prolonged sound.

     私語    sī yǔ    intimate whisper.

30. 閒關    jiān guān    sound of birds chirping (閒 is the same as 間).

31. 幽咽    yōu yè    the sobbing sound of rapids.

32. 冷澀    lěng sè    like water freezing gradually so that currents slow down, i.e., the musical sounds become low and slow.

     凝絕    níng jué    frozen and still.

33. 乍    zhà    all of a sudden.

     迸    bèng    bursting out.

34. 鐵騎    tiě jì    armored cavalry.

     裂帛    liè bó    tearing a silk fabric.

35. 舫    fǎng    a relatively large boat.

36. 沉吟    chén yín    in a meditative mood; pensive.

37. 斂容    liǎn róng    to put on a sober mien.

38. 蝦蟆陵    Hámálíng    a place near Chang'an, famous for producing beauties and good wine.

39. 教坊    jiào fāng    a ward in the imperial city where musicians and dancers lived.

40. 秋娘    qiū niáng    beautiful women.

41. 武陵年少    Wǔlíng nián shào    young men of rich or noble families. 武陵, an area where rich and noble families resided.

     纏頭    chán tóu    money and gifts given to entertainers.

42. 紅綃    hóng xiāo    red raw silk, usually used as 纏頭.

43. 鈿頭銀篦    diàn tóu yín bì    a silver comb decorated with gold ornamentation at both ends. 篦, a fine-toothed comb.

44. 羅裙    luó qún    skirt made of thin silk.

45. 等閒    děng xián    idly, as if of no importance.

46. 暮去朝來    mù qù zhāo lái    time passes. 暮, dusk; 朝, dawn.

     顏色故    yán sè gù    the appearance has aged.

47. 浮梁    Fúliáng    a place famous for its tea market, in present-day Jiangxi.

48. 夢啼妝淚紅闌干    mèng tí zhuāng lèi hóng lán gān    sobbing in dreams so tears smeared the make-up. 闌干 here means "crisscross".

49. 唧唧    jī jī    sound of sighing.

50. 天涯淪落人    tiān yá lún luò rén    people who are neglected and lonely in a land far away from home.

51. 終歲    zhōng suì    the whole year.

|  | 絲竹聲 | sī zhú shēng | the sound of music. |
|---|---|---|---|
| 52. | 低溼 | dī shī | low-lying and damp. |
| 53. | 杜鵑啼血<br>猿哀鳴 | dù juān tí xuè<br>yuán āi míng | the cuckoos cry bitterly and the gibbons scream<br>sorrowfully. |
| 54. | 春江花朝<br>秋月夜 | chūn jiāng<br>huā zhāo qiū<br>yuè yè | good weather and beautiful scenery. (Literally,<br>a morning with flowers by the river in spring and<br>a night with the autumn moon.) |
| 55. | 獨傾 | dú qīng | pouring wine for oneself, i.e., drinking alone. |
| 56. | 嘔哑嘲哳 | ōu yǎ zhāo<br>zhā | inharmonious noise. |
| 57. | 卻坐 | què zuò | to retreat to one's seat. |
| 58. | 向前 | xiàng qián | previous. (Both 向 and 前 mean "earlier".) |
| 59. | 掩泣 | yǎn qì | to cover one's face and weep. |
| 60. | 青衫 | qīng shān | dark blue coat (the type worn by low ranking<br>officials). |

# 三十七.《岳陽樓記》[1]

## 范仲淹 (989–1052) [2]

## 📖 課文 (Text)

慶曆四年春，³滕子京謫守巴陵郡。⁴越明年，⁵政通人和，⁶百廢具興，⁷乃重修岳陽樓，⁸增其舊制，⁹刻唐賢今人詩賦於其上；¹⁰屬予作文以記之。¹¹

予觀夫巴陵勝狀，¹²在洞庭一湖。¹³銜遠山，¹⁴吞長江，¹⁵浩浩湯湯，¹⁶橫無際涯；¹⁷朝暉夕陰，¹⁸氣象萬千；¹⁹此則岳陽樓之大觀也，²⁰前人之述備矣。²¹然則北通巫峽，²²南極瀟湘，²³遷客騷人，²⁴多會於此，覽物之情，得無異乎？²⁵

## 📝 註 釋 (Annotations)

| | | |
|---|---|---|
| 1. 岳陽樓 | Yuèyánglóu | a building in Yueyang, in present-day Hunan province. |
| 2. 范仲淹 | Fàn Zhòngyān | a high official and famous writer of the Song Dynasty. |
| 3. 慶曆 | Qìnglì | name of a reign period (1041–1048) in the reign of Emperor Rénzōng 仁宗 of the Song Dynasty. |
| 4. 滕子京 | Téng Zǐjīng | name of a person. |
| 謫 | zhé | to relegate a high official to a minor post in an outlying district. |
| 守 | shǒu | the magistrate of a prefecture; here used as a verb, meaning "to serve as a magistrate". |
| 巴陵 | Bālíng | ancient name of Yuèzhōu 岳州. (In the Song Dynasty, a prefecture was called 州, not 郡, but the author chose to use the older term.) |

5. 越　　　　yuè　　　　after. (A preposition.) (Note that this 越 does not mean "to surpass".)

　　明年　　míng nián　　the following year, i.e., 慶曆五年.

6. 政通　　zhèng tōng　　there are no obstacles to the conduct of government affairs.

　　人和　　rén hé　　harmony among the people.

7. 百廢　　bǎi fèi　　all neglected tasks.

　　具興　　jù xīng　　all have been erected or rebuilt (of buildings); reinstated (of tasks).

8. 重修　　chóng xiū　　to renovate.

9. 增　　　　zēng　　　　to add to; to extend.

　　制　　　　zhì　　　　scale.

10. 唐賢　　Táng xián　　worthy men of the Tang Dynasty.

　　賦　　　　fù　　　　a type of Classical Chinese verse.

11. 屬　　　　zhǔ　　　　to entrust.

12. 勝狀　　shèng zhuàng　　beautiful scenery.

13. 洞庭　　Dòngtíng　　name of a lake. 岳陽樓 is located on the banks of the Dongting Lake.

14. 銜　　　　xián　　　　to hold in the mouth; here, to contain.

　　遠山　　yuǎn shān　　Jūnshān 君山, in the Dongting Lake.

15. 吞　　　　tūn　　　　to swallow; here it means "to drain; to be the outlet of".

16. 浩浩湯湯　hào hào shāng shāng　　(of water) vast and mighty.

17. 橫　　　　héng　　　　vast.

| | | |
|---|---|---|
| 際 | jì | edge. |
| 涯 | yá | margin; limit. |
| 18. 朝 | zhāo | morning; daybreak. |
| 暉 | huī | sunlight. |
| 夕 | xī | evening; sunset. |
| 陰 | yīn | gloom; dusk. |
| 19. 氣象 | qì xiàng | view; scene. |
| 萬千 | wàn qiān | multifarious; here, spectacular. |
| 20. 大觀 | dà guān | magnificent view. |
| 21. 述 | shù | to state; to describe. |
| 備 | bèi | complete; thorough. |
| 22. 然則 | rán zé | but; however. (Here equivalent to 然而.) |
| 巫峽 | Wūxiá | the Wu gorge, one of the three Yangtze River Gorges. |
| 23. 極 | jí | the farthest point; here used as a verb meaning "to lead ultimately to". |
| 瀟 | Xiāo | name of a river which flows into the 湘 river. |
| 湘 | Xiāng | name of a river which flows into the Dongting Lake. |
| 24. 遷 | qiān | to move; but here synonymous with 謫, to relegate to. |
| 遷客 | qiān kè | one who is relegated to an outlying post. |
| 騷 | sāo | the abbreviated form for the *Lísāo*《離騷》, a famous poem by Qū Yuán 屈原. |
| 騷人 | sāo rén | poet. |

25. 覽　　　　　lǎn　　　　　to view.

得無　　　　dé wú　　　　could there be no ... ? (Used in combination with
　　　　　　　　　　　　　　乎 at the end of the sentence to form a rhetorical
　　　　　　　　　　　　　　courtesy inquiry.)

📖 課 文—續 (Text — Continued)

若夫霪雨霏霏，²⁶ 連月不開；²⁷ 陰風怒號，²⁸ 濁浪排空；²⁹ 日星隱耀，³⁰ 山岳潛形；³¹ 商旅不行，³² 檣傾楫摧，³³ 薄暮冥冥，³⁴ 虎嘯猿啼；³⁵ 登斯樓也，³⁶ 則有去國懷鄉，³⁷ 憂讒畏譏，³⁸ 滿目蕭然，³⁹ 感極而悲者矣！⁴⁰

至若春和景明，⁴¹ 波瀾不驚，⁴² 上下天光，⁴³ 一碧萬頃；⁴⁴ 沙鷗翔集，⁴⁵ 錦鱗游泳，⁴⁶ 岸芷汀蘭，⁴⁷ 郁郁青青。⁴⁸ 而或長煙一空，⁴⁹ 皓月千里，⁵⁰ 浮光躍金，⁵¹ 靜影沉璧，⁵² 漁歌互答，⁵³ 此樂何極！⁵⁴ 登斯樓也，則有心曠神怡，⁵⁵ 寵辱皆忘、⁵⁶ 把酒臨風，⁵⁷ 其喜洋洋者矣！⁵⁸

嗟夫！⁵⁹ 予嘗求古仁人之心，或異二者之為，⁶⁰ 何哉？⁶¹ 不以物喜，⁶² 不以己悲，⁶³ 居廟堂之高，⁶⁴ 則憂其民；處江湖之遠，⁶⁵ 則憂其君。是進亦憂，⁶⁶ 退亦憂；⁶⁷ 然則何時而樂耶？其必曰：「先天下之憂而憂，後天下之樂而樂歟？」噫！微斯人，⁶⁸ 吾誰與歸！⁶⁹ 時六年九月十五日。

## 📖 註釋 (Annotations)

| | | | |
|---|---|---|---|
| 26. | 若夫 | ruò fú | roughly meaning "as for". (An initial expression.) |
| | 霪雨 | yín yǔ | rain that has been falling for several days running. |
| | 霏霏 | fēi fēi | (of snow or rain) falling thick and fast. |
| 27. | 連月 | lián yuè | for several months running. |
| | 開 | kāi | here it means "to clear". |
| 28. | 陰風 | yīn fēng | cold wind. |
| | 怒號 | nù háo | to howl. |
| 29. | 濁浪 | zhuó làng | turbid waves. |
| | 排 | pái | to beat; to push at. |
| | 空 | kōng | sky. |
| 30. | 隱 | yǐn | to hide. |
| | 耀 | yào | light (of sun or star). |
| 31. | 岳 | yuè | high mountain. |
| | 潛 | qián | to hide. |
| | 形 | xíng | shape. |
| | 潛形 | qián xíng | to vanish from sight. |
| 32. | 商旅 | shāng lǚ | merchant. |
| 33. | 檣 | qiáng | mast. |
| | 傾 | qīng | to topple. |
| | 楫 | jí | oar. |
| | 摧 | cuī | to break. |

34. 薄暮　　bó mù　　dusk.

　　冥冥　　míng míng　　dark; gloomy.

35. 嘯　　xiào　　to roar.

　　猿　　yuán　　monkey.

　　啼　　tí　　to cry.

36. 登　　dēng　　to go up.

37. 去　　qù　　to leave.

　　國　　guó　　capital.

　　懷　　huái　　to yearn for.

　　鄉　　xiāng　　one's native place.

38. 憂　　yōu　　to worry about.

　　讒　　chán　　to slander; here, being slandered.

　　畏　　wèi　　to fear.

　　譏　　jī　　to ridicule or to censure; here, being ridiculed or censured.

39. 滿目　　mǎn mù　　to meet the eye on every side—everywhere one turns, one sees ....

　　蕭然　　xiāo rán　　desolate.

40. 感極　　gǎn jí　　to feel keenly.

41. 至若　　zhì ruò　　as to.

　　和　　hé　　warm.

　　景　　jǐng　　sunlight. (This is the original meaning of 景.)

42. 波瀾　　bō lán　　wave.

　　不驚　　bù jīng　　undisturbed; here, calm.

43. 上下天光    shàng xià    the bright sky and its reflection mirrored by the
           tiān guāng      lake.

44. 一        yī         all.

     碧       bì         blue-green.

     頃       qǐng       a unit of area (6.667 hectares).

     一碧萬頃    yī bì wàn qǐng    a boundless expanse of blue-green.

45. 沙鷗     shā ōu     gull.

     翔       xiáng     to circle in the air.

     集       jí        to perch.

46. 鱗       lín        (fish) scales.

     錦鱗     jǐn lín     shiny and colorful fish.

     游       yóu      to swim or play in water.

     泳       yǒng     to swim.

47. 芷       zhǐ       a kind of iris or other sweetgrass plant.

     汀       tīng      level land along the water.

     蘭       lán       orchid or similar fragrant plants.

48. 郁郁     yù yù      (of fragrance) to pervade.

49. 長煙     cháng yān    mist in the vast sky.

     空       kōng      empty; here, dispelled or cleared.

50. 皓       hào       bright.

51. 浮光     fú guāng    floating light; here, the moonlight reflected on the
                        waves.

     浮光躍金    fú guāng    (when there is wind) the moonlight reflected on
             yuè jīn      the waves looks like glittering gold.

| 52. | 影 | yǐng | reflection. |
|---|---|---|---|
| | 沉 | chén | to sink. |
| | 璧 | bì | a flat jade disc with a hole in its center. |
| | 靜影沉璧 | jìng yǐng chén bì | (when there is no wind) the reflection of the moon looks like a jade disc under water. |
| 53. | 漁歌 | yú gē | fishermen's song. |
| | 答 | dá | to reply; here, to sing in reply. |
| 54. | 極 | jí | limit. |
| 55. | 心曠神怡 | xīn kuàng shén yí | cheerful and carefree. |
| 56. | 寵 | chǒng | honor. |
| | 辱 | rǔ | humiliation. |
| 57. | 把 | bǎ | to hold; to take. |
| 58. | 洋洋 | yáng yáng | jubilant. |
| 59. | 嗟夫 | jiē fú | exclamation, roughly equivalent to 嗟乎. (See Lesson 30.) |
| 60. | 二者之為 | èr zhě zhī wéi | the manifestation of these two moods (sadness or jubilation). |
| 61. | 何哉 | hé zāi | why? |
| 62. | 物 | wù | here referring to the weather and scenery. |
| 63. | 己 | jǐ | self; one's own circumstances. |
| 64. | 廟堂 | miào táng | royal court; here, high office. |
| 65. | 江湖 | jiāng hú | rivers and lakes; a metaphor for being out of office and away from the central government. |
| 66. | 進 | jìn | to go forward; here, to be an official. |

| | | |
|---|---|---|
| 憂 | yōu | to worry. |
| 67. 退 | tuì | to move back; here, to withdraw from government office. |
| 68. 微 | wēi | but for. |
| 斯 | sī | this. |
| 69. 歸 | guī | to go back to; to be with. |
| 吾誰與歸 | wú shéi yǔ guī | who shall I go back with; who shall I follow? |

## ☀ 文法闡釋 (Grammar Notes)

### I. 覽物之情，得無異乎？

覽物之情 is the subject of the sentence, 得無異乎 is the predicate. 覽物 is a modifier for the head noun 情, so the phrase means "(their) moods when looking at the things". As an adverb, 得 means "by any chance" (coming from its verbal meaning "to get a chance"), so the phrase 得無異乎 means "to have no difference by any chance?" Thus this sentence can be rendered as: "Wouldn't their moods upon viewing the scenery be different by any chance?"

### II. 微斯人，吾誰與歸！

微 is a negative particle used specifically for subjunctive clauses, so 微斯人 means "if it were not (with) this person". In the rhetorical question 吾誰與歸，誰 is the object of the co-verb 與, and the verb 歸 always implies "to go to the place where one belongs". Therefore, this sentence can be translated as: "If it were not with such a person, with whom should I then associate?"

# 三十八.《醉翁亭記》

## 歐陽修 (1007–1072)

## 📖 課文 (Text)

　　環滁皆山也。² 其西南諸峰，³ 林壑尤美。⁴ 望之蔚然而深秀者，⁵ 瑯琊也。⁶ 山行六七里，⁷ 漸聞水聲潺潺，⁸ 而瀉出於兩峰之間者，⁹ 釀泉也。¹⁰ 峰回路轉，¹¹ 有亭翼然臨於泉上者，¹² 醉翁亭也。作亭者誰？山之僧智僊也。¹³ 名之者誰？¹⁴ 太守自謂也。¹⁵ 太守與客來飲於此，飲少輒醉，¹⁶ 而年又最高，故自號曰「醉翁」也。¹⁷ 醉翁之意不在酒，¹⁸ 在乎山水之間也。山水之樂，得之心而寓之酒也。¹⁹

　　若夫日出而林霏開，²⁰ 雲歸而巖穴暝，²¹ 晦明變化者，²² 山間之朝暮也。野芳發而幽香，²³ 佳木秀而繁陰，²⁴ 風霜高潔，²⁵ 水落而石出者，²⁶ 山間之四時也。²⁷ 朝而往，暮而歸，四時之景不同，²⁸ 而樂亦無窮也。²⁹

## 📝 註釋 (Annotations)

1. 醉翁　　zuì wēng　　drunken old man.

　　亭　　tíng　　pavilion.

2. 環　　huán　　to surround.

　　滁　　Chú　　a Song prefecture, in present-day Ānhuī 安徽 province.

3. 峰　　fēng　　peak.

4. 壑　　hè　　gully.

5. 蔚然　　　wèi rán　　　luxuriant (of a plant).

深秀　　　shēn xiù　　　secluded and lovely.

6. 瑯琊　　　Lángyé　　　name of a mountain.

7. 山行　　　shān xíng　　　to walk in the mountains.

8. 潺潺　　　chán chán　　　murmur of water. (An onomatopoeia.)

9. 瀉　　　xiè　　　to flow swiftly.

10. 釀　　　niàng　　　to make wine.

泉　　　quán　　　spring.

釀泉　　　Niàngquán　　　name of a spring which is said to be good for making wine.

11. 回　　　huí　　　to make a turn.

12. 翼然　　　yì rán　　　like a bird spreading its wings.

13. 僧　　　sēng　　　Buddhist monk.

智僊　　　Zhìxiān　　　name of a monk.

14. 名　　　míng　　　name; here used as a verb, meaning "to name".

15. 太守　　　tài shǒu　　　magistrate of a prefecture. (See Lesson 26). During the Song Dynasty, the magistrate of a prefecture was called a 知州 zhī zhǒu. Here the pre-Song title is used. 歐陽修 was the magistrate at that time.

謂　　　wèi　　　to call.

太守自謂也　　　tài shǒu zì wèi yě　　　It is the magistrate who named the pavilion 醉翁亭 after himself.

16. 輒　　　zhé　　　immediately; always.

17. 號　　　hào　　　appellation; here used as a verb, meaning "to give an appellation to".

| | | |
|---|---|---|
| 18. 意 | yì | intention; here, interest. |
| 19. 寓之 | yù zhī | to entrust it to; to let it be expressed in. |
| 20. 林霏 | lín fēi | mist in the forest. |
| 開 | kāi | to open up; to be dispelled. |
| 21. 巖穴 | yán xué | rock cave. |
| 暝 | míng | dim. |
| 22. 晦 | huì | dim; gloomy. |
| 23. 芳 | fāng | fragrant; here used as a noun, meaning "flowers". |
| 發 | fā | here, to bloom. |
| 幽香 | yōu xiāng | delicately fragrant. |
| 24. 佳 | jiā | fine; beautiful. |
| 秀 | xiù | to grow; to be abundant. |
| 繁陰 | fán yīn | luxuriantly shaded. |
| 25. 高潔 | gāo jié | (the sky becomes) high and clear. |
| 26. 水落 | shuǐ luò | the water subsides. |
| 石出 | shí chū | the stones emerge. |
| 27. 四時 | sì shí | the four seasons. (In the lines above, 野芳, 佳木, 風霜, 水落 describe scenes of the four seasons.) |
| 28. 景 | jǐng | scene. |
| 29. 無窮 | wú qióng | to be without end; to be inexhaustible. |

## 課 文—續 (Text — Continued)

　　至於負者歌於塗，[30] 行者休於樹，前者呼，後者應，[31] 傴僂提攜，[32] 往來而不絕者，滁人遊也。臨谿而漁，[33] 谿深而魚肥；釀泉為酒，泉香而酒冽；[34] 山肴野蔌，[35] 雜然而前陳者，[36] 太守宴也。[37] 宴酣之樂，[38] 非絲非竹，[39] 射者中，[40] 弈者勝，[41] 觥籌交錯，[42] 起坐而諠譁者，[43] 眾賓讙也。[44] 蒼顏白髮，[45] 頹然乎其間者，[46] 太守醉也。

　　已而夕陽在山，[47] 人影散亂，太守歸而賓客從也。樹林陰翳，[48] 鳴聲上下，遊人去而禽鳥樂也。然而禽鳥知山林之樂，而不知人之樂；人知從太守遊而樂，而不知太守之樂其樂也。醉能同其樂，醒能述其文者，[49] 太守也。太守謂誰？廬陵歐陽修也。[50]

## 註 釋 (Annotations)

30. 至於　zhì yú　as to; as for.

　　負　fù　to carry on the back.

　　塗　tú　road. (Same as 途.)

31. 應　yìng　to respond.

32. 傴僂　yǔ lǚ　to bend one's back; here used as a noun, referring to "old men". (A sound-related disyllabic word.)

|  | 提攜 | tí xié | to lead by the hand; here used as a noun, meaning "children". |
| 33. | 谿 | xī | stream. |
|  | 漁 | yú | to fish. |
| 34. | 洌 | liè | clear. |
| 35. | 肴 | yáo | dishes of meat. |
|  | 山肴 | shān yáo | game. |
|  | 蔌 | sù | vegetables. (This word is normally written as 蔬 shū.) |
| 36. | 雜然 | zá rán | mixed. |
|  | 陳 | chén | to place; to display. |
| 37. | 宴 | yàn | a banquet; here, to give a banquet. |
| 38. | 酣 | hān | to carouse. |
| 39. | 絲 | sī | silk string; here, stringed musical instruments or the music they produce. |
|  | 竹 | zhú | bamboo; here, musical pipes or the music they produce. |
| 40. | 射 | shè | to shoot; here referring to 投壺 tóu hú, an ancient game where arrows are pitched into a pitcher. |
|  | 中 | zhòng | to hit. (See Lesson 24.) |
| 41. | 弈 | yì | to play chess. |
| 42. | 觥 | gōng | a kind of goblet. |
|  | 籌 | chóu | bamboo chips; here, the bamboo chips with which the number of drinks is counted. |
|  | 交錯 | jiāo cuò | to crisscross; here, to be passed around. |

43. 諠譁　　xuān huá　　to talk uproariously.

44. 賓　　bīn　　guest.

譁　　huān　　cheering. (A variant form of 歡.)

45. 蒼顏　　cāng yán　　dark complexion.

46. 頹然　　tuí rán　　dejected; tired. Here, to rest quietly in a chair.

47. 已而　　yǐ ér　　afterward. (Originally, 已 meant "to stop" and 而 was a conjunction, but they later became a compound.)

48. 翳　　yì　　to shade; here used as an adjective, meaning "shadowy".

49. 述　　shù　　to describe; to narrate.

50. 廬陵　　Lúlíng　　name of a place in present-day Jiangxi province which is the author's home town.

# 三十九.《遊褒禪山記》[1]

## 王安石（1021–1086）

📖 課文 (Text)

　　褒禪山，亦謂之華山。[2] 唐浮圖慧褒始舍於其址，[3] 而卒葬之，[4] 以故其後名之曰褒禪。[5] 今所謂慧空禪院者，[6] 褒之廬冢也。[7] 距其院東五里，[8] 所謂華陽洞者，以其在華山之陽名之也。[9] 距洞百餘步，有碑仆道，[10] 其文漫滅，[11] 獨其為文猶可識，[12] 曰：「花山。」今言「華」如「華實」之「華」者，[13] 蓋音謬也。[14] 其下平曠，有泉側出，[15] 而記遊者甚眾，[16] 所謂前洞也。由山以上五六里，有穴窈然，[17] 入之甚寒，問其深，則其好遊者不能窮也，謂之後洞。

　　予與四人擁火以入，[18] 入之愈深，其進愈難，而其見愈奇。有怠而出者，[19] 曰：「不出，火且盡。」遂與之俱出。蓋予所至，[20] 比好遊者尚不能十一，[21] 然視其左右，來而記之者已少。蓋其又深，則其至又加少矣。[22] 方是時，予之力尚足以入，火尚足以明也。既其出，則或咎其欲出者，[23] 而予亦悔其隨之，而不得極乎遊之樂也。

## 🗒 註 釋 (Annotations)

1. 褒禪山　　Bāochánshān　name of a hill in Jiāngsū 江蘇 province.

2. 華山　　　Huáshān　　another name for Baochanshan. As Wang Anshi argues in the text later on, 華 here should be regarded as a synonym of 花 and should thus be pronounced in the first tone as huā.

3. 浮圖　　　fú tú　　　　Buddhist monk.

   慧褒　　　Huìbāo　　name of a monk.

   舍　　　　shè　　　　to reside.

   址　　　　zhǐ　　　　foot of a mountain.

4. 卒　　　　zú　　　　　at last; at death.

5. 禪　　　　chán　　　*dhyana* (meditation) in Sanskrit and *zen* in Japanese.

6. 慧空禪院　Huìkōng Chán　the Huikong Buddhist Hall.
   　　　　　Yuàn

7. 廬　　　　lú　　　　　hut; cottage.

   冢　　　　zhǒng　　　grave.

8. 距　　　　jù　　　　　a certain distance from.

9. 陽　　　　yáng　　　　the south side of a mountain or the north side of a river.

10. 碑　　　　bēi　　　　stele; stone tablet.

    仆　　　　pū　　　　　to fall down.

11. 文　　　　wén　　　　writing; inscription.

    漫滅　　　màn miè　　to be blurred.

| 12. | 其為文 | qí wéi wén | literally, their being written (referring to the title characters of the stele). |
|-----|--------|------------|----------------------------------------------------------------------------------|
| 13. | 華實 | huá shí | flowers and fruit. |
| 14. | 蓋 | gài | roughly; probably. (A sentence-initial particle.) |
|     | 音 | yīn | pronunciation. |
|     | 謬 | miù | wrong; mistaken. |
| 15. | 側出 | cè chū | to come out from the side. |
| 16. | 記遊者 | jì yóu zhě | people who commemorated their trip; here referring to the writings left by the tourists on the cliff wall. |
| 17. | 窈然 | yǎo rán | deep and far. |
| 18. | 擁 | yōng | to hold. |
|     | 火 | huǒ | torch. |
| 19. | 怠 | dài | idle; lazy. |
| 20. | 蓋 | gài | now; well. (A sentence-initial particle.) |
| 21. | 尚 | shàng | even; still. (Corresponding to 還 in Modern Chinese.) |
|     | 十一 | shíyī | one tenth. |
|     | 尚不能十一 | shàng bù néng shí yī | cannot even measure up to a tenth. |
| 22. | 加 | jiā | to make (something or some quality) even more so. (Note that in Modern Chinese this word means "to add", but in Classical Chinese, it can be used before both 多 and 少 to mean "to make it more" and "to make it less" respectively.) |
| 23. | 咎 | jiù | to blame; to find fault with. |

📖 **課文—續 (Text — Continued)**

　　於是予有歎焉。古人之觀於天地、山川、草木、蟲魚、鳥獸，往往有得，[24] 以其求思之深而無不在也。[25] 夫夷以近，[26] 則遊者眾；險以遠，則至者少。而世之奇偉瑰怪非常之觀，[27] 常在於險遠，而人之所罕至焉。[28] 故非有志者不能至也。有志矣，不隨以止也，[29] 然力不足者，亦不能至也。有志與力，而又不隨以怠，至於幽暗昏惑，[30] 而無物以相之，[31] 亦不能至也。然力足以至焉而不至，於人為可譏，而在己為有悔。盡吾志也，而不能至者，可以無悔矣。其孰能譏之乎？此予之所得也！

　　余於仆碑，又以悲夫古書之不存，後世之謬其傳而莫能名者，[32] 何可勝道也哉？[33] 此所以學者不可以不深思而慎取之也。

　　四人者：廬陵蕭君圭君玉，[34] 長樂王回深父，[35] 余弟安國平父、安上純父。至和元年七月某日，[36] 臨川王某記。[37]

## 📝 註釋 (Annotations)

24. 得              dé              gains.

25. 無不在          wú bú zài       there was nothing in which (their minds) did not
                                    reside, i.e., they pondered everything.

26. 以              yǐ              equivalent to 而. (A conjunction.) (See 文法闡
                                    釋 I.)

27. 奇偉            qí wěi          extraordinary.

    瑰              guī             beautiful.

    非常            fēi cháng       unusual.

    觀              guān            sight; scene.

28. 罕              hǎn             seldom.

29. 隨以止          suí yǐ zhǐ      to stop like the others.

30. 幽暗昏惑        yōu àn hūn huò  confused and blurred in the dark.

31. 相              xiàng           to assist; here, to encourage.

32. 謬其傳          miù qí chuán    to spread an error.

    莫能名          mò néng míng    no one can name it (correctly).

33. 何可勝道        hé kě shēng     how can we fully explain or describe this?
                    dào

34. 蕭君圭          Xiāo Jūnguī     蕭君圭, whose courtesy name is 君玉.
    君玉            Jūnyù

35. 長樂王          Chánglè Wáng    王回 from 長樂, whose courtesy name is 深父.
    回深父          Huí Shēnfù      The two other names in the next line should be
                                    understood in the same way, i.e., (Wáng) Ānguó
                                    (王) 安國, whose courtesy name is Píngfǔ 平
                                    父, and (Wáng) Ānshàng (王) 安上, whose
                                    courtesy name is Chúnfǔ 純父.

| 36. | 至和 | Zhìhé | a reign period (1054–1056) of Emperor Rénzōng 仁宗. |
| | 某日 | mǒu rì | on a certain day. |
| 37. | 臨川 | Línchuān | a place in Jiangxi; also the birthplace of 王安石. |
| | 某 | mǒu | a substitute for the author's personal name. |

## 文法闡釋 (Grammar Note)

夫夷以近，則遊者眾；險以遠，則至者少。

The only issue concerning these two sentences is the rather unusual use of the particle 以 in a place where 而 is normally expected. This is seen in some very old texts, and some Classical Chinese prose writers of later ages deliberately imitated that. As we have said, when two clauses (or verb phrases) are connected by 而, the first one is subordinated to the second one. But sometimes the subordination may not be very obvious, so the two clauses may seem to be equally ranked. Roughly speaking, in cases like that, we can expect the interchangeable use of the two particles which can then simply be translated as "and". So these two sentences can be translated as: "Now, if a place is easy (to reach) and nearby, tourists will be numerous; if it is hard (to reach) and far away, visitors will be few".

# 四十.《留侯論》[1]

## 蘇軾 (1037–1101)[2]

## 📖 課文 (Text)

古之所謂豪傑之士者，必有過人之節。[3] 人情有所不能忍者，[4] 匹夫見辱，[5] 拔劍而起，挺身而鬥，[6] 此不足為勇也。天下有大勇者，卒然臨之而不驚，[7] 無故加之而不怒，[8] 此其所挾持者甚大，[9] 而其志甚遠也。[10]

夫子房受書於圯上之老人也，[11] 其事甚怪；然亦安知其非秦之世，有隱君子者，[12] 出而試之。觀其所以微見其意者，[13] 皆聖賢相與警戒之義；[14] 而世不察，[15] 以為鬼物，[16] 亦已過矣。[17] 且其意不在書。

當韓之亡，秦之方盛也，[18] 以刀鋸鼎鑊待天下之士。[19] 其平居無罪夷滅者，[20] 不可勝數。[21] 雖有賁、育，[22] 無所復施。[23] 夫持法太急者，[24] 其鋒不可犯，[25] 而其末可乘。[26] 子房不忍忿忿之心，[27] 以匹夫之力而逞於一擊之間，[28] 當此之時，子房之不死者，其間不能容髮，[29] 蓋亦已危矣。千金之子[30] 不死於盜賊。何者？[31] 其身之可愛，[32] 而盜賊之不足以死也。子房以蓋世之材，[33] 不為伊尹、太公之謀，[34] 而特出於荊軻、聶政之計，[35] 以僥倖於不死，[36] 此圯上老人之所為深惜者也。[37] 是故倨傲鮮腆而深折之，[38] 彼其能有所忍也，然後可以就大事，[39] 故曰：「孺子可教也。」

## 📑 註釋 (Annotations)

1. 留侯　　　　Liúhóu　　　　the Marquis of Liu. The title conferred on Zhang Liang. (See Lesson 24.)

2. 蘇軾　　　　Sū Shì　　　　a writer of the Song Dynasty, whose courtesy name is Zǐzhān 子瞻. He is also known as Dōngpō jūshì 東坡居士.

3. 過　　　　　guò　　　　　to surpass.

   節　　　　　jié　　　　　moral principle; here, moral character.

4. 忍　　　　　rěn　　　　　to endure; to bear.

5. 匹夫　　　　pǐ fū　　　　an ordinary person.

   見辱　　　　jiàn rǔ　　　　to be insulted.

6. 挺身　　　　tǐng shēn　　　to stand erect; to stand up to.

7. 卒然　　　　cù rán　　　　suddenly.

   臨　　　　　lín　　　　　(of some incident) to befall; to happen to.

8. 無故　　　　wú gù　　　　without reason.

   加　　　　　jiā　　　　　to impose.

9. 挾持　　　　xié chí　　　　to hold something under one's arm; here, to have in mind; to harbor.

   所挾持者　　suǒ xié chí zhě　what is on his mind, i.e., ambition or a cause.

10. 志　　　　　zhì　　　　　ambition.

    遠　　　　　yuǎn　　　　far-reaching; lofty.

11. 子房　　　　Zǐfáng　　　　Zhang Liang's courtesy name.

    圯上之老人　yí shàng zhī lǎo rén　the old man on the bridge. (See Lesson 24.)

12. 隱君子　　　yǐn jūn zǐ　　　hermit.

| 13. 觀 | guān | to observe. (觀 is the main verb of the sentence, with the long clause following as its object. Its implied subject is "you" or "we". So it can be translated as "Note that …".) |
| 見 | xiàn | to reveal; to show. (Same as 現, a causative verb.) |
| 微見其意 | wēi xiàn qí yì | subtly revealing his intention. |
| 14. 相與警戒 | xiāng yǔ jǐng jiè | to give warning and advice to each other. |
| 15. 察 | chá | to observe; to have an insight. |
| 16. 鬼物 | guǐ wù | ghost; demon. |
| 17. 過 | guò | excessive; to miss the mark. |
| 18. 盛 | shèng | strong; prosperous; flourishing. |
| 19. 鋸 | jù | saw. |
| 鼎 | dǐng | ancient cooking vessel with three legs. |
| 鑊 | huò | cauldron. |
| 刀鋸鼎鑊 | dāo jù dǐng huò | four ancient instruments of torture. |
| 20. 平居 | píng jū | to stay at home. |
| 夷滅 | yí miè | to kill a person's family members and relatives; here used in the passive sense. |
| 21. 不可勝數 | bù kě shēng shǔ | too numerous to count. |
| 22. 賁 | Bēn | Mèng Bēn 孟賁, a brave man of the Zhou Dynasty. |
| 育 | Yù | Xià Yù 夏育, a brave man of the Zhou Dynasty. |

| 23. | 施 | shī | to put to good use; here, to put their strength to good use. |
|---|---|---|---|
| 24. | 持法 | chí fǎ | to enforce the law. |
| | 急 | jí | in a hurry; intense; harsh. |
| 25. | 鋒 | fēng | the sharp point of a sword or knife; here, initial stage; momentum. |
| | 犯 | fàn | equivalent to 觸 chù "to touch"; here, to go up against. |
| 26. | 末 | mò | the end; here, decline. |
| | 乘 | chéng | to take advantage of. |
| 27. | 忿忿 | fèn fèn | indignant; angry. |
| 28. | 逞 | chěng | satisfied. |
| | 一擊之間 | yì jī zhī jiān | at the moment of hitting (Qin Shihuang). (See Lesson 24.) |
| 29. | 其間 | qí jiān | the space between (life and death). |
| | 容 | róng | to contain. |
| | 子房之不死者，其間不能容髮 | Zǐfáng zhī bù sǐ zhě, qí jiān bù néng róng fà | there was not a hair's breadth between life and death for Zhang Liang. |
| 30. | 千金之子 | qiān jīn zhī zǐ | sons of the rich people. |
| 31. | 何者 | hé zhě | why? (Equivalent to 何哉.) |
| 32. | 可愛 | kě ài | should be cherished. |
| 33. | 材 | cái | abilities; talents. (This character is used in place of 才.) |

| 34. 伊尹 | Yī Yǐn | a minister of Tāng 湯 who helped him overthrow the Xià 夏 Dynasty and establish the Shang Dynasty. |
| 太公 | Tàigōng | referring to Jiāng Tàigōng 姜太公. (See Lesson 17.) |
| 35. 特 | tè | only; merely. |
| 出於⋯之計 | chū yú ... zhī jì | following the strategies of. |
| 荊軻 | Jīng Kē | an assassin of the Warring States period. |
| 聶政 | Niè Zhèng | an assassin of the Warring States period. |
| 36. 僥倖 | jiǎo xìng | to trust one's luck; to take a chance. |
| 37. 惜 | xī | to feel sorry about. |
| 38. 倨傲 | jù ào | haughty; arrogant. |
| 鮮腆 | xiān tiǎn | full of oneself. |
| 折 | zhé | to frustrate; to humble. |
| 39. 就 | jiù | to accomplish. |

## 📖 課 文—續 (Text — Continued)

楚莊王伐鄭，⁴⁰鄭伯肉袒牽羊以逆，⁴¹莊王曰：「其
主能下人，⁴²必能信用其民矣。」遂舍之。⁴³句踐之困於
會稽，⁴⁴而歸臣妾於吳者，⁴⁵三年而不倦。⁴⁶且夫有報
人之志，而不能下人者，⁴⁷是匹夫之剛也。⁴⁸夫老人
者，以為子房才有餘，而憂其度量之不足，⁴⁹故深折其

少年剛銳之氣，[50] 使之忍不忿而就大謀。何則？[51] 非有生平之素，[52] 卒然相遇於草野之間，[53] 而命以僕妾之役，[54] 油然而不怪者，[55] 此固秦皇之所不能驚，[56] 而項籍之所不能怒也。

觀夫高祖之所以勝，而項籍之所以敗者，在能忍與不能忍之間而已矣。[57] 項籍唯不能忍，是以百戰百勝，而輕用其鋒；高祖忍之，養其全鋒，以待其弊，[58] 此子房教之也。當淮陰破齊，[59] 而欲自王，[60] 高祖發怒，[61] 見於詞色。[62] 由此觀之，猶有剛強不能忍之氣，[63] 非子房其誰全之？[64]

太史公疑子房以為魁梧奇偉，[65] 而其狀貌乃如婦人女子，[66] 不稱其志氣。[67] 而愚以為此其所以為子房歟？[68]

## 📑 註釋 (Annotations)

| | | |
|---|---|---|
| 40. 楚莊王 | Chǔ Zhuāng-wáng | King Zhuang of Chu. |
| 鄭 | Zhèng | a state during the Zhou Dynasty. |
| 41. 鄭伯 | Zhèng Bó | the Earl of Zheng. |
| 肉袒 | ròu tǎn | to bare one's chest and back. |
| 逆 | nì | to welcome; to go forward to meet. |
| 42. 下人 | xià rén | to humble oneself before others. (下人 is a shortened form of 下於人.) |

| 43. | 舍 | shě | to release; to free. |
|---|---|---|---|
| 44. | 句踐 | Gōu Jiàn | the king of the state of Yue. (See Lesson 9.) (句 is the original form of 勾.) |
| | 困 | kùn | to fall into dire straits; to be restricted. |
| 45. | 臣 | chén | male slave. |
| | 妾 | qiè | female slave. |
| | 歸臣妾於吳者 | guī chén qiè yú Wú zhě | returned to Wu (with the King of Wu) and served as a slave there. (Note that 臣妾 form a compound meaning "slave" in general; and are used here as a verb, meaning "to serve as a slave".) |
| 46. | 不倦 | bú juàn | not tired; never neglected his duty. |
| 47. | 報 | bào | to take revenge on. |
| 48. | 剛 | gāng | firm; indomitable. |
| 49. | 度量 | dù liàng | broadmindedness. |
| 50. | 銳 | ruì | sharp; here, vigorous. |
| | 氣 | qì | spirit. |
| 51. | 何則 | hé zé | why? (Equivalent to 何哉.) |
| 52. | 生平 | shēng píng | all one's life; here, it means "in the past". |
| | 素 | sù | friendship; acquaintance. |
| 53. | 草野 | cǎo yě | wilderness; countryside. |
| 54. | 命 | mìng | to order. |
| | 役 | yì | labor. |
| 55. | 油然 | yóu rán | free from affectation. |
| | 怪 | guài | here, it means "to find it strange". |

| 56. | 驚 | jīng | to startle; to frighten (here used as causative verb. 怒 in the next sentence is also a causative verb). |
| 57. | 間 | jiān | here, it means "the difference between". |
| 58. | 待 | dài | to wait. |
| | 弊 | bì | decline; weakening. |
| 59. | 淮陰 | Huáiyīn | referring to the Marquis of Huaiyin (淮陰侯 Huáiyīnhóu), the title conferred on Hán Xìn 韓信 who was Gaozu's (the founder of the Han Dynasty) leading general. |
| 60. | 王 | wàng | to rule as king. (A verb.) (See Lesson 23.) |
| 61. | 發怒 | fā nù | to get angry. |
| 62. | 詞色 | cí sè | speech and countenance. |
| 63. | 猶 | yóu | still. |
| 64. | 其 | qí | particle expressing the mode of non-assertion. (An adverb.) |
| | 全 | quán | to help somebody achieve his aim. (According to the *Shiji*, when Han Xin requested to be made the King of Qi 齊, Gaozu became angry at first. Zhang Liang quickly suggested that he should accede to the request, otherwise Han Xin would revolt against him. Gaozu accepted this advice.) |
| 65. | 太史公 | Tài Shǐ Gōng | the Grand Historian, i.e., Sima Qian. |
| | 疑 | yí | to suspect; to suppose. |
| | 以為 | yǐ wéi | 以 is redundant here. Only 為 is needed. |
| | 魁梧 | kuí wú | stalwart in appearance. |
| 66. | 狀貌 | zhuàng mào | stature and appearance. |
| 67. | 稱 | chèn | to fit; to match. |

|        |        |                                              |
|--------|--------|----------------------------------------------|
| 志氣    | zhì qì | spirit.                                       |
| 68. 愚  | yú     | humble term of reference to oneself.         |
| 歟      | yú     | interrogative particle for equational sentences. |

---

## ☀ 文法闡釋 (Grammar Note)

### 人情有所不能忍者

The underlying form of this sentence is 有人情所不能忍者, that is, with 有 "there is or are" as the verb and 人情所不能忍者 "what the human mind or heart cannot bear" as its object. So this sentence can be translated as: "There are indeed things which human minds or hearts cannot bear". Syntactically, this sentence is independent, but semantically related to the following sentence, 匹夫見辱, 拔劍而起, which is provided to illustrate the sentence in question. Moreover, our claim that 人情 is not really the subject of 有 is based on the fact that sentences that start with 有 or 無 or 非 in most cases have the subject of their predicate clause at the beginning of the sentence. For example, 汝有所不解 "there is something you do not understand"; 彼無所不知 "there is nothing he does not know"; and 吾非愛其財而易之以羊也 "it is not [true] that I used a goat to replace it because I cared about its [greater] value".

# Appendix I:
# Grammar Summary

## The Major Structural Patterns and Usages Covered in
### *Classical Chinese Primer*

### I.  Common Classical Chinese Personal Pronouns 常見古文人稱代詞

| Common personal pronouns | | | | |
|---|---|---|---|---|
| 1st person pronouns | 2nd person pronouns | 3rd person pronouns | Other person pronouns | Indefinite pronouns |
| 我<br>吾<br>余<br>予 | 女<br>汝<br>爾<br>而<br>若 | 其 (pronoun substitute for N + 之)<br>之 | 寡人 (I, me: humble self used by a king)<br>不穀 (I, me: humble self used by a king or prince)<br>朕 (I, me: used only by emperor from the Qin Dynasty onwards)<br>君 (an honorific form for "you")<br>子 (another honorific form for "you")<br>臣 ("your servant", i.e., "I": used when speaking to a king or prince ) | 他 (other)<br>人 (other people)<br>或 (someone, something) |

Examples:

(1)  吾聞漢購我頭千金，邑萬戶，吾為若德。〔23.《史記‧項羽本紀》(節)〕

(2)  昔召康公命我先君大公曰：五侯九伯，女實征之，以夾輔周室，賜我先君履。
    (17.《左傳‧僖公四年》：齊桓公伐楚)

(3)  爾貢包茅不入，王祭不共，無以縮酒，寡人是徵；昭王南征而不復，寡人是問。
    (17.《左傳‧僖公四年》：齊桓公伐楚)

(4)  若非吾故人乎？〔23.《史記‧項羽本紀》(節)〕

(5)  齊侯曰：「豈不穀是為？先君之好是繼，與不穀同好，如何？」(17.《左傳‧僖公四年》：齊桓公伐楚)

(6) <u>君</u>若以德綏諸侯，誰敢不服。〔17.《左傳‧僖公四年》：齊桓公伐楚〕

(7) 渤海廢亂，<u>朕</u>甚憂之。<u>君</u>欲何以息其盜賊，有稱<u>朕</u>意？〔27.《漢書‧循吏傳》：龔遂傳(節)〕

(8) 蛇固無足，<u>子</u>安能為之足。〔1. 寓言選(上)：(丁)畫蛇添足〕

(9) <u>臣</u>聞治亂民猶治亂繩，不可急也。〔27.《漢書‧循吏傳》：龔遂傳(節)〕

(10) 豈有<u>他</u>哉？避水火也？〔7.《孟子‧梁惠王下》(節)〕

(11) <u>人</u>皆弔<u>之</u>。〔2. 寓言選(下)：(丙)塞翁失馬〕

(12) <u>或</u>謂<u>寡人</u>勿取，<u>或</u>謂<u>寡人</u>取<u>之</u>。〔7.《孟子‧梁惠王下》(節)〕

## II. Common Classical Chinese Interrogative Pronouns 常見古文疑問代詞

| |
|---|
| (a) mainly used for persons: 誰 (who); 孰 (which; who) |
| (b) mainly used for things: 何 (what); 奚 (why); 胡 (why); 盍 (why not) |
| (c) others: 安 (how; by what; from where); 焉 (for what; why) |
| Examples: |
| (1) 王<u>誰</u>與為善？〔8.《孟子‧滕文公下》(節)〕 |
| (2) 此<u>何</u>遽不為福乎？〔2.《寓言選(下)：(丙)塞翁失馬〕 |
| (3) 君長有齊，<u>奚</u>以薛為？〔20.《戰國策‧齊策一》：靖郭君將城薛〕 |
| (4) 子曰：「<u>盍</u>各言爾志？」〔4.《論語》選(中)〕 |
| (5) 蛇固無足，子<u>安</u>能為之足？〔1. 寓言選(上)：(丁)畫蛇添足〕 |
| (6) 割雞<u>焉</u>用牛刀？〔5.《論語》選(下)〕 |

## III. **Common Classical Chinese Adverbs** 常見古文副詞

| Adverbs | Some examples |
|---|---|
| 時間副詞：<br>始、卒、今、<br>將、且、遂、<br>業、已、既、<br>嘗、時、忽、<br>初、尋、先、<br>後、終、即、<br>向、乃、因 | (1) 環滁皆山也。其西南諸峰，林壑尤美。(38. 歐陽修：《醉翁亭記》)<br>　　(皆: all; 尤: especially)<br><br>(2) 褒禪山，亦謂之華山。唐浮圖慧褒始舍於其址，而卒葬之，以故其<br>　　後名之曰褒禪。今所謂慧空禪院者，褒之廬冢也。(39. 王安石：<br>　　《遊褒禪山記》)<br>　　(亦: also; 始: at first; 卒: at last, finally; 今: now)<br><br>(3) 予與四人擁火以入，入之愈深，其進愈難，而其見愈奇。有怠而出<br>　　者，曰：「不出，火且盡。」遂與之俱出。(39. 王安石：《遊褒禪山<br>　　記》)<br>　　(愈: more; 且: about to; 遂: then; 俱: all)<br><br>(4) 予嘗求古仁人之心。(37. 范仲淹：《岳陽樓記》)<br>　　(嘗: once)<br><br>(5) 其必曰。(37. 范仲淹：《岳陽樓記》)<br>　　(必: must)<br><br>(6) 「蛇固無足，子安能為之足？」遂飲其酒。為蛇足者，終亡其酒。<br>　　〔1. 寓言選 (上)：(丁) 畫蛇添足〕<br>　　(固: absolutely; 遂: then; 終: finally)<br><br>(7) 良業為取履，因長跪履之。〔24.《史記‧留侯世家》(節)〕<br>　　(業: already; 因: thereupon)<br><br>(8) 村中聞有此人，咸來問訊。…未果，尋病終。後遂無問津者。<br>　　(30. 陶淵明：《桃花源記》)<br>　　(咸: all; 尋: later; 後: afterward) |
| 程度副詞：<br>甚、愈、極、<br>尤 | |
| 性態副詞：<br>亦、猶、尚、<br>又、必、誠、<br>固、殊、復、<br>相 | |
| 範圍副詞：<br>各、具、俱、<br>悉、咸、並、<br>皆 | |

## IV. **Common Classical Chinese Exclamatories** 常見古文感嘆詞

| Exclamatories | Features | Examples |
|---|---|---|
| 噫 | corresponding to "ah" in English. | 噫！形之龐也，類有德，聲之宏也，類有能。<br>(34. 柳宗元：《黔之驢》) |
| 夫 | (particle) used at the end of a sentence to indicate exclamation. | 今若是焉，悲夫！(34. 柳宗元：《黔之驢》) |
| 嗟乎 | corresponding to "alas" in English. | 嗟乎！師道之不傳也久矣！(33. 韓愈：《師說》) |
| 嗚呼 | corresponding to "alas" in English. | 嗚呼！師道之不復可知矣。(33. 韓愈：《師說》)<br>嗚呼！其真無馬邪？其真不知馬也！<br>(32. 韓愈：《雜說四》) |

## V. Common Classical Chinese Negative Particles 常見古文否定詞

| Negative particles | Features | Examples |
|---|---|---|
| 不 | "not"<br>不 + Verb | 宋人有閔其苗之<u>不</u>長而揠之者。<br>〔1. 寓言選（上）：（甲）揠苗助長〕 |
| 毋 | "don't" | <u>毋</u>妄言！族矣。〔23.《史記・項羽本紀》（節）〕 |
| 無 | "there is no …";<br>opposite of 有 | 雖有舟輿，<u>無</u>所乘之；雖有甲兵，<u>無</u>所陳之。<br>（10.《老子》選） |
| 非 | "is not; are not";<br>非 + Noun | 是葉公<u>非</u>好龍也，好夫似龍而<u>非</u>龍者也。<br>〔2. 寓言選（下）：（丁）葉公好龍〕<br>是<u>非</u>君子之言也。（9.《禮記》選） |
| 莫 | negative pronoun;<br>"no one; nothing;<br>nobody; in no case" | 天下<u>莫</u>柔弱於水，而攻堅強者<u>莫</u>之能勝，以其無以<br>易之。弱之勝強，柔之勝剛，天下<u>莫</u>不知，<u>莫</u>能<br>行。（10.《老子》選） |
| 未 | "not yet" | <u>未</u>成，一人之蛇成，奪其卮曰。〔1. 寓言選（上）：<br>（丁）畫蛇添足〕<br><u>未</u>有仁而遺其親者也，<u>未</u>有義而後其君者也。<br>〔6.《孟子・梁惠王上》（節）〕 |
| 勿 | imperative negative;<br>"do not" (fusion of<br>毋之) | 或謂寡人<u>勿</u>取，或謂寡人取之。…取之而燕民不<br>悅，則<u>勿</u>取。〔7.《孟子・梁惠王下》（節）〕 |
| 弗 | "not it" (fusion of<br>不之) | 衣食所安，<u>弗</u>敢專也，必以分人。（16.《左傳・莊<br>公十年》：曹劌論戰） |
| 微 | negative particle<br>used specifically in<br>the subjunctive clause | <u>微</u>斯人，吾誰與歸！（37. 范仲淹：《岳陽樓記》） |

## VI. Common Classical Chinese Passive Sense Constructions 常見古文被動句式

| Some common passive constructions | Examples |
| --- | --- |
| 為 + N + (所) + Vt<br><br>The construction "為 + N + (所) + Vt" often seems to carry a passive sense. | 身為宋國笑。〔1. 寓言選 (上)：(丙) 守株待兔〕 |
| 於 | 郤克傷於矢。(《左傳・成公二年》)<br>(郤克: was wounded by an arrow)<br>昔者吾舅死於虎。(9.《禮記》選) |
| 見 + V | 吾長見笑於大方之家。〔12.《莊子・秋水》(節)〕<br>"(if it had not been that I came to your door,) I would have always been laughed at by the great enlightened masters". |

## VII. Common Unusual Patterns of Classical Chinese Grammar 常見的特殊古文句式

1.  Subjectless sentence is very common in Classical Chinese. The undertsood subject can be comprehended from the context.
    Examples:
    齊宣王使人吹竽，(it) 必三百人。〔1. 寓言選 (上)：(乙) 濫竽充數〕
    宣王說之，(king) 廩食以數百人。〔1. 寓言選 (上)：(乙) 濫竽充數〕
    (Anybody) 學而時習之。〔3.《論語》選 (上)〕

    * Sometimes, other elements of sentences can be omitted too.

2.  Flexible usage of "parts of speech" is commonly seen in Classical Chinese. For example, noun can serve as an adverb.
    Example:
    宣王說之，廩食以數百人。〔1. 寓言選 (上)：(乙) 濫竽充數〕
    (廩 "government granary" is a noun but functions here as an adverb modifying the verb 食 "to feed".)

3.  Causative usage is another feature in Classical Chinese. Intransitive verbs (or nouns, adjectives) are used before nouns to make its object perform the function of the verb (or nouns, or adjectives).
    Examples:
    苟為後義而先利，不奪不饜。〔6.《孟子・梁惠王上》(節)〕
    小國寡民。(10.《老子》選)
    ("Make your state small and your subjects few".)

4. Putative usage means to regard (or "assume") its object as that noun.

   Examples:

   不恥下問。〔3.《論語》選 (上)〕

   (not to regard 下問 as a shame".)

   甘其食，美其服，安其居，樂其俗。(10.《老子》選)

   ("[Make your subjects] regard their food delicious, their clothes beautiful, their home comfortable, and their way of living enjoyable".)

5. Many modal particles are used to indicate the speakers' mood or attitude.

   (1) Sentence-end particles: 也, 矣, 耳, 乎, 哉

        Examples:

        小人學道則易使也。〔5.《論語》選 (下)〕

        抑為之不厭，誨人不倦，則可謂云爾已矣。〔3.《論語》選 (上)〕

        二三子，偃之言是也，前言戲之耳。〔5.《論語》選 (下)〕

        與朋友交而不信乎？〔3.《論語》選 (上)〕

        夫子之云不亦宜乎？〔5.《論語》選 (下)〕

        求劍若此，不亦惑乎？〔2. 寓言選 (下)：(乙) 刻舟求劍〕

        豈有他哉？〔7.《孟子・梁惠王下》(節)〕

        甚哉！(9.《禮記》選) (哉: sentence-end particle, indicating exclamation.)

   (2) Sentence-initial particles: 夫

        Example:

        夫不忍麑，又且忍吾子乎？〔15.《韓非子・説林上》(節)〕

        (As an initial modal particle for sentences, 夫 can perhaps be rendered as something like "Now (you listen)". So the sentence can be translated as "Now, if he cannot even bear to hurt a fawn, will he then bear to hurt my son?")

## VIII. Common Grammar Particles Review 常見的古文語法詞復習

1. Conjunctions: 而, 則
   - 願車馬衣輕裘與朋友共，敝之<u>而</u>無憾。〔4.《論語》選 (中)〕
   - 君子學道<u>則</u>愛人，小人學道<u>則</u>易使也。〔5.《論語》選 (下)〕

2. Prepositions (Co-verbs): 於, 以, 為, 自, 與
   - 窺頭<u>於</u>牖，施尾<u>於</u>堂。〔2. 寓言選 (下)：(丁) 葉公好龍〕
   - 鉤<u>以</u>寫龍，鑿<u>以</u>寫龍，屋室雕文<u>以</u>寫龍。〔2. 寓言選 (下)：(丁) 葉公好龍〕
   - 賜其舍人 (以-with) 卮酒。〔1. 寓言選 (上)：(丁) 畫蛇添足〕
   - 子<u>以</u>我<u>為</u>不信，吾<u>為</u>子先行。〔2. 寓言選 (下)：(甲) 狐假虎威〕
   - 子服景伯<u>以</u>告子貢。〔5.《論語》選 (下)〕
   - 吾能<u>為</u>之足。〔1.. 寓言選 (上)：(丁) 畫蛇添足〕
   - 願車馬衣輕裘<u>與</u>朋友共，敝之而無憾。〔4.《論語》選 (中)〕

3. Nominalizers: 者, 所, and 所…者
   - 老者安之，朋友信之，少者懷之。〔4.《論語》選（中）〕

   (When 者 is attached to the end of a verb or verb phrase, it turns the whole phrase into a nominal expression. Such an expression usually means, "one who does (or those who do) something".

   - 是吾劍之所從墜。〔2. 寓言選（下）：（乙）刻舟求劍〕

   (所 is a nominalizer of the verb or verb phrase that follows it.)

   - 其所契者。〔2. 寓言選（下）：（乙）刻舟求劍〕

   (者 is sometimes used in coordination with 所.)

4. Conditional sentence expressions: 若…則
   - 若聖與仁，則吾豈敢？〔3.《論語》選（上）〕

   (若 and 則 are two conjunctions often used in coordination to form what is generally called a conditional sentence, and can thus be translated "If …, then ".)

   \* A conditional sentence may be without a marker. For example,
   - 不取，必有天殃。〔7.《孟子・梁惠王下》（節）〕
   - 苟為後義而先利，不奪不饜。〔6.《孟子・梁惠王上》（節）〕
   - 大道廢，有仁義。（10.《老子》選）

   (Though with no marker, these sentences are conditional. The first clause should, therefore, be translated with "if" or "when".)

5. The grammatical functions and meanings of "之":
   之 can be used as a verb, a pronoun, a possessive marker, or a marker for the subordination of a simple sentence as a relative clause.

   之 as a verb
   - 子之武城，聞弦歌之聲。〔5.《論語》選（下）〕

   (之 as a verb & possessive marker respectively)

   之 as a pronoun
   - 其子趨而往視之，苗則槁矣。〔1. 寓言選（上）：（甲）揠苗助長〕

   之 as a marker for the subordination of a simple sentence
   - 宋人有閔其苗之不長而揠之者。〔1. 寓言選（上）：（甲）揠苗助長〕

   (之 as a marker and pronoun respectively.)

   之 as a possessive marker
   - 鄰國之民不加少；寡人之民不加多。（《孟子・梁惠王》）
   - 有子之言似夫子也。（9.《禮記》選）

   (The possessive particle 之 turns 有子言 into a nominal phrase as 有子之言)

6. The grammatical functions and meanings of "於":

   於 as a verb
   – 寡人之於國也。(《孟子・梁惠王》) (於: deal with)

   於 as a preposition
   – 移其民於河東。(《孟子・梁惠王》) (於: to)
   – 叔孫武叔語大夫於朝曰。〔5.《論語》選 (下)〕(於: in)
   – 子於是日哭，則不歌。(《論語》) (於: in)

   於 in a sentence of comparison
   – 苛政猛於虎。(9.《禮記》選) (於: comparison)
   – 子貢賢於仲尼。〔5.《論語》選 (下)〕(於: comparison)

   於 in a passive sense sentence
   – 郤克傷於矢。(郤克: was wounded by an arrow) (《左傳・成公二年》)
   – 昔者吾舅死於虎。(9.《禮記》選)

7. Comparison usage:
   "A + Adj. + 於 B", meaning "A is _____er than B".
   – 子貢賢於仲尼。〔5.《論語》選 (下)〕
   – 苛政猛於虎。(9.《禮記》選)
   – 天下莫柔弱於水。(10.《老子》選)

   "A 不如 B"
   – 若是其靡也！死不如速朽之愈也。(9.《禮記》選)

8. The grammatical functions and meanings of "以":

   以 as a preposition: with
   – 鉤以寫龍。〔2. 寓言選 (下)：(丁) 葉公好龍〕

   以 as a conjunction providing reason
   – 天下莫柔弱於水，而攻堅強者莫之能勝，以其無以易之。(10.《老子》選)

   以 in 以…為 pattern
   – 子以我為不信。〔2. 寓言選 (下)：(甲) 狐假虎威〕
   ("以 A 為 B" means "regard A as B" or "think A to be B".)

9. Word fusions: 諸, 盍, 焉
   諸 is the fused form of the pronoun 之 with the question particle 乎 or the co-verb 於.
   – 如之何，聞斯行諸？〔4.《論語》選 (中)〕(諸：之+乎)
   – 參也聞諸夫子也。(9.《禮記》選) (諸：之+於)

   焉 is the fused form of 於 and 之.
   – 萬取千焉，千取百焉。〔6.《孟子・梁惠王上》(節)〕(焉：於+之)

   盍 is the fusion of 何 and 不, meaning "why not".
   – 盍各言爾志？〔4.《論語》選 (中)〕

10. Inverted sentence:

– 甚哉，有子之言似夫子也！(9.《禮記》選)

(This is an inverted sentence, with its predicate 甚哉 put before its subject which is a complex clause. The sentence can, therefore, be rendered as "It is to the extreme, indeed, that Youzi talks just like the Master!")

– 若是其靡也！(9.《禮記》選)

(This is an inverted sentence with its predicate 若是 appearing before its subject 其靡. The sentence means "It's like that, his extravagance!")

# Appendix II:
# Simplified Character Texts with Pinyin

ᕃᕃᕃᕃᕃᕃᕃᕃᕃᕃᕃᕃᕃᕃᕃᕃ
## 1. Ancient Fables (Part 1: A–D)

一 · 寓 言 选 （ 上 ）
yī　　yù yán xuǎn　　shàng

（甲） 揠 苗 助 长
jiǎ　　yà miáo zhù zhǎng

宋 人 有 闵 其 苗 之 不 长 而 揠 之 者 ，
sòng rén yǒu mǐn qí miáo zhī bù zhǎng ér yà zhī zhě

芒 芒 然 归 ， 谓 其 人 曰 ：「 今 日 病 矣 ，
máng máng rán guī　　wèi qí rén yuē　　jīn rì bìng yǐ

予 助 苗 长 矣 ！」 其 子 趋 而 往 视 之 ，
yú zhù miáo zhǎng yǐ　　qí zǐ qū ér wǎng shì zhī

苗 则 槁 矣 。 天 下 之 不 助 苗 长 者 寡
miáo zé gǎo yǐ　　tiān xià zhī bù zhù miáo zhǎng zhě guǎ

矣 ！ 以 为 无 益 而 舍 之 者 ， 不 耘 苗
yǐ　　yǐ wéi wú yì ér shě zhī zhě　　bù yún miáo

者 也 ； 助 之 长 者 ， 揠 苗 者 也 ； 非 徒
zhě yě　　zhù zhī zhǎng zhě　　yà miáo zhě yě　　fēi tú

无 益 ， 而 又 害 之 。
wú yì　　ér yòu hài zhī

《 孟 子 · 公 孙 丑 上 》
mèng zǐ　　gōng sūn chǒu shàng

（乙） 滥 竽 充 数
yǐ   làn   yú   chōng   shù

齐 宣 王 使 人 吹 竽 ， 必 三 百 人 。
qí   xuān   wáng   shǐ   rén   chuī   yú ， bì   sān   bǎi   rén 。

南 郭 处 士 请 为 王 吹 竽 ， 宣 王 说 之 ，
nán   guō   chǔ   shì   qǐng   wèi   wáng   chuī   yú ， xuān   wáng   yuè   zhī ，

廪 食 以 数 百 人 。 宣 王 死 ， 湣 王 立 ，
lǐn   sì   yǐ   shù   bǎi   rén 。 xuān   wáng   sǐ ， mǐn   wáng   lì ，

好 一 一 听 之 ， 处 士 逃 。
hào   yī   yī   tīng   zhī ， chǔ   shì   táo 。

《 韩 非 子 · 内 储 说 上 》
hán   fēi   zǐ · nèi   chǔ   shuō   shàng

（丙） 守 株 待 兔
bǐng   shǒu   zhū   dài   tù

宋 人 有 耕 者 ， 田 中 有 株 ， 兔 走
sòng   rén   yǒu   gēng   zhě ， tián   zhōng   yǒu   zhū ， tù   zǒu

触 株 ， 折 颈 而 死 。 因 释 其 耒 而 守
chù   zhū ， zhé   jǐng   ér   sǐ 。 yīn   shì   qí   lěi   ér   shǒu

株 ， 冀 复 得 兔 。 兔 不 可 复 得 ， 而 身
zhū ， jì   fù   dé   tù 。 tù   bù   kě   fù   dé ， ér   shēn

为 宋 国 笑 。
wéi   sòng   guó   xiào 。

《 韩 非 子 · 五 蠹 》
hán   fēi   zǐ · wǔ   dù

（丁） 画 蛇 添 足
dīng   huà   shé   tiān   zú

楚 有 祠 者 ， 赐 其 舍 人 卮 酒 。 舍
chǔ   yǒu   cí   zhě ， cì   qí   shè   rén   zhī   jiǔ 。 shè

人 相 谓 曰： 「 数 人 饮 之 不 足， 一 人
rén xiāng wèi yuē　　　shù rén yǐn zhī bù zú　　　yì rén

饮 之 有 余 。 请 画 地 为 蛇， 先 成 者
yǐn zhī yǒu yú　　qǐng huà dì wéi shé　　xiān chéng zhě

饮 酒 。」 一 人 蛇 先 成， 引 酒 且 饮 之，
yǐn jiǔ　　yī rén shé xiān chéng　　yǐn jiǔ qiě yǐn zhī

乃 左 手 持 卮， 右 手 画 蛇 曰： 「 吾 能
nǎi zuǒ shǒu chí zhī　　yòu shǒu huà shé yuē　　　wú néng

为 之 足 。」 未 成， 一 人 之 蛇 成， 夺
wèi zhī zú　　　wèi chéng　　yì rén zhī shé chéng　　duó

其 卮 曰： 「 蛇 固 无 足， 子 安 能 为 之
qí zhī yuē　　　shé gù wú zú　　zǐ ān néng wèi zhī

足 ？」 遂 饮 其 酒 。 为 蛇 足 者， 终 亡
zú　　　suì yǐn qí jiǔ　　wéi shé zú zhě　　zhōng wú

其 酒 。
qí jiǔ

《 战 国 策 · 齐 策 》
zhàn guó cè　　qí cè

꜀꜀꜀꜀꜀꜀꜀꜀꜀꜀꜀꜀꜀꜀꜀꜀꜀

## 2. Ancient Fables (Part 2: A–D)

二 ． 寓 言 选 （ 下 ）
èr　　yù yán xuǎn　　xià

（甲） 狐 假 虎 威
jiǎ　　hú jiǎ hǔ wēi

虎 求 百 兽 而 食 之， 得 狐 。 狐 曰：
hǔ qiú bǎi shòu ér shí zhī　　dé hú　　hú yuē

「 子 无 敢 食 我 也 ！ 天 帝 使 我 长 百
zǐ wú gǎn shí wǒ yě　　tiān dì shǐ wǒ zhǎng bǎi

兽，今子食我，是逆天帝命也。子
shòu　jīn zǐ shí wǒ　shì nì tiān dì mìng yě　zǐ

以我为不信，吾为子先行，子随
yǐ wǒ wéi bù xìn　wú wèi zǐ xiān xíng　zǐ suí

我后，观百兽之见我而敢不走乎？」
wǒ hòu　guān bǎi shòu zhī jiàn wǒ ér gǎn bù zǒu hū

虎以为然，故遂与之行，兽见之
hǔ yǐ wéi rán　gù suì yǔ zhī xíng　shòu jiàn zhī

皆走，虎不知兽畏己而走也，以
jiē zǒu　hǔ bù zhī shòu wèi jǐ ér zǒu yě　yǐ

为畏狐也。
wéi wèi hú yě

《 战 国 策 · 楚 策 》
zhàn guó cè　chǔ cè

（乙） 刻 舟 求 剑
yǐ　kè zhōu qiú jiàn

楚人有涉江者，其剑自舟中坠
chǔ rén yǒu shè jiāng zhě　qí jiàn zì zhōu zhōng zhuì

于水，遽契其舟曰：「是吾剑之所
yú shuǐ　jù qì qí zhōu yuē　shì wú jiàn zhī suǒ

从坠。」舟止。从其所契者入水求
cóng zhuì　zhōu zhǐ　cóng qí suǒ qì zhě rù shuǐ qiú

之，舟已行矣，而剑不行，求剑若
zhī　zhōu yǐ xíng yǐ　ér jiàn bù xíng　qiú jiàn ruò

此，不亦惑乎？
cǐ　bú yì huò hū

《 吕 氏 春 秋 · 察 今 》
lǔ shì chūn qiū　chá jīn

（丙）塞 翁 失 马
bǐng sài wēng shī mǎ

近 塞 上 之 人 有 善 术 者 ， 马 无 故
jìn sài shàng zhī rén yǒu shàn shù zhě mǎ wú gù

亡 而 入 胡 ， 人 皆 吊 之 。 其 父 曰 ：「 此
wáng ér rù hú rén jiē diào zhī qí fù yuē cǐ

何 遽 不 为 福 乎 ？」 居 数 月 ， 其 马 将
hé jù bù wéi fú hū jū shù yuè qí mǎ jiāng

胡 骏 马 而 归 ， 人 皆 贺 之 ， 其 父 曰 ：
hú jùn mǎ ér guī rén jiē hè zhī qí fù yuē

「 此 何 遽 不 能 为 祸 乎 ？」 家 富 良 马 ，
cǐ hé jù bù néng wéi huò hū jiā fù liáng mǎ

其 子 好 骑 ， 坠 而 折 其 髀 ， 人 皆 吊
qí zǐ hào qí zhuì ér zhé qí bì rén jiē diào

之 。 其 父 曰 ：「 此 何 遽 不 为 福 乎 ？」
zhī qí fù yuē cǐ hé jù bù wéi fú hū

居 一 年 ， 胡 人 大 入 塞 ， 丁 壮 者 引
jū yī nián hú rén dà rù sài dīng zhuàng zhě yǐn

弦 而 战 。 近 塞 上 之 人 ， 死 者 十 九 。
xián ér zhàn jìn sài shàng zhī rén sǐ zhě shí jiǔ

此 独 以 跛 之 故 ， 父 子 相 保 。 故 福
cǐ dú yǐ bǒ zhī gù fù zǐ xiāng bǎo gù fú

之 为 祸 ， 祸 之 为 福 ， 化 不 可 极 ， 深
zhī wéi huò huò zhī wéi fú huà bù kě jí shēn

不 可 测 也 。
bù kě cè yě

《 淮 南 子 · 人 间 训 》
huái nán zǐ rén jiān xùn

（丁）叶公好龙
dīng shè gōng hào lóng

叶公子高好龙，钩以写龙，凿
shè gōng zǐ gāo hào lóng, gōu yǐ xiě lóng, záo

以写龙，屋室雕文以写龙，于是
yǐ xiě lóng, wū shì diāo wén yǐ xiě lóng, yú shì

天龙闻而下之，窥头于牖，施尾
tiān lóng wén ér xià zhī, kuī tóu yú yǒu, yì wěi

于堂。叶公见之，弃而还走，失其
yú táng. Shè gōng jiàn zhī, qì ér huán zǒu, shī qí

魂魄，五色无主。是叶公非好龙
hún pò, wǔ sè wú zhǔ. shì shè gōng fēi hào lóng

也，好夫似龙而非龙者也。
yě, hào fú sì lóng ér fēi lóng zhě yě.

《新序·杂事第五》
xīn xù zá shì dì wǔ

## 3. Selections from the *Lunyu* (Part 1)

三.《论语》选（上）
sān lún yǔ xuǎn shàng

（甲）子曰：「学而时习之，不亦说
jiǎ zǐ yuē xué ér shí xí zhī, bú yì yuè

乎？有朋自远方来，不亦乐乎？人
hū yǒu péng zì yuǎn fāng lái, bú yì lè hū rén

不知而不愠，不亦君子乎？」
bù zhī ér bú yùn, bú yì jūn zǐ hū

〈学而〉
xué ér

（乙） 曾 子 曰 ：「 吾 日 三 省 吾 身 ： 为
　　　 zēng zǐ yuē 　　 wú rì sān xǐng wú shēn 　 wèi

人 谋 而 不 忠 乎 ？ 与 朋 友 交 而 不 信
rén móu ér bù zhōng hū 　 yǔ péng yǒu jiāo ér bú xìn

乎 ？ 传 不 习 乎 ？」
hū 　 chuán bù xí hū

〈 学 而 〉
　 xué ér

（丙） 子 贡 曰 ：「 孔 文 子 ， 何 以 谓 之
　　 bǐng zǐ gòng yuē 　 kǒng wén zǐ 　 hé yǐ wèi zhī

文 也 ？」 子 曰 ：「 敏 而 好 学 ， 不 耻
wén yě 　　 zǐ yuē 　　 mǐn ér hào xué 　 bù chǐ

下 问 ， 是 以 谓 之 文 也 。」
xià wèn 　 shì yǐ wèi zhī wén yě

〈 公 冶 长 〉
　 gōng yě cháng

（丁） 子 曰 ：「 若 圣 与 仁 ， 则 吾 岂 敢 ？
　　 dīng zǐ yuē 　 ruò shèng yǔ rén 　 zé wú qǐ gǎn

抑 为 之 不 厌 ， 诲 人 不 倦 ， 则 可 谓
yì wéi zhī bú yàn 　 huì rén bú juàn 　 zé kě wèi

云 尔 已 矣 ！」 公 西 华 曰 ：「 正 唯 弟
yún ěr yǐ yǐ 　　 gōng xī huá yuē 　 zhèng wéi dì

子 不 能 学 也 。」
zǐ bù néng xué yě

〈 述 而 〉
　 shù ér

# 4. Selections from the *Lunyu* (Part 2)

四．《论语》选（中）
sì　　 lún yǔ xuǎn zhōng

（甲）颜 渊 季 路 侍 ，子 曰 ：「 盍 各 言
jiǎ　yán yuān jì lù shì　　　 zǐ yuē　　　　 hé gè yán

尔 志 ？」子 路 曰 ：「 愿 车 马 衣 轻 裘
ér zhì　　　 zǐ lù yuē　　　 yuàn chē mǎ yī qīng qiú

与 朋 友 共 ，敝 之 而 无 憾 。」颜 渊 曰 ：
yǔ péng yǒu gòng　 bì zhī ér wú hàn　　　 yán yuān yuē

「 无 伐 善 ，无 施 劳 。」子 路 曰 ：「 愿
wú fá shàn　 wú shī láo　　　 zǐ lù yuē　　　 yuàn

闻 子 之 志 。」子 曰 ：「 老 者 安 之 ，
wén zǐ zhī zhì　　　 zǐ yuē　　　 lǎo zhě ān zhī

朋 友 信 之 ，少 者 怀 之 。」
péng yǒu xìn zhī　 shào zhě huái zhī

〈 公 冶 长 〉
gōng yě cháng

（乙）子 路 问 ：「 闻 斯 行 诸 ？」子 曰 ：
yǐ　zǐ lù wèn　　　 wén sī xíng zhū　　　 zǐ yuē

「 有 父 兄 在 ，如 之 何 其 闻 斯 行 之 ？」
yǒu fù xiōng zài　 rú zhī hé qí wén sī xíng zhī

冉 有 问 ：「 闻 斯 行 诸 ？」子 曰 ：「 闻
rǎn yǒu wèn　　 wén sī xíng zhū　　　 zǐ yuē　　　 wén

斯 行 之 。」公 西 华 曰 ：「 由 也 问 ：
sī xíng zhī　　　 gōng xī huá yuē　　　 yóu yě wèn

『 闻 斯 行 诸 ？』；子 曰 ：『 有 父 兄
wén sī xíng zhū　　　 zǐ yuē　　　 yǒu fù xiōng

在 。』求 也 问 ：『 闻 斯 行 诸 ？』；子
zài　　　 qiú yě wèn　　 wén sī xíng zhū　　　 zǐ

曰 ： 『 闻 斯 行 之 。 』 赤 也 惑 ， 敢 问 。 」
yuē wén sī xíng zhī chì yě huò gǎn wèn

子 曰 ： 「 求 也 退 ， 故 进 之 。 由 也 兼
zǐ yuē qiú yě tuì gù jìn zhī yóu yě jiān

人 ， 故 退 之 。 」
rén gù tuì zhī

〈 先 进 〉
xiān jìn

## 5. Selections from the *Lunyu* (Part 3)

五 . 《 论 语 》 选 （ 下 ）
wǔ lún yǔ xuǎn xià

（甲） 子 之 武 城 ， 闻 弦 歌 之 声 。 夫 子
jiǎ zǐ zhī wǔ chéng wén xián gē zhī shēng fū zǐ

莞 尔 而 笑 。 曰 ： 「 割 鸡 焉 用 牛 刀 ？ 」
wǎn ěr ér xiào yuē gē jī yān yòng niú dāo

子 游 对 曰 ： 「 昔 者 偃 也 闻 诸 夫 子
zǐ yóu duì yuē xī zhě yǎn yě wén zhū fū zǐ

曰 ： 『 君 子 学 道 则 爱 人 ， 小 人 学 道
yuē jūn zǐ xué dào zé ài rén xiǎo rén xué dào

则 易 使 也 。 』 」 子 曰 ： 「 二 三 子 ，
zé yì shǐ yě zǐ yuē èr sān zǐ

偃 之 言 是 也 。 前 言 戏 之 耳 。 」
yǎn zhī yán shì yě qián yán xì zhī ěr

〈 阳 货 〉
yáng huò

（乙）叔孙武叔语大夫于朝曰：「子
(yǐ) shū sūn wǔ shū yù dà fū yú cháo yuē zǐ

贡贤于仲尼。」子服景伯以告子
gòng xián yú zhòng ní zǐ fú jǐng bó yǐ gào zǐ

贡。子贡曰：「譬之宫墙，赐之墙
gòng zǐ gòng yuē pì zhī gōng qiáng cì zhī qiáng

也及肩，窥见室家之好。夫子之
yě jí jiān kuī jiàn shì jiā zhī hǎo fū zǐ zhī

墙数仞，不得其门而入，不见宗
qiáng shù rèn bù dé qí mén ér rù bú jiàn zōng

庙之美，百官之富。得其门者或
miào zhī měi bǎi guān zhī fù dé qí mén zhě huò

寡矣。夫子之云，不亦宜乎？」
guǎ yǐ fū zǐ zhī yún bú yì yí hū

〈子张〉
zǐ zhāng

## 6. Selection from the *Mengzi* (Part 1)

六．《孟子·梁惠王上》（节）
liù mèng zǐ liáng huì wáng shàng jié

孟子见梁惠王。王曰：「叟！不
mèng zǐ jiàn liáng huì wáng wáng yuē sǒu bù

远千里而来，亦将有以利吾国乎？」
yuǎn qiān lǐ ér lái yì jiāng yǒu yǐ lì wú guó hū

孟子对曰：「王何必曰利？亦有
mèng zǐ duì yuē wáng hé bì yuē lì yì yǒu

仁义而已矣。」王曰：「何以利吾
rén yì ér yǐ yǐ wáng yuē hé yǐ lì wú

国 ？ 」 大 夫 曰 ： 「 何 以 利 吾 家 ？ 」
guó dà fū yuē hé yǐ lì wú jiā

士 庶 人 曰 ： 「 何 以 利 吾 身 ？ 上 下 交
shì shù rén yuē hé yǐ lì wú shēn shàng xià jiāo

征 利 而 国 危 矣 。 万 乘 之 国 ， 弑 其
zhēng lì ér guó wēi yǐ wàn shèng zhī guó shì qí

君 者 ， 必 千 乘 之 家 ； 千 乘 之 家 ， 弑
jūn zhě bì qiān shèng zhī jiā qiān shèng zhī jiā shì

其 君 者 ， 必 百 乘 之 家 。 万 取 千 焉 ，
qí jūn zhě bì bǎi shèng zhī jiā wàn qǔ qiān yān

千 取 百 焉 ， 不 为 不 多 矣 。 苟 为 后
qiān qǔ bǎi yān bù wéi bù duō yǐ gǒu wéi hòu

义 而 先 利 ， 不 夺 不 餍 。 未 有 仁 而
yì ér xiān lì bù duó bú yàn wèi yǒu rén ér

遗 其 亲 者 也 ， 未 有 义 而 后 其 君 者
yí qí qīn zhě yě wèi yǒu yì ér hòu qí jūn zhě

也 。 王 亦 曰 仁 义 而 已 矣 ， 何 必 曰
yě wáng yì yuē rén yì ér yǐ yǐ hé bì yuē

利 ？ 」
lì

ꆃꆃꆃꆃꆃꆃꆃꆃꆃꆃꆃꆃꆃ

# 7. Selection from the *Mengzi* (Part 2)

七 . 《 孟 子 · 梁 惠 王 下 》 （ 节 ）
qī mèng zǐ liáng huì wáng xià jié

齐 人 伐 燕 ， 胜 之 。 宣 王 问 曰 ： 「 或
qí rén fá yān shèng zhī xuān wáng wèn yuē huò

谓 寡 人 勿 取 ， 或 谓 寡 人 取 之 。 以
wèi guǎ rén wù qǔ huò wèi guǎ rén qǔ zhī yǐ

万 乘 之 国 伐 万 乘 之 国 ， 五 旬 而 举
wàn shèng zhī guó fá wàn shèng zhī guó wǔ xún ér jǔ

之 ， 人 力 不 至 于 此 。 不 取 ， 必 有 天
zhī rén lì bù zhì yú cǐ bù qǔ bì yǒu tiān

殃 。 取 之 何 如 ？」 孟 子 对 曰 ：「 取
yāng qǔ zhī hé rú mèng zǐ duì yuē qǔ

之 而 燕 民 悦 ， 则 取 之 。 古 之 人 有
zhī ér yàn mín yuè zé qǔ zhī gǔ zhī rén yǒu

行 之 者 ， 武 王 是 也 。 取 之 而 燕 民
xíng zhī zhě wǔ wáng shì yě qǔ zhī ér yàn mín

不 悦 ， 则 勿 取 。 古 之 人 有 行 之 者 ，
bú yuè zé wù qǔ gǔ zhī rén yǒu xíng zhī zhě

文 王 是 也 。 以 万 乘 之 国 伐 万 乘 之
wén wáng shì yě yǐ wàn shèng zhī guó fá wàn shèng zhī

国 ， 箪 食 壶 浆 以 迎 王 师 ， 岂 有 他
guó dān sì hú jiāng yǐ yíng wáng shī qǐ yǒu tā

哉 ？ 避 水 火 也 。 如 水 益 深 ， 如 火 益
zāi bì shuǐ huǒ yě rú shuǐ yì shēn rú huǒ yì

热 ， 亦 运 而 已 矣 。」
rè yì yùn ér yǐ yǐ

## 8. Selection from the *Mengzi*

八 .《 孟 子 · 滕 文 公 下 》（ 节 ）
bā mèng zǐ téng wén gōng xià jié

孟 子 谓 戴 不 胜 曰 ：「 子 欲 子 之
mèng zǐ wèi dài bú shèng yuē zǐ yù zǐ zhī

王 之 善 与 ？ 我 明 告 子 。 有 楚 大 夫
wáng zhī shàn yú wǒ míng gào zǐ yǒu chǔ dà fū

于 此 ， 欲 其 子 之 齐 语 也 ， 则 使 齐
yú cǐ yù qí zǐ zhī qí yǔ yě zé shǐ qí

人 傅 诸 ？ 使 楚 人 傅 诸 ？ 」 曰 ： 「 使
rén fù zhū shǐ chǔ rén fù zhū yuē shǐ

齐 人 傅 之 。 」 曰 ： 「 一 齐 人 傅 之 ，
qí rén fù zhī yuē yī qí rén fù zhī

众 楚 人 咻 之 ， 虽 日 挞 而 求 其 齐 也 ，
zhòng chǔ rén xiū zhī suī rì tà ér qiú qí qí yě

不 可 得 矣 ； 引 而 置 之 庄 岳 之 间 数
bù kě dé yǐ yǐn ér zhì zhī zhuāng yuè zhī jiān shù

年 ， 虽 日 挞 而 求 其 楚 ， 不 可 得 矣 。
nián suī rì tà ér qiú qí chǔ bù kě dé yǐ

子 谓 薛 居 州 善 士 也 ， 使 之 居 于 王
zǐ wèi xuē jū zhōu shàn shì yě shǐ zhī jū yú wáng

所 。 在 于 王 所 者 ， 长 幼 卑 尊 皆 薛
suǒ zài yú wáng suǒ zhě zhǎng yòu bēi zūn jiē xuē

居 州 也 ， 王 谁 与 为 不 善 ？ 在 王 所
jū zhōu yě wáng shéi yǔ wéi bú shàn zài wáng suǒ

者 ， 长 幼 卑 尊 皆 非 薛 居 州 也 ， 王
zhě zhǎng yòu bēi zūn jiē fēi xuē jū zhōu yě wáng

谁 与 为 善 ？ 一 薛 居 州 ， 独 如 宋 王
shéi yǔ wéi shàn yī xuē jū zhōu dú rú sòng wáng

何 ？ 」
hé

# 9. Selections from the *Liji*

九 . 《礼 记》选
jiǔ      lǐ   jì   xuǎn

（甲）有 子 之 言 似 夫 子
jiǎ    yǒu zǐ zhī yán sì fū zǐ

有 子 问 于 曾 子 曰：「问 丧 于 夫
yǒu zǐ wèn yú zēng zǐ yuē wèn sàng yú fū

子 乎 ？」曰：「闻 之 矣。『丧 欲 速
zǐ hū yuē wén zhī yǐ sàng yù sù

贫，死 欲 速 朽。』」有 子 曰：「是
pín sǐ yù sù xiǔ yǒu zǐ yuē shì

非 君 子 之 言 也。」曾 子 曰：「参 也
fēi jūn zi zhī yán yě zēng zǐ yuē shēn yě

闻 诸 夫 子 也。」有 子 又 曰：「是 非
wén zhū fū zǐ yě yǒu zǐ yòu yuē shì fēi

君 子 之 言 也。」曾 子 曰：「参 也 与
jūn zi zhī yán yě zēng zǐ yuē shēn yě yǔ

子 游 闻 之。」有 子 曰：「然。然 则
zǐ yóu wén zhī yǒu zǐ yuē rán rán zé

夫 子 有 为 言 之 也。」
fū zǐ yǒu wéi yán zhī yě

曾 子 以 斯 言 告 于 子 游。子 游 曰：
zēng zǐ yǐ sī yán gào yú zǐ yóu zǐ yóu yuē

「甚 哉，有 子 之 言 似 夫 子 也！昔 者
shèn zāi yǒu zǐ zhī yán sì fū zǐ yě xī zhě

夫 子 居 于 宋，见 桓 司 马 自 为 石 椁。
fū zǐ jū yú sòng jiàn huán sī mǎ zì wéi shí guǒ

三 年 而 不 成。夫 子 曰：『若 是 其 靡
sān nián ér bù chéng fū zǐ yuē ruò shì qí mǐ

也 ！ 死 不 如 速 朽 之 愈 也 。 』 死 之 欲
yě　　sǐ　bù　rú　sù　xiǔ　zhī　yù　yě　　　　　sǐ　zhī　yù

速 朽 ， 为 桓 司 马 言 之 也 。 南 宫 敬
sù　xiǔ　　wèi　huán　sī　mǎ　yán　zhī　yě　　nán　gōng　jìng

叔 反 ， 必 载 宝 而 朝 。 夫 子 曰 ： 『 若
shū　fǎn　　bì　zài　bǎo　ér　cháo　　fū　zǐ　yuē　　　　ruò

是 其 货 也 ， 丧 不 如 速 贫 之 愈 也 。 』
shì　qí　huò　yě　　sàng　bù　rú　sù　pín　zhī　yù　yě

丧 之 欲 速 贫 ， 为 敬 叔 言 之 也 。 」
sàng　zhī　yù　sù　pín　　wèi　jìng　shū　yán　zhī　yě

〈 檀 弓 上 〉
tán　gōng　shàng

（乙） 苛 政 猛 于 虎
yǐ　　kē　zhèng　měng　yú　hǔ

孔 子 过 泰 山 侧 ， 有 妇 人 哭 于 墓
kǒng　zǐ　guò　tài　shān　cè　　yǒu　fù　rén　kū　yú　mù

者 而 哀 。 夫 子 式 而 听 之 。 使 子 路
zhě　ér　āi　　fū　zǐ　shì　ér　tīng　zhī　　shǐ　zǐ　lù

问 之 曰 ： 「 子 之 哭 也 ， 壹 似 重 有 忧
wèn　zhī　yuē　　zǐ　zhī　kū　yě　　yī　sì　chóng　yǒu　yōu

者 ？ 」 而 曰 ： 「 然 。 昔 者 吾 舅 死 于
zhě　　ér　yuē　　rán　　xī　zhě　wú　jiù　sǐ　yú

虎 ， 吾 夫 又 死 焉 ， 今 吾 子 又 死 焉 。 」
hǔ　　wú　fū　yòu　sǐ　yān　　jīn　wú　zǐ　yòu　sǐ　yān

夫 子 曰 ： 「 何 为 不 去 也 ？ 」 曰 ： 「 无
fū　zǐ　yuē　　hé　wèi　bú　qù　yě　　　yuē　　wú

苛　政。」夫　子　曰：「小　子　识　之，苛
kě　zhèng　　　　fū　zǐ　yuē　　　xiǎo　zǐ　zhì　zhī　　　kě

政　猛　于　虎　也。」
zhèng　měng　yú　hǔ　yě

〈　檀　弓　下　〉
tán　gōng　xià

## 10. Selection from the *Laozi*

十．《老　子》选
shí　　　lǎo　zǐ　xuǎn

大　道　废，有　仁　义。慧　智　出，有　大
dà　dào　fèi　　yǒu　rén　yì　　huì　zhì　chū　　yǒu　dà

伪。六　亲　不　和，有　孝　慈。国　家　昏　乱，
wěi　　liù　qīn　bù　hé　　yǒu　xiào　cí　　guó　jiā　hūn　luàn

有　忠　臣。
yǒu　zhōng　chén

天　下　莫　柔　弱　于　水，而　攻　坚　强　者
tiān　xià　mò　róu　ruò　yú　shuǐ　　ér　gōng　jiān　qiáng　zhě

莫　之　能　胜，以　其　无　以　易　之。弱　之
mò　zhī　néng　shèng　　yǐ　qí　wú　yǐ　yì　zhī　　ruò　zhī

胜　强，柔　之　胜　刚，天　下　莫　不　知，莫
shèng　qiáng　　róu　zhī　shèng　gāng　　tiān　xià　mò　bù　zhī　　mò

能　行。是　以　圣　人　云：「受　国　之　垢，
néng　xíng　　shì　yǐ　shèng　rén　yún　　shòu　guó　zhī　gòu

是　谓　社　稷　主；受　国　不　祥，是　为　天
shì　wèi　shè　jì　zhǔ　　shòu　guó　bù　xiáng　　shì　wéi　tiān

下　王。」正　言　若　反。
xià　wáng　　zhèng　yán　ruò　fǎn

小 国 寡 民 ， 使 有 什 佰 之 器 而 不
xiǎo guó guǎ mín　　shǐ yǒu shí bǎi zhī qì ér bú

用 ， 使 民 重 死 而 不 远 徙 。 虽 有 舟
yòng　　shǐ mín zhòng sǐ ér bù yuǎn xǐ　　suī yǒu zhōu

舆 ， 无 所 乘 之 ； 虽 有 甲 兵 ， 无 所 陈
yú　　wú suǒ chéng zhī　　suī yǒu jiǎ bīng　　wú suǒ chén

之 ； 使 人 复 结 绳 而 用 之 。 甘 其 食 ，
zhī　　shǐ rén fù jié shéng ér yòng zhī　　gān qí shí

美 其 服 ， 安 其 居 ， 乐 其 俗 。 邻 国 相
měi qí fú　　ān qí jū　　lè qí sú　　lín guó xiāng

望 ， 鸡 犬 之 声 相 闻 ， 民 至 老 死 不
wàng　　jī quǎn zhī shēng xiāng wén　　mín zhì lǎo sǐ bù

相 往 来 。
xiāng wǎng lái

## 11. Selection from the *Mozi*

十 一 . 《 墨 子 · 公 输 》： 墨 子 说 公 输 盘
shí yī　　mò zǐ gōng shū　　mò zǐ shuì gōng shū pán

公 输 盘 为 楚 造 云 梯 之 械 ， 成 ，
gōng shū pán wèi chǔ zào yún tī zhī xiè　　chéng

将 以 攻 宋 。 子 墨 子 闻 之 ， 起 于 齐 ，
jiāng yǐ gōng sòng　　zǐ mò zǐ wén zhī　　qǐ yú qí

行 十 日 十 夜 而 至 于 郢 。 见 公 输 盘 。
xíng shí rì shí yè ér zhì yú yǐng　　jiàn gōng shū pán

公 输 盘 曰 ： 「 夫 子 何 命 焉 为 ？ 」 子
gōng shū pán yuē　　　　fū zǐ hé mìng yān wéi　　　zǐ

墨 子 曰 ： 「 北 方 有 侮 臣 （ 者 ） ， 愿
mò zǐ yuē　　　　běi fāng yǒu wǔ chén　　zhě　　　yuàn

藉 子 杀 之 。」 公 输 盘 不 说 。 子 墨 子
jiè zǐ shā zhī　　　　gōng shū pán bú yuè　　zǐ mò zǐ

曰：「 请 献 十 金 。」 公 输 盘 曰：「 吾
yuē　　　qǐng xiàn shí jīn　　　gōng shū pán yuē　　　wú

义 固 不 杀 人 。」 子 墨 子 起 ， 再 拜 曰：
yì gù bù shā rén　　zǐ mò zǐ qǐ　　zài bài yuē

「 请 说 之 。 吾 从 北 方 ， 闻 子 为 梯 ，
qǐng shuō zhī　　wú cóng běi fāng　　wén zǐ wéi tī

将 以 攻 宋 。 宋 何 罪 之 有 ？ 荆 国 有
jiāng yǐ gōng sòng　　sòng hé zuì zhī yǒu　　jīng guó yǒu

余 于 地 ， 而 不 足 于 民 。 杀 所 不 足
yú yú dì　　ér bù zú yú mín　　shā suǒ bù zú

而 争 所 有 余 ， 不 可 谓 智 ； 宋 无 罪
ér zhēng suǒ yǒu yú　　bù kě wèi zhì　　sòng wú zuì

而 攻 之 ， 不 可 谓 仁 ； 知 而 不 争 ， 不
ér gōng zhī　　bù kě wèi rén　　zhī ér bù zhēng　　bù

可 谓 忠 ； 争 而 不 得 ， 不 可 谓 强 。 义
kě wèi zhōng　　zhēng ér bù dé　　bù kě wèi qiáng　　yì

不 杀 少 而 杀 众 ， 不 可 谓 知 类 。」 公
bù shā shǎo ér shā zhòng　　bù kě wèi zhī lèi　　gōng

输 盘 服 。
shū pán fú

## 12.　Selection from the *Zhuangzi* (No. 1)

十 二 .《 庄 子 · 秋 水 》（ 节 ）
shí èr　　zhuāng zǐ qiū shuǐ　　jié

秋 水 时 至 ， 百 川 灌 河 。 泾 流 之
qiū shuǐ shí zhì　　bǎi chuān guàn hé　　jīng liú zhī

大 ， 两 涘 渚 崖 之 间 ， 不 辩 牛 马 。 于
dà　　liǎng sì zhǔ yá zhī jiān　　bú biàn niú mǎ　　yú

是 焉 河 伯 欣 然 自 喜 ， 以 天 下 之 美
shì yān hé bó xīn rán zì xǐ　　yǐ tiān xià zhī měi

为 尽 在 己 。 顺 流 而 东 行 ， 至 于 北
wéi jìn zài jǐ　　shùn liú ér dōng xíng　　zhì yú běi

海 ； 东 面 而 视 ， 不 见 水 端 。
hǎi　　dōng miàn ér shì　　bú jiàn shuǐ duān

于 是 焉 河 伯 始 旋 其 面 目 ， 望 洋
yú shì yān hé bó shǐ xuán qí miàn mù　　wàng yáng

向 若 而 叹 曰 ： 「 野 语 有 之 曰 ： 『 闻
xiàng ruò ér tàn yuē　　yě yǔ yǒu zhī yuē　　wén

道 百 ， 以 为 莫 己 若 』 者 ， 我 之 谓 也 。
dào bǎi　　yǐ wéi mò jǐ ruò　　zhě　　wǒ zhī wèi yě

且 夫 我 尝 闻 少 仲 尼 之 闻 ， 而 轻 伯
qiě fú wǒ cháng wén shǎo zhòng ní zhī wén　　ér qīng bó

夷 之 义 者 ， 始 吾 弗 信 ， 今 我 睹 子
yí zhī yì zhě　　shǐ wú fú xìn　　jīn wǒ dǔ zǐ

之 难 穷 也 ， 吾 非 至 于 子 之 门 ， 则
zhī nán qióng yě　　wú fēi zhì yú zǐ zhī mén　　zé

殆 矣 ， 吾 长 见 笑 于 大 方 之 家 。 」
dài yǐ　　wú cháng jiàn xiào yú dà fāng zhī jiā

---

# 13. Selection from the *Zhuangzi* (No. 2)

十 三 . 《 庄 子 · 徐 无 鬼 》： 运 斤 成 风
shí sān　　zhuāng zǐ　　xú wú guǐ　　yùn jīn chéng fēng

庄 子 送 葬 ， 过 惠 子 之 墓 。 顾 谓
zhuāng zǐ sòng zàng　　guò huì zǐ zhī mù　　gù wèi

从者曰：「郢人垩慢其鼻端，若蝇
cóng zhě yuē yǐng rén è màn qí bí duān ruò yíng

翼。使匠石斲之。匠石运斤成风，
yì shǐ jiàng shí zhuó zhī jiàng shí yùn jīn chéng fēng

听而斲之，尽垩而鼻不伤。郢人
tīng ér zhuó zhī jìn è ér bí bù shāng yǐng rén

立不失容。宋元君闻之，召匠石
lì bù shī róng sòng yuán jūn wén zhī zhào jiàng shí

曰：『尝试为寡人为之。』匠石曰：
yuē cháng shì wèi guǎ rén wéi zhī jiàng shí yuē

『臣则尝能斲之，虽然，臣之质死
chén zé cháng néng zhuó zhī suī rán chén zhī zhì sǐ

久矣！』自夫子之死也，吾无以为
jiǔ yǐ zì fū zǐ zhī sǐ yě wú wú yǐ wéi

质矣！吾无与言之矣！」
zhì yǐ wú wú yǔ yán zhī yǐ

# 14. Selection from the *Xunzi*

十四．《荀子·劝学》（节）
shí sì xún zǐ quàn xué jié

君子曰：学不可以已。青，取之
jūn zǐ yuē xué bù kě yǐ yǐ qīng qǔ zhī

于蓝，而青于蓝；冰，水为之，而
yú lán ér qīng yú lán bīng shuǐ wéi zhī ér

寒于水。木直中绳，鞣以为轮，其
hán yú shuǐ mù zhí zhòng shéng róu yǐ wéi lún qí

曲中规，虽有槁暴，不复挺者，鞣
qū zhòng guī suī yǒu gǎo pù bù fù tǐng zhě róu

使 之 然 也 。 故 木 受 绳 则 直 ， 金 就
shǐ zhī rán yě gù mù shòu shéng zé zhí jīn jiù

砺 则 利 ， 君 子 博 学 而 日 参 省 乎 己 ，
lì zé lì jūn zǐ bó xué ér rì cān xíng hū jǐ

则 知 明 而 行 无 过 矣 。 故 不 登 高 山 ，
zé zhì míng ér xíng wú guò yǐ gù bù dēng gāo shān

不 知 天 之 高 也 ； 不 临 深 谿 ， 不 知
bù zhī tiān zhī gāo yě bù lín shēn xī bù zhī

地 之 厚 也 ； 不 闻 先 王 之 遗 言 ， 不
dì zhī hòu yě bù wén xiān wáng zhī yí yán bù

知 学 问 之 大 也 。 干 、 越 、 夷 、 貉 之
zhī xué wèn zhī dà yě gān yuè yí mò zhī

子 ， 生 而 同 声 ， 长 而 异 俗 ， 教 使 之
zǐ shēng ér tóng shēng zhǎng ér yì sú jiào shǐ zhī

然 也 。 …
rán yě

积 土 成 山 ， 风 雨 兴 焉 ； 积 水 成
jī tǔ chéng shān fēng yǔ xīng yān jī shuǐ chéng

渊 ， 蛟 龙 生 焉 ； 积 善 成 德 ， 而 神 明
yuān jiāo lóng shēng yān jī shàn chéng dé ér shén míng

自 得 ， 圣 心 备 焉 。 故 不 积 颐 步 ， 无
zì dé shèng xīn bèi yān gù bù jī kuī bù wú

以 至 千 里 ； 不 积 小 流 ， 无 以 成 江
yǐ zhì qiān lǐ bù jī xiǎo liú wú yǐ chéng jiāng

海 。 骐 骥 一 跃 ， 不 能 十 步 ； 驽 马 十
hǎi qí jì yí yuè bù néng shí bù nú mǎ shí

驾 ， 功 在 不 舍 。 锲 而 舍 之 ， 朽 木 不
jià gōng zài bù shě qiè ér shě zhī xiǔ mù bù

折 ； 锲 而 不 舍 ， 金 石 可 镂 。 蚓 无 爪
zhé qiè ér bù shě jīn shí kě lòu yǐn wú zhuǎ

牙 之 利 ， 筋 骨 之 强 ， 上 食 埃 土 ， 下
yá zhī lì   jīn gǔ zhī qiáng   shàng shí āi tǔ   xià

饮 黄 泉 ， 用 心 一 也 。 蟹 六 跪 而 二
yǐn huáng quán   yòng xīn yī yě   xiè liù guì ér èr

螯 ， 非 蛇 蟺 之 穴 无 可 寄 托 者 ， 用
áo   fēi shé shàn zhī xué wú kě jì tuō zhě   yòng

心 躁 也 。 是 故 无 冥 冥 之 志 者 ， 无
xīn zào yě   shì gù wú míng míng zhī zhì zhě   wú

昭 昭 之 明 ； 无 惛 惛 之 事 者 ， 无 赫
zhāo zhāo zhī míng   wú hūn hūn zhī shì zhě   wú hè

赫 之 功 。
hè zhī gōng

# 15. Selection from the *Han Feizi*

十 五 . 《 韩 非 子 · 说 林 上 》： 巧 诈 不 如 拙 诚
shí wǔ   hán fēi zǐ · shuō lín shàng   qiǎo zhà bù rú zhuó chéng

乐 羊 为 魏 将 而 攻 中 山 ， 其 子 在
yuè yáng wéi wèi jiàng ér gōng zhōng shān   qí zǐ zài

中 山 ， 中 山 之 君 烹 其 子 而 遗 之 羹 ，
zhōng shān   zhōng shān zhī jūn pēng qí zǐ ér wèi zhī gēng

乐 羊 坐 于 幕 下 而 啜 之 ， 尽 一 杯 ，
yuè yáng zuò yú mù xià ér chuò zhī   jìn yì bēi

文 侯 谓 堵 师 赞 曰 ： 「 乐 羊 以 我 故
wén hóu wèi dǔ shī zàn yuē   yuè yáng yǐ wǒ gù

而 食 其 子 之 肉 。 」 答 曰 ： 「 其 子 而
ér shí qí zǐ zhī ròu   dá yuē   qí zǐ ér

食 之 ， 且 谁 不 食 ？」 乐 羊 罢 中 山 ，
shí zhī qiě shéi bù shí yuè yáng bà zhōng shān

文 侯 赏 其 功 而 疑 其 心 。
wén hóu shǎng qí gōng ér yí qí xīn

孟 孙 猎 得 麑 ， 使 秦 西 巴 持 之 归 ，
mèng sūn liè dé ní shǐ qín xī bā chí zhī guī

其 母 随 之 而 啼 ， 秦 西 巴 弗 忍 而 与
qí mǔ suí zhī ér tí qín xī bā fú rěn ér yǔ

之 ， 孟 孙 归 ， 至 而 求 麑 ， 答 曰 ：「 余
zhī mèng sūn guī zhì ér qiú ní dá yuē yú

弗 忍 而 与 其 母 。」 大 怒 ， 逐 之 ， 居
fú rěn ér yǔ qí mǔ dà nù zhú zhī jū

三 月 ， 复 召 以 为 其 子 傅 ， 其 御 曰 ：
sān yuè fù zhào yǐ wéi qí zǐ fù qí yù yuē

「 曩 将 罪 之 ， 今 召 以 为 子 傅 ， 何 也 ？」
náng jiāng zuì zhī jīn zhào yǐ wéi zǐ fù hé yě

孟 孙 曰 ：「 夫 不 忍 麑 ， 又 且 忍 吾 子
mèng sūn yuē fú bù rěn ní yòu qiě rěn wú zǐ

乎 ？」
hū

故 曰 ：「 巧 诈 不 如 拙 诚 。」 乐 羊
gù yuē qiǎo zhà bù rú zhuó chéng yuè yáng

以 有 功 见 疑 ， 秦 西 巴 以 有 罪 益 信 。
yǐ yǒu gōng jiàn yí qín xī bā yǐ yǒu zuì yì xìn

# 16. Selection from the *Zuozhuan* (No. 1)

十六．《左传·庄公十年》：曹刿论战
shí liù　　　zuǒ zhuàn zhuāng gōng shí nián　　cáo guì lùn zhàn

十 年 春， 齐 师 伐 我 。 公 将 战， 曹
shí nián chūn　 qí shī fá wǒ　 gōng jiāng zhàn　 cáo

刿 请 见 。 其 乡 人 曰：「 肉 食 者 谋 之，
guì qǐng jiàn　 qí xiāng rén yuē　 ròu shí zhě móu zhī

又 何 间 焉 ？」 刿 曰 ：「 肉 食 者 鄙，
yòu hé jiàn yān　　 guì yuē　　 ròu shí zhě bǐ

未 能 远 谋 。」 乃 入 见 。 问 何 以 战 ？
wèi néng yuǎn móu　 nǎi rù jiàn　 wèn hé yǐ zhàn

公 曰 ：「 衣 食 所 安， 弗 敢 专 也， 必
gōng yuē　 yī shí suǒ ān　 fú gǎn zhuān yě　 bì

以 分 人 。」 对 曰 ：「 小 惠 未 偏， 民
yǐ fēn rén　 duì yuē　 xiǎo huì wèi biàn　 mín

弗 从 也 。」 公 曰 ：「 牺 牲 玉 帛， 弗
fú cóng yě　 gōng yuē　 xī shēng yù bó　 fú

敢 加 也， 必 以 信 。」 对 曰 ：「 小 信
gǎn jiā yě　 bì yǐ xìn　 duì yuē　 xiǎo xìn

未 孚， 神 弗 福 也 。」 公 曰 ：「 小 大
wèi fú　 shén fú fú yě　 gōng yuē　 xiǎo dà

之 狱， 虽 不 能 察， 必 以 情 。」 对 曰 ：
zhī yù　 suī bù néng chá　 bì yǐ qíng　 duì yuē

「 忠 之 属 也， 可 以 一 战， 战 则 请 从 。」
zhōng zhī shǔ yě　 kě yǐ yí zhàn　 zhàn zé qǐng cóng

公 与 之 乘， 战 于 长 勺， 公 将 鼓 之 。
gōng yǔ zhī chéng　 zhàn yú cháng sháo　 gōng jiāng gǔ zhī

刿 曰 ：「 未 可 。」 齐 人 三 鼓， 刿 曰 ：
guì yuē　 wèi kě　 qí rén sān gǔ　 guì yuē

「可 矣 。」 齐 师 败 绩 ， 公 将 驰 之 ，
kě yǐ qí shī bài jī gōng jiāng chí zhī

刿 曰 ： 「 未 可 。」 下 视 其 辙 ， 登 轼
guì yuē wèi kě xià shì qí zhé dēng shì

而 望 之 ， 曰 ： 「 可 矣 。」 遂 逐 齐 师 。
ér wàng zhī yuē kě yǐ suì zhú qí shī

既 克 ， 公 问 其 故 。 对 曰 ： 「 夫 战 ，
jì kè gōng wèn qí gù duì yuē fú zhàn

勇 气 也 。 一 鼓 作 气 ， 再 而 衰 ， 三 而
yǒng qì yě yī gǔ zuò qì zài ér shuāi sān ér

竭 。 彼 竭 我 盈 ， 故 克 之 。 夫 大 国 ，
jié bǐ jié wǒ yíng gù kè zhī fú dà guó

难 测 也 。 惧 有 伏 焉 。 吾 视 其 辙 乱 ，
nán cè yě jù yǒu fú yān wú shì qí zhé luàn

望 其 旗 靡 ， 故 逐 之 。」
wàng qí qí mǐ gù zhú zhī

## 17. Selection from the *Zuozhuan* (No. 2)

十 七 . 《 左 传 · 僖 公 四 年 》： 齐 桓 公 伐 楚
shí qī zuǒ zhuàn xī gōng sì nián qí huán gōng fá chǔ

四 年 春 ， 齐 侯 以 诸 侯 之 师 侵 蔡 。
sì nián chūn qí hóu yǐ zhū hóu zhī shī qīn cài

蔡 溃 ， 遂 伐 楚 。 楚 子 使 与 师 言 曰 ：
cài kuì suì fá chǔ chǔ zǐ shǐ yǔ shī yán yuē

「 君 处 北 海 ， 寡 人 处 南 海 ， 唯 是 风
jūn chǔ běi hǎi guǎ rén chǔ nán hǎi wéi shì fēng

马 牛 不 相 及 也 。 不 虞 君 之 涉 吾 地
mǎ niú bù xiāng jí yě bù yú jūn zhī shè wú dì

也，何故？」管仲对曰：「昔召康公命我先君大公曰：五侯九伯，女实征之，以夹辅周室。赐我先君履：东至于海，西至于河，南至于穆陵，北至于无棣。尔贡包茅不入，王祭不共，无以缩酒，寡人是征；昭王南征而不复，寡人是问。」对曰：「贡之不入，寡君之罪也，敢不共给？昭王之不复，君其问诸水滨！」师进，次于陉。

夏，楚子使屈完如师。师退，次于召陵。齐侯陈诸侯之师，与屈完乘而观之。齐侯曰：「岂不谷是为？先君之好是继！与不谷同好，如何？」对曰：「君惠徼福于敝邑

之 社 稷 ， 辱 收 寡 君 ， 寡 君 之 愿 也 。」
zhī shè jì rǔ shōu guǎ jūn guǎ jūn zhī yuàn yě

齐 侯 曰 ：「 以 此 众 战 ， 谁 能 御 之 ？
qí hóu yuē yǐ cǐ zhòng zhàn shéi néng yù zhī

以 此 攻 城 ， 何 城 不 克 ？」 对 曰 ：「 君
yǐ cǐ gōng chéng hé chéng bú kè duì yuē jūn

若 以 德 绥 诸 侯 ， 谁 敢 不 服 。 君 若
ruò yǐ dé suí zhū hóu shéi gǎn bù fú jūn ruò

以 力 ， 楚 国 方 城 以 为 城 ， 汉 水 以
yǐ lì chǔ guó fāng chéng yǐ wéi chéng hàn shuǐ yǐ

为 池 ， 虽 众 ， 无 所 用 之 ！」 屈 完 及
wéi chí suī zhòng wú suǒ yòng zhī qū wán jí

诸 侯 盟 。
zhū hóu méng

# 18. Selection from the *Zuozhuan* (No. 3)

十 八 .《 左 传 · 襄 公 三 十 一 年 》： 子 产 论 治
shí bā zuǒ zhuàn xiāng gōng sān shí yī nián zǐ chǎn lùn zhì

子 皮 欲 使 尹 何 为 邑 ， 子 产 曰 ：
zǐ pí yù shǐ yǐn hé wéi yì zǐ chǎn yuē

「 少 ， 未 知 可 否 。」 子 皮 曰 ：「 愿 ，
shào wèi zhī kě fǒu zǐ pí yuē yuàn

吾 爱 之 ， 不 吾 叛 也 。 使 夫 往 而 学
wú ài zhī bù wú pàn yě shǐ fú wǎng ér xué

焉 ， 夫 亦 愈 知 治 矣 。」 子 产 曰 ：「 不
yān fú yì yù zhī zhì yǐ zǐ chǎn yuē bù

可 。 人 之 爱 人 ， 求 利 之 也 。 今 吾 子
kě rén zhī ài rén qiú lì zhī yě jīn wú zǐ

爱人则以政，犹未能操刀而使割
ài rén zé yǐ zhèng yóu wèi néng cāo dāo ér shǐ gē

也，其伤实多。子之爱人，伤之而
yě qí shāng shí duō zǐ zhī ài rén shāng zhī ér

已。其谁敢求爱于子，子于郑国，
yǐ qí shéi gǎn qiú ài yú zǐ zǐ yú zhèng guó

栋也。栋折榱崩，侨将厌焉，敢不
dòng yě dòng zhé cuī bēng qiáo jiāng yā yān gǎn bù

尽言。子有美锦，不使人学制焉。
jìn yán zǐ yǒu měi jǐn bù shǐ rén xué zhì yān

大官大邑，身之所庇也，而使学
dà guān dà yì shēn zhī suǒ bì yě ér shǐ xué

者制焉。其为美锦不亦多乎？侨
zhě zhì yān qí wéi měi jǐn bú yì duō hū qiáo

闻学而后入政，未闻以政学者也。
wén xué ér hòu rù zhèng wèi wén yǐ zhèng xué zhě yě

若果行此，必有所害。譬如田猎，
ruò guǒ xíng cǐ bì yǒu suǒ hài pì rú tián liè

射御贯则能获禽，若未尝登车射
shè yù guàn zé néng huò qín ruò wèi cháng dēng chē shè

御，则败绩厌覆是惧，何暇思获？」
yù zé bài jī yā fù shì jù hé xiá sī huò

子皮曰：「善哉！虎不敏，吾闻君
zǐ pí yuē shàn zāi hǔ bù mǐn wú wén jūn

子务知大者远者，小人务知小者
zǐ wù zhī dà zhě yuǎn zhě xiǎo rén wù zhī xiǎo zhě

近者。我小人也。衣服附在吾身，
jìn zhě wǒ xiǎo rén yě yī fu fù zài wú shēn

我知而慎之。大官大邑所以庇身
wǒ zhī ér shèn zhī dà guān dà yì suǒ yǐ bì shēn

也 ， 我 远 而 慢 之 。 微 子 之 言 ， 吾 不
yě 　 wǒ yuǎn ér màn zhī 　 wēi zǐ zhī yán 　 wú bù

知 也 … 。 」
zhī yě

## 19. Selection from the *Guoyu*

十 九 . 《 国 语 · 越 语 上 》： 句 践 治 越
shí jiǔ 　 guó yǔ 　 yuè yǔ shàng 　 gōu jiàn zhì yuè

句 践 之 地 ， 南 至 于 句 无 ， 北 至
gōu jiàn zhī dì 　 nán zhì yú gōu wú 　 běi zhì

于 御 儿 ， 东 至 于 鄞 ， 西 至 于 姑 蔑 ，
yú yù ér 　 dōng zhì yú yín 　 xī zhì yú gū miè

广 运 百 里 。 乃 致 其 父 母 昆 弟 而 誓
guǎng yùn bǎi lǐ 　 nǎi zhì qí fù mǔ kūn dì ér shì

之 曰 ： 「 寡 人 闻 ， 古 之 贤 君 ， 四 方
zhī yuē 　 guǎ rén wén 　 gǔ zhī xián jūn 　 sì fāng

之 民 归 之 ， 若 水 之 归 下 也 。 今 寡
zhī mín guī zhī 　 ruò shuǐ zhī guī xià yě 　 jīn guǎ

人 不 能 ， 将 帅 二 三 子 夫 妇 以 蕃 。 」
rén bù néng 　 jiàng shuài èr sān zǐ fū fù yǐ fán

令 壮 者 无 取 老 妇 ， 令 老 者 无 取 壮
lìng zhuàng zhě wú qǔ lǎo fù 　 lìng lǎo zhě wú qǔ zhuàng

妻 。 女 子 十 七 不 嫁 ， 其 父 母 有 罪 ；
qī 　 nǚ zǐ shí qī bù jià 　 qí fù mǔ yǒu zuì

丈 夫 二 十 不 取 ， 其 父 母 有 罪 。 将
zhàng fū èr shí bù qǔ 　 qí fù mǔ yǒu zuì 　 jiāng

免者以告，公令醫守之。生丈夫，
二壺酒，一犬；生女子，二壺酒，
一豚。生三人，公與之母；生二人，
公與之餼。當室者死，三年釋其
政；支子死，三月釋其政。必哭泣
葬埋之，如其子。令孤子、寡婦、
疾疹、貧病者，納宦其子。其達士，
潔其居，美其服，飽其食，而摩厲
之于義。四方之士來者，必廟禮
之。句踐載稻與脂于舟以行，國
之孺子之游者，無不哺也，無不
歠也，必問其名。非其身之所種
則不食，非其夫人之所織則不衣，
十年不收于國，民俱有三年之食。

᠁᠁᠁᠁᠁᠁᠁᠁᠁᠁᠁᠁᠁᠁

# 20. Selection from the *Zhanguo ce* (No. 1)

二十．《战 国 策 · 齐 策 一》： 靖 郭 君 将 城 薛
èr shí　　zhàn guó cè　 qí cè yī　　　　jìng guō jūn jiāng chéng xuē

靖 郭 君 将 城 薛 ， 客 多 以 谏 。 靖
jìng guō jūn jiāng chéng xuē 　 kè duō yǐ jiàn 。 jìng

郭 君 谓 谒 者 ， 无 为 客 通 。 齐 人 有
guō jūn wèi yè zhě 　 wú wèi kè tōng 。 qí rén yǒu

请 者 曰 ： 「 臣 请 三 言 而 已 矣 ！ 益 一
qǐng zhě yuē 　 chén qǐng sān yán ér yǐ yǐ 　 yì yī

言 ， 臣 请 烹 。 」 靖 郭 君 因 见 之 。 客
yán 　 chén qǐng pēng 。 　 jìng guō jūn yīn jiàn zhī 。 kè

趋 而 进 曰 ： 「 海 大 鱼 。 」 因 反 走 。
qū ér jìn yuē 　 hǎi dà yú 。 　 yīn fǎn zǒu 。

君 曰 ： 「 客 ， 有 于 此 。 」 客 曰 ： 「 鄙
jūn yuē 　 kè 　 yǒu yú cǐ 。 　 kè yuē 　 bǐ

臣 不 敢 以 死 为 戏 。 」 君 曰 ： 「 亡 ，
chén bù gǎn yǐ sǐ wéi xì 。 　 jūn yuē 　 wú

更 言 之 。 」 对 曰 ： 「 君 不 闻 大 鱼 乎 ？
gèng yán zhī 。 　 duì yuē 　 jūn bù wén dà yú hū 。

网 不 能 止 ， 钩 不 能 牵 ， 荡 而 失 水 ，
wǎng bù néng zhǐ 　 gōu bù néng qiān 　 dàng ér shī shuǐ 　

则 蝼 蚁 得 意 焉 。 今 夫 齐 亦 君 之 水
zé lóu yǐ dé yì yān 。 jīn fú qí yì jūn zhī shuǐ

也 。 君 长 有 齐 ， 奚 以 薛 为 ？ 夫 齐 ，
yě 。 jūn cháng yǒu qí 　 xī yǐ xuē wéi 。 fū qí 　

虽 隆 薛 之 城 到 于 天 ， 犹 之 无 益 也 。 」
suī lóng xuē zhī chéng dào yú tiān 　 yóu zhī wú yì yě 。 　

君 曰 ： 「 善 。 」 乃 辍 城 薛 。
jūn yuē 　 shàn 。 　 nǎi chuò chéng xuē 。

## 21. Selection from the *Zhanguo ce* (No. 2)

二十一．《战国策·齐策四》：冯谖客孟尝君
èr shí yī　　　zhàn guó cè　qí cè sì　　　féng xuān kè mèng cháng jūn

齐　人　有　冯　谖　者，贫　乏　不　能　自　存，
qí　rén　yǒu　féng　xuān　zhě　　pín　fá　bù　néng　zì　cún

使　人　属　孟　尝　君，愿　寄　食　门　下。孟
shǐ　rén　zhǔ　mèng　cháng　jūn　　yuàn　jì　shí　mén　xià　　mèng

尝　君　曰：「客　何　好？」　曰：「客　无　好
cháng　jūn　yuē　　kè　hé　hào　　　yuē　　kè　wú　hào

也。」曰：「客　何　能？」曰：「客　无
yě　　　yuē　　kè　hé　néng　　yuē　　kè　wú

能　也。」孟　尝　君　笑　而　受　之　曰：「诺。」
néng　yě　　mèng　cháng　jūn　xiào　ér　shòu　zhī　yuē　　nuò

左　右　以　君　贱　之　也，食　以　草　具。
zuǒ　yòu　yǐ　jūn　jiàn　zhī　yě　　sì　yǐ　cǎo　jù

居　有　顷，倚　柱　弹　其　剑，歌　曰：「长
jū　yǒu　qǐng　　yǐ　zhù　tán　qí　jiàn　　gē　yuē　　cháng

铗　归　来　乎，食　无　鱼！」左　右　以　告。
jiá　guī　lái　hū　　shí　wú　yú　　zuǒ　yòu　yǐ　gào

孟　尝　君　曰：「食　之，比　门　下　之　客。」
mèng　cháng　jūn　yuē　　sì　zhī　　bǐ　mén　xià　zhī　kè

居　有　顷，复　弹　其　铗，歌　曰：「长　铗
jū　yǒu　qǐng　　fù　tán　qí　jiá　　gē　yuē　　cháng　jiá

归　来　乎，出　无　车！」左　右　皆　笑　之，
guī　lái　hū　　chū　wú　chē　　zuǒ　yòu　jiē　xiào　zhī

以　告。孟　尝　君　曰：「为　之　驾，比　门
yǐ　gào　　mèng　cháng　jūn　yuē　　wèi　zhī　jià　　bǐ　mén

下　之　车　客。」于　是　乘　其　车，揭　其　剑，
xià　zhī　chē　kè　　yú　shì　chéng　qí　chē　　jiē　qí　jiàn

过其友曰：「孟尝君客我。」后有
guò qí yǒu yuē mèng cháng jūn kè wǒ hòu yǒu

顷，复弹其剑铗，歌曰：「长铗归
qǐng fù tán qí jiàn jiá gē yuē cháng jiá guī

来乎，无以为家！」左右皆恶之，
lái hū wú yǐ wéi jiā zuǒ yòu jiē wù zhī

以为贪而不知足。孟尝君问：「冯
yǐ wéi tān ér bù zhī zú mèng cháng jūn wèn féng

公有亲乎？」对曰：「有老母。」
gōng yǒu qīn hū duì yuē yǒu lǎo mǔ

孟尝君使人给其食用，无使乏。
mèng cháng jūn shǐ rén gěi qí shí yòng wú shǐ fá

于是冯谖不复歌。
yú shì féng xuān bú fù gē

后孟尝君出记，问门下诸客：
hòu mèng cháng jūn chū jì wèn mén xià zhū kè

「谁习计会，能为文收责于薛者
shéi xí jì kuài néng wèi wén shōu zhài yú xuē zhě

乎？」冯谖署曰：「能。」孟尝君
hū féng xuān shǔ yuē néng mèng cháng jūn

怪之，曰：「此谁也？」左右曰：
guài zhī yuē cǐ shéi yě zuǒ yòu yuē

「乃歌夫长铗归来者也。」孟尝君
nǎi gē fú cháng jiá guī lái zhě yě mèng cháng jūn

笑曰：「客果有能也，吾负之，未
xiào yuē kè guǒ yǒu néng yě wú fù zhī wèi

尝见也。」请而见之，谢曰：「文
cháng jiàn yě qǐng ér jiàn zhī xiè yuē wén

倦于事，愦于忧，而性懧愚，沉于
juàn yú shì kuì yú yōu ér xìng nuò yú chén yú

国家之事，开罪于先生。先生不羞，乃有意欲为收责于薛乎？」冯谖曰：「愿之。」于是约车治装，载券契而行，辞曰：「责毕收，以何市而反？」孟尝君曰：「视吾家所寡有者。」

驱而之薛，使吏召诸民当偿者，悉来合券。券遍合，起，矫命以责赐诸民，因烧其券，民称万岁。

长驱到齐，晨而求见。孟尝君怪其疾也，衣冠而见之，曰：「责毕收乎？来何疾也！」曰：「收毕矣。」「以何市而反？」冯谖曰：「君云『视吾家所寡有者』。臣窃计君宫中积珍宝，狗马实外厩，

美 人 充 下 陈 。 君 家 所 寡 有 者 以 义
měi rén chōng xià chén jūn jiā suǒ guǎ yǒu zhě yǐ yì

耳 ！ 窃 以 为 君 市 义 。 」 孟 尝 君 曰 ：
ěr qiè yǐ wèi jūn shì yì mèng cháng jūn yuē

「 市 义 奈 何 ？ 」 曰 ： 「 今 君 有 区 区
shì yì nài hé yuē jīn jūn yǒu qū qū

之 薛 ， 不 拊 爱 子 其 民 ， 因 而 贾 利
zhī xuē bù fǔ ài zǐ qí mín yīn ér gǔ lì

之 。 臣 窃 矫 君 命 ， 以 责 赐 诸 民 ， 因
zhī chén qiè jiǎo jūn mìng yǐ zhài cì zhū mín yīn

烧 其 券 ， 民 称 万 岁 。 乃 臣 所 以 为
shāo qí quàn mín chēng wàn suì nǎi chén suǒ yǐ wèi

君 市 义 也 。 」 孟 尝 君 不 说 ， 曰 ： 「 诺 ，
jūn shì yì yě mèng cháng jūn bú yuè yuē nuò

先 生 休 矣 ！ 」
xiān shēng xiū yǐ

后 期 年 ， 齐 王 谓 孟 尝 君 曰 ： 「 寡
hòu jī nián qí wáng wèi mèng cháng jūn yuē guǎ

人 不 敢 以 先 王 之 臣 为 臣 。 」 孟 尝
rén bù gǎn yǐ xiān wáng zhī chén wéi chén mèng cháng

君 就 国 于 薛 ， 未 至 百 里 ， 民 扶 老
jūn jiù guó yú xuē wèi zhì bǎi lǐ mín fú lǎo

携 幼 ， 迎 君 道 中 。 孟 尝 君 顾 谓 冯
xié yòu yíng jūn dào zhōng mèng cháng jūn gù wèi féng

谖 ： 「 先 生 所 为 文 市 义 者 ， 乃 今 日
xuān xiān shēng suǒ wèi wén shì yì zhě nǎi jīn rì

见 之 。 」
jiàn zhī

# 22. Selection from the *Zhanguo ce* (No. 3)

二十二．《战国策·燕策一》：燕昭王 收破燕后即位
èr shí èr　　zhàn guó cè　yān cè yī　　yān zhāo wáng shōu pò yān hòu jí wèi

燕 昭 王 收 破 燕 后 即 位 ， 卑 身 厚
yān zhāo wáng shōu pò yān hòu jí wèi　bēi shēn hòu

币 以 招 贤 者 ， 欲 将 以 报 雠 。 故 往
bì yǐ zhāo xián zhě　　yù jiāng yǐ bào chóu　　gù wǎng

见 郭 隗 先 生 曰 ： 「 齐 因 孤 国 之 乱
jiàn guō wěi xiān shēng yuē　　qí yīn gū guó zhī luàn

而 袭 破 燕 。 孤 极 知 燕 小 力 少 不 足
ér xí pò yān　gū jí zhī yān xiǎo lì shǎo bù zú

以 报 。 然 得 贤 士 与 共 国 ， 以 雪 先
yǐ bào　rán dé xián shì yǔ gòng guó　　yǐ xuě xiān

王 之 耻 ， 孤 之 愿 也 。 敢 问 以 国 报
wáng zhī chǐ　gū zhī yuàn yě　　gǎn wèn yǐ guó bào

雠 者 奈 何 ？ 」
chóu zhě nài hé

郭 隗 先 生 对 曰 ： 「 … 王 诚 博 选
guō wěi xiān shēng duì yuē　　… wáng chéng bó xuān

国 中 之 贤 者 而 朝 其 门 下 ， 天 下 闻
guó zhōng zhī xián zhě ér cháo qí mén xià　　tiān xià wén

王 朝 其 贤 臣 ， 天 下 之 士 必 趋 于 燕
wáng cháo qí xián chén　　tiān xià zhī shì bì qū yú yān

矣 。 」
yǐ

昭 王 曰 ： 「 寡 人 将 谁 朝 而 可 ？ 」
zhāo wáng yuē　　guǎ rén jiāng shéi cháo ér kě

郭 隗 先 生 曰 ： 「 臣 闻 古 之 君 人 ， 有
guō wěi xiān shēng yuē　　chén wén gǔ zhī jūn rén　　yǒu

以 千 金 求 千 里 马 者，三 年 不 能 得。
yǐ qiān jīn qiú qiān lǐ mǎ zhě sān nián bù néng dé

涓 人 言 于 君 曰：『 请 求 之。』 君 遣
juān rén yán yú jūn yuē qǐng qiú zhī jūn qiǎn

之。三 月 得 千 里 马，马 已 死，买 其
zhī sān yuè dé qiān lǐ mǎ mǎ yǐ sǐ mǎi qí

首 五 百 金，反 以 报 君。君 大 怒 曰：
shǒu wǔ bǎi jīn fǎn yǐ bào jūn jūn dà nù yuē

『 所 求 者 生 马，安 事 死 马 而 捐 五
suǒ qiú zhě shēng mǎ ān shì sǐ mǎ ér juān wǔ

百 金？』 涓 人 对 曰：『 死 马 且 买 之
bǎi jīn juān rén duì yuē sǐ mǎ qiě mǎi zhī

五 百 金，况 生 马 乎？天 下 必 以 王
wǔ bǎi jīn kuàng shēng mǎ hū tiān xià bì yǐ wáng

为 能 市 马，马 今 至 矣。』 于 是 不 能
wéi néng shì mǎ mǎ jīn zhì yǐ yú shì bù néng

期 年，千 里 之 马 至 者 三。今 王 诚
jī nián qiān lǐ zhī mǎ zhì zhě sān jīn wáng chéng

欲 致 士，先 从 隗 始；隗 且 见 事，况
yù zhì shì xiān cóng wěi shǐ wěi qiě jiàn shì kuàng

贤 于 隗 者 乎？岂 远 千 里 哉？』 于 是
xián yú wěi zhě hū qǐ yuǎn qiān lǐ zāi yú shì

昭 王 为 隗 筑 宫 而 师 之。乐 毅 自 魏
zhāo wáng wěi wěi zhù gōng ér shī zhī yuè yì zì wèi

往，邹 衍 自 齐 往，剧 辛 自 赵 往，士
wǎng zōu yǎn zì qí wǎng jù xīn zì zhào wǎng shì

争 凑 燕 …。
zhēng còu yān

# 23. Selection from the *Shiji* (No. 1)

二十三．《史记·项羽本纪》（节）
èr shí sān　shǐ jì　xiàng yǔ běn jì　　jié

项 王 军 壁 垓 下 ， 兵 少 食 尽 ， 汉
xiàng wáng jūn bì gāi xià　bīng shǎo shí jìn　hàn

军 及 诸 侯 兵 围 之 数 重 。 夜 闻 汉 军
jūn jí zhū hóu bīng wéi zhī shù chóng　yè wén hàn jūn

四 面 皆 楚 歌 ， 项 王 乃 大 惊 曰 ： 「 汉
sì miàn jiē chǔ gē　xiàng wáng nǎi dà jīng yuē　hàn

皆 已 得 楚 乎 ？ 是 何 楚 人 之 多 也 ！ 」
jiē yǐ dé chǔ hū　shì hé chǔ rén zhī duō yě

项 王 则 夜 起 ， 饮 帐 中 。 有 美 人 名
xiàng wáng zé yè qǐ　yǐn zhàng zhōng　yǒu měi rén míng

虞 ， 常 幸 从 ； 骏 马 名 骓 ， 常 骑 之 。
yú　cháng xìng cóng　jùn mǎ míng zhuī　cháng qí zhī

于 是 项 王 乃 悲 歌 忼 慨 ， 自 为 诗 曰 ：
yú shì xiàng wáng nǎi bēi gē kāng kǎi　zì wéi shī yuē

「 力 拔 山 兮 气 盖 世 ， 时 不 利 兮 骓
lì bá shān xī qì gài shì　shí bú lì xī zhuī

不 逝 。 骓 不 逝 兮 可 奈 何 ， 虞 兮 虞
bú shì　zhuī bú shì xī kě nài hé　yú xī yú

兮 奈 若 何 ！ 」 歌 数 阕 ， 美 人 和 之 。
xī nài ruò hé　gē shù què　měi rén hè zhī

项 王 泣 数 行 下 ， 左 右 皆 泣 ， 莫 能
xiàng wáng qì shù háng xià　zuǒ yòu jiē qì　mò néng

仰 视 。
yǎng shì

于 是 项 王 乃 上 马 骑 ， 麾 下 壮 士
yú shì xiàng wáng nǎi shàng mǎ jì　huī xià zhuàng shì

骑 从 者 八 百 余 人 ， 直 夜 溃 围 南 出 ，
jì cóng zhě bā bǎi yú rén zhí yè kuì wéi nán chū

驰 走 。 平 明 ， 汉 军 乃 觉 之 ， 令 骑 将
chí zǒu píng míng hàn jūn nǎi jué zhī lìng jì jiàng

灌 婴 以 五 千 骑 追 之 。 项 王 渡 淮 ，
guàn yīng yǐ wǔ qiān jì zhuī zhī xiàng wáng dù huái

骑 能 属 者 百 余 人 耳 。 项 王 至 阴 陵 ，
jì néng zhǔ zhě bǎi yú rén ěr xiàng wáng zhì yīn líng

迷 失 道 ， 问 一 田 父 ， 田 父 绐 曰 ：「 左 。」
mí shī dào wèn yì tián fù tián fù dài yuē zuǒ

左 ， 乃 陷 大 泽 中 。 以 故 汉 追 及 之 。
zuǒ nǎi xiàn dà zé zhōng yǐ gù hàn zhuī jí zhī

项 王 乃 复 引 兵 而 东 ， 至 东 城 ，
xiàng wáng nǎi fù yǐn bīng ér dōng zhì dōng chéng

乃 有 二 十 八 骑 。 汉 骑 追 者 数 千 人 。
nǎi yǒu èr shí bā jì hàn jì zhuī zhě shù qiān rén

项 王 自 度 不 得 脱 ， 谓 其 骑 曰 ：「 吾
xiàng wáng zì duò bù dé tuō wèi qí jì yuē wú

起 兵 至 今 八 岁 矣 ， 身 七 十 余 战 ，
qǐ bīng zhì jīn bā suì yǐ shēn qī shí yú zhàn

所 当 者 破 ， 所 击 者 服 ， 未 尝 败 北 ，
suǒ dāng zhě pò suǒ jī zhě fú wèi cháng bài běi

遂 霸 有 天 下 ； 然 今 卒 困 于 此 ， 此
suì bà yǒu tiān xià rán jīn zú kùn yú cǐ cǐ

天 之 亡 我 ， 非 战 之 罪 也 。 今 日 固
tiān zhī wáng wǒ fēi zhàn zhī zuì yě jīn rì gù

决 死 ， 愿 为 诸 君 快 战 ， 必 三 胜 之 ，
jué sǐ yuàn wèi zhū jūn kuài zhàn bì sān shèng zhī

为 诸 君 溃 围 ， 斩 将 ， 刈 旗 ， 令 诸 君
wèi zhū jūn kuì wéi zhǎn jiàng yì qí lìng zhū jūn

知 天 亡 我，非 战 之 罪 也。」乃 分 其
zhī tiān wáng wǒ fēi zhàn zhī zuì yě nǎi fēn qí

骑 以 为 四 队，四 向。汉 军 围 之 数
jì yǐ wéi sì duì sì xiàng hàn jūn wéi zhī shù

重。项 王 谓 其 骑 曰：「吾 为 公 取 彼
chóng xiàng wáng wèi qí jì yuē wú wèi gōng qǔ bǐ

一 将。」令 四 面 骑 驰 下，期 山 东 为
yī jiàng lìng sì miàn jì chí xià qī shān dōng wéi

三 处。
sān chù

于 是 项 王 大 呼 驰 下，汉 军 皆 披
yú shì xiàng wáng dà hū chí xià hàn jūn jiē pī

靡，遂 斩 汉 一 将。是 时，赤 泉 侯 为
mí suì zhǎn hàn yī jiàng shì shí chì quán hóu wéi

骑 将，追 项 王，项 王 嗔 目 而 叱 之，
jì jiàng zhuī xiàng wáng xiàng wáng chēn mù ér chì zhī

赤 泉 侯 人 马 俱 惊，辟 易 数 里。与
chì quán hóu rén mǎ jū jīng bì yì shù lǐ yǔ

其 骑 会 为 三 处。汉 军 不 知 项 王 所
qí jì huì wéi sān chù hàn jūn bù zhī xiàng wáng suǒ

在，乃 分 军 为 三，复 围 之。项 王 乃
zài nǎi fēn jūn wéi sān fù wéi zhī xiàng wáng nǎi

驰，复 斩 汉 一 都 尉，杀 数 十 百 人，
chí fù zhǎn hàn yī dū wèi shā shù shí bǎi rén

复 聚 其 骑，亡 其 两 骑 耳。乃 谓 其
fù jù qí jì wáng qí liǎng jì ěr nǎi wèi qí

骑 曰：「何 如？」骑 皆 伏 曰：「如
jì yuē hé rú jì jiē fú yuē rú

大 王 言。」
dài wáng yán

是 项 王 乃 欲 东 渡 乌 江 。 乌 江 亭
shì xiàng wáng nǎi yù dōng dù wū jiāng wū jiāng tíng

长 檥 船 待 ， 谓 项 王 曰 ： 「 江 东 虽 小 ，
zhǎng yǐ chuán dài wèi xiàng wáng yuē jiāng dōng suī xiǎo

地 方 千 里 ， 众 数 十 万 人 ， 亦 足 王
dì fāng qiān lǐ zhòng shù shí wàn rén yì zú wàng

也 。 愿 大 王 急 渡 。 今 独 臣 有 船 ， 汉
yě yuàn dài wáng jí dù jīn dú chén yǒu chuán hàn

军 至 ， 无 以 渡 。 」 项 王 笑 曰 ： 「 天
jūn zhì wú yǐ dù xiàng wàng xiào yuē tiān

之 亡 我 ， 我 何 渡 为 ！ 且 籍 与 江 东
zhī wáng wǒ wǒ hé dù wéi qiě jí yǔ jiāng dōng

子 弟 八 千 人 渡 江 而 西 ， 今 无 一 人
zǐ dì bā qiān rén dù jiāng ér xī jīn wú yī rén

还 ， 纵 江 东 父 兄 怜 而 王 我 ， 我 何
huán zòng jiāng dōng fù xiōng lián ér wàng wǒ wǒ hé

面 目 见 之 ？ 纵 彼 不 言 ， 籍 独 不 愧
miàn mù jiàn zhī zòng bǐ bù yán jí dú bú kuì

于 心 乎 ？ 」 乃 谓 亭 长 曰 ： 「 吾 知 公
yú xīn hū nǎi wèi tíng zhǎng yuē wú zhī gōng

长 者 。 吾 骑 此 马 五 岁 ， 所 当 无 敌 ，
zhǎng zhě wú qí cǐ mǎ wǔ suì suǒ dāng wú dí

尝 一 日 行 千 里 ， 不 忍 杀 之 ， 以 赐
cháng yī rì xíng qiān lǐ bù rěn shā zhī yǐ cì

公 ！ 」 乃 令 骑 皆 下 马 步 行 ， 持 短 兵
gōng nǎi lìng jì jiē xià mǎ bù xíng chí duǎn bīng

接 战 。 独 籍 所 杀 汉 军 数 百 人 。 项
jiē zhàn dú jí suǒ shā hàn jūn shù bǎi rén xiàng

王 身 亦 被 十 余 创 。 顾 见 汉 骑 司 马
wáng shēn yì bèi shí yú chuāng gù jiàn hàn jì sī mǎ

吕马童，曰：「若非吾故人乎？」
lǚ mǎ tóng　yuē　　ruò fēi wú gù rén hū

马童面之，指王翳曰：「此项王也！」
mǎ tóng miàn zhī　zhǐ wáng yì yuē　　cǐ xiàng wáng yě

项王乃曰：「吾闻汉购我头千金，
xiàng wáng nǎi yuē　　wú wén hàn gòu wǒ tóu qiān jīn

邑万户，吾为若德。」乃自刭而死。
yì wàn hù　wú wèi ruò dé　　nǎi zì wěn ér sǐ

## 24. Selection from the *Shiji* (No. 2)

二十四．《史记·留侯世家》（节）
èr shí sì　　shǐ jì　liú hóu shì jiā　　jié

留侯张良者，其先韩人也。大
liú hóu zhāng liáng zhě　qí xiān hán rén yě　　dà

父开地，相韩昭侯、宣惠王、襄哀
fù kāi dì　xiàng hán zhāo hóu　xuān huì wáng　xiāng āi

王；父平，相釐王、悼惠王。悼惠
wáng　fù píng　xiàng xī wáng　dào huì wáng　dào huì

王二十三年，平卒。卒二十岁，秦
wáng èr shí sān nián　píng zú　zú èr shí suì　qín

灭韩。良年少，未宦事韩。韩破，
miè hán　liáng nián shào　wèi huàn shì hán　hán pò

良家僮三百人，弟死不葬，悉以
liáng jiā tóng sān bǎi rén　dì sǐ bú zàng　xī yǐ

家财求客刺秦王，为韩报仇，以
jiā cái qiú kè cì qín wáng　wèi hán bào chóu　yǐ

大父、父五世相韩故。
dà fù　fù wǔ shì xiàng hán gù

良 尝 学 礼 淮 阳 ， 东 见 仓 海 君 ，
liáng cháng xué lǐ huái yáng dōng jiàn cāng hǎi jūn

得 力 士 ， 为 铁 椎 重 百 二 十 斤 。 秦
dé lì shì wéi tiě chuí zhòng bǎi èr shí jīn qín

皇 帝 东 游 ， 良 与 客 狙 击 秦 皇 帝 博
huáng dì dōng yóu liáng yǔ kè jū jī qín huáng dì bó

浪 沙 中 ， 误 中 副 车 。 秦 皇 帝 大 怒 ，
làng shā zhōng wù zhòng fù chē qín huáng dì dà nù

大 索 天 下 ， 求 贼 急 甚 ， 为 张 良 故
dà suǒ tiān xià qiú zéi jí shèn wèi zhāng liáng gù

也 。 良 乃 更 名 姓 ， 亡 匿 下 邳 。
yě liáng nǎi gēng míng xìng wáng nì xià péi

良 尝 闲 从 容 步 游 下 邳 圯 上 ， 有
liáng cháng xián cōng róng bù yóu xià péi yí shàng yǒu

一 老 父 ， 衣 褐 ， 至 良 所 ， 直 堕 其 履
yī lǎo fù yì hè zhì liáng suǒ zhí duò qí lǚ

圯 下 ， 顾 谓 良 曰 ：「 孺 子 下 取 履 ！」
yí xià gù wèi liáng yuē rú zǐ xià qǔ lǚ

良 鄂 然 ， 欲 殴 之 。 为 其 老 ， 强 忍 ，
liáng è rán yù ōu zhī wèi qí lǎo qiáng rěn

下 取 履 。 父 曰 ：「 履 我 ！」 良 业 为
xià qǔ lǚ fù yuē lǚ wǒ liáng yè wèi

取 履 ， 因 长 跪 履 之 。 父 以 足 受 ， 笑
qǔ lǚ yīn cháng guì lǚ zhī fù yǐ zú shòu xiào

而 去 。 良 殊 大 惊 ， 随 目 之 。 父 去 里
ér qù liáng shū dà jīng suí mù zhī fù qù lǐ

所 ， 复 还 ， 曰 ：「 孺 子 可 教 矣 ！ 后
suǒ fù huán yuē rú zǐ kě jiào yǐ hòu

五 日 平 明 ， 与 我 会 此 。」 良 因 怪 之 ，
wǔ rì píng míng yǔ wǒ huì cǐ liáng yīn guài zhī

跪 曰 ：「 诺 。」
guì yuē　　　　　 nuò

五 日 平 明 ， 良 往 。 父 已 先 在 ， 怒
wǔ rì píng míng， liáng wǎng。 fù yǐ xiān zài， nù

曰 ：「 与 老 人 期 ， 后 ， 何 也 ？」 去 ，
yuē 　 yǔ lǎo rén jī， hòu， hé yě？ qù，

曰 ：「 后 五 日 早 会 ！」 五 日 鸡 鸣 ，
yuē 　 hòu wǔ rì zǎo huì！ wǔ rì jī míng，

良 往 ， 父 又 先 在 ， 复 怒 曰 ：「 后 ，
liáng wǎng， fù yòu xiān zài， fù nù yuē 　 hòu，

何 也 ？」 去 ， 曰 ：「 后 五 日 复 早 来 ！」
hé yě？ qù， yuē 　 hòu wǔ rì fù zǎo lái！

五 日 ， 良 夜 未 半 往 。 有 顷 ， 父 亦 来 ，
wǔ rì， liáng yè wèi bàn wǎng。 yǒu qǐng， fù yì lái，

喜 曰 ：「 当 如 是 。」 出 一 编 书 ， 曰 ：
xǐ yuē 　 dāng rú shì。 chū yī biān shū， yuē

「 读 此 则 为 王 者 师 矣 ！ 后 十 年 ， 兴 。
dú cǐ zé wéi wáng zhě shī yǐ！ hòu shí nián， xīng

十 三 年 ， 孺 子 见 我 ， 济 北 谷 城 山
shí sān nián， rú zǐ jiàn wǒ， jì běi gǔ chéng shān

下 黄 石 ， 即 我 矣 。」 遂 去 ， 无 他 言 ，
xià huáng shí， jí wǒ yǐ。 suì qù， wú tā yán，

不 复 见 。
bù fù jiàn

旦 日 视 其 书 ， 乃 太 公 兵 法 也 。
dàn rì shì qí shū， nǎi tài gōng bīng fǎ yě

良 因 异 之 ， 常 习 诵 读 之 。
liáng yīn yì zhī， cháng xí sòng dú zhī

# 25. Selection from the *Shiji* (No. 3)

二十五．《史记·魏公子列传》（节）
èr shí wǔ　　shǐ jì　wèi gōng zǐ liè zhuàn　　jié

魏 有 隐 士 曰 侯 嬴，年 七 十，家
wèi yǒu yǐn shì yuē hóu yíng nián qī shí jiā

贫，为 大 梁 夷 门 监 者。公 子 闻 之，
pín wéi dà liáng yí mén jiān zhě gōng zǐ wén zhī

往 请，欲 厚 遗 之。不 肯 受。公 子 于
wǎng qǐng yù hòu wèi zhī bù kěn shòu gōng zǐ yú

是 乃 置 酒 大 会 宾 客。坐 定，公 子
shì nǎi zhì jiǔ dà huì bīn kè zuò dìng gōng zǐ

从 车 骑，虚 左，自 迎 夷 门 侯 生。侯
cóng chē jì xū zuǒ zì yíng yí mén hóu shēng hóu

生 摄 敝 衣 冠，直 上 载 公 子 上 坐，
shēng shè bì yī guān zhí shàng zài gōng zǐ shàng zuò

不 让，欲 以 观 公 子。公 子 执 辔 愈
bù ràng yù yǐ guān gōng zǐ gōng zǐ zhí pèi yù

恭。侯 生 又 谓 公 子 曰：「臣 有 客 在
gōng hóu shēng yòu wèi gōng zǐ yuē chén yǒu kè zài

市 屠 中，愿 枉 车 骑 过 之。」公 子 引
shì tú zhōng yuàn wǎng chē jì guò zhī gōng zǐ yǐn

车 入 市，侯 生 下 见 其 客 朱 亥，俾
chē rù shì hóu shēng xià jiàn qí kè zhū hài bì

倪 故 久 立，与 其 客 语，微 察 公 子。
nì gù jiǔ lì yǔ qí kè yǔ wēi chá gōng zǐ

公 子 颜 色 愈 和。当 是 时，魏 将 相
gōng zǐ yán sè yù hé dāng shì shí wèi jiàng xiàng

宗 室 宾 客 满 堂，待 公 子 举 酒，市
zōng shì bīn kè mǎn táng dài gōng zǐ jǔ jiǔ shì

人 皆 观 公 子 执 辔 。 从 骑 皆 窃 骂 侯
rén jiē guān gōng zǐ zhí pèi cóng jì jiē qiè mà hóu

生 。 侯 生 视 公 子 色 终 不 变 ， 乃 谢
shēng hóu shēng shì gōng zǐ sè zhōng bú biàn nǎi xiè

客 就 车 。 至 家 ， 公 子 引 侯 生 坐 上
kè jiù chē zhì jiā gōng zǐ yǐn hóu shēng zuò shàng

坐 ， 遍 赞 宾 客 ， 宾 客 皆 惊 … 。 侯 生
zuò biàn zàn bīn kè bīn kè jiē jīng hóu shēng

遂 为 上 客 … 。
suì wéi shàng kè

魏 安 厘 王 二 十 年 ， 秦 昭 王 已 破
wèi ān lí wáng èr shí nián qín zhāo wáng yǐ pò

赵 长 平 军 ， … 围 邯 郸 。 公 子 姊 为
zhào cháng píng jūn wéi hán dān gōng zǐ zǐ wéi

赵 惠 文 王 弟 平 原 君 夫 人 ， 数 遗 魏
zhào huì wén wáng dì píng yuán jūn fū rén shù wèi wèi

王 及 公 子 书 ， 请 救 于 魏 。 魏 王 使
wáng jí gōng zǐ shū qǐng jiù yú wèi wèi wáng shǐ

将 军 晋 鄙 将 十 万 众 救 赵 。 … 留 军
jiāng jūn jìn bǐ jiāng shí wàn zhòng jiù zhào liú jūn

壁 邺 ， 名 为 救 赵 ， 实 持 两 端 以 观
bì yè míng wéi jiù zhào shí chí liǎng duān yǐ guān

望 。 平 原 君 使 者 冠 盖 相 属 于 魏 ，
wàng píng yuán jūn shǐ zhě guān gài xiāng zhǔ yú wèi

… 公 子 患 之 ， 数 请 魏 王 ， 及 宾 客
gōng zǐ huàn zhī shù qǐng wèi wáng jí bīn kè

辩 士 说 王 万 端 。 魏 王 畏 秦 ， 终 不
biàn shì shuì wáng wàn duān wèi wáng wèi qín zhōng bù

听 … 。 公 子 … 乃 请 宾 客 ， 约 车 骑
tīng gōng zǐ nǎi qǐng bīn kè yuē chē jì

百 余 乘 ， 欲 赴 秦 军 ， 与 赵 俱 死 。
bǎi yú shèng yù fù qín jūn yǔ zhào jù sǐ

行 过 夷 门 ， 见 侯 生 ， … 侯 生 曰 ：
xíng guò yí mén jiàn hóu shēng hóu shēng yuē

「公 子 勉 之 矣 ， 老 臣 不 能 从 。」 公
gōng zǐ miǎn zhī yǐ lǎo chén bù néng cóng gōng

子 行 数 里 ， … 复 引 车 还 ， 问 侯 生 。
zǐ xíng shù lǐ fù yǐn chē huán wèn hóu shēng

侯 生 笑 曰 ：「臣 固 知 公 子 之 还 也 。」
hóu shēng xiào yuē chén gù zhī gōng zǐ zhī huán yě

… 乃 屏 人 闲 语 曰 ：「嬴 闻 晋 鄙 之
nǎi bǐn rén jiàn yǔ yuē yíng wén jìn bǐ zhī

兵 符 常 在 王 卧 内 ， 而 如 姬 最 幸 ，
bīng fú cháng zài wáng wò nèi ér rú jī zuì xìng

出 入 王 卧 内 ， 力 能 窃 之 。 嬴 闻 如
chū rù wáng wò nèi lì néng qiè zhī yíng wén rú

姬 父 为 人 所 杀 ， … 如 姬 为 公 子 泣 ，
jī fù wéi rén suǒ shā rú jī wèi gōng zǐ qì

公 子 使 客 斩 其 仇 头 ， 敬 进 如 姬 。
gōng zǐ shǐ kè zhǎn qí chóu tóu jìng jìn rú jī

如 姬 之 欲 为 公 子 死 ， 无 所 辞 … 。
rú jī zhī yù wèi gōng zǐ sǐ wú suǒ cí

公 子 诚 一 开 口 请 如 姬 ， 如 姬 必 许
gōng zǐ chéng yì kāi kǒu qǐng rú jī rú jī bì xǔ

诺 。 …」 公 子 从 其 计 ， 请 如 姬 。 如
nuò gōng zǐ cóng qí jì qǐng rú jī rú

姬 果 盗 晋 鄙 兵 符 与 公 子 。
jī guǒ dào jìn bǐ bīng fú yǔ gōng zǐ

公 子 行 ， 侯 生 曰 ：「… 晋 鄙 不 授
gōng zǐ xíng hóu shēng yuē jìn bǐ bú shòu

公子兵而复请之，事必危矣。臣客屠者朱亥可与俱，此人力士。晋鄙听，大善；不听，可使击之。」…于是公子请朱亥。…朱亥遂与公子俱。公子过谢侯生。侯生曰：「臣宜从，老不能。请数公子行日，以至晋鄙军之日，北乡自刭以送公子。」公子遂行。至邺，矫魏王令代晋鄙。晋鄙合符，疑之，…欲无听。朱亥袖四十斤铁椎，椎杀晋鄙，公子遂将晋鄙军…。秦军解去…。公子与侯生决，至军，侯生果北乡自刭。

# Reference Text — Wang Wei: "The Yimen Song"

参 考 篇 章 — 王 维：《夷 门 歌》
cān kǎo piān zhāng　wáng wéi　　yí mén gē

七 雄 雄 雌 犹 未 分 ，
qī xióng xióng cí yóu wèi fēn

攻 城 杀 将 何 纷 纷 ？
gōng chéng shā jiàng hé fēn fēn

秦 兵 益 围 邯 郸 急 ，
qín bīng yì wéi hán dān jí

魏 王 不 救 平 原 君 。
wèi wáng bú jiù píng yuán jūn

公 子 为 嬴 停 驷 马 ，
gōng zǐ wèi yíng tíng sì mǎ

执 辔 愈 恭 意 愈 下 。
zhí pèi yù gōng yì yù xià

亥 为 屠 肆 鼓 刀 人 ，
hài wéi tú sì gǔ dāo rén

嬴 乃 夷 门 抱 关 者 。
yíng nǎi yí mén bào guān zhě

非 但 慷 慨 献 奇 谋 ，
fēi dàn kāng kǎi xiàn qí móu

意 气 兼 将 身 命 酬 。
yì qì jiān jiāng shēn mìng chóu

向 风 刎 颈 送 公 子 ，
xiàng fēng wěn jǐng sòng gōng zǐ

七 十 老 翁 何 所 求 ？
qī shí lǎo wēng hé suǒ qiú

# 26. Selection from the *Shiji* (No. 4)

二十六 .《史记·李将军列传》（节）
èr shí liù　　shǐ jì　lǐ jiāng jūn liè zhuàn　　jié

匈 奴 大 入 上 郡 ， 天 子 使 中 贵 人
xiōng nú dà rù shàng jùn　tiān zǐ shǐ zhōng guì rén

从 广 勒 习 兵 击 匈 奴 。 中 贵 人 将 骑
cóng guǎng lè xí bīng jí xiōng nú　zhōng guì rén jiàng jì

数 十 纵 ， 见 匈 奴 三 人 ， 与 战 ； 三 人
shù shí zòng　jiàn xiōng nú sān rén　yǔ zhàn　sān rén

还 射 ， 伤 中 贵 人 ， 杀 其 骑 且 尽 。 中
huán shè　shāng zhōng guì rén　shā qí jì qiě jìn　zhōng

贵 人 走 广 。 广 曰 ：「 是 必 射 雕 者 也 。」
guì rén zǒu guǎng　guǎng yuē　shì bì shè diāo zhě yě

广 乃 遂 从 百 骑 往 驰 三 人 。 三 人 亡
guǎng nǎi suì cóng bǎi jì wǎng chí sān rén　sān rén wáng

马 步 行 ， 行 数 十 里 。 广 令 其 骑 张
mǎ bù xíng　xíng shù shí lǐ　guǎng lìng qí jì zhāng

左 右 翼 ， 而 广 身 自 射 彼 三 人 者 ，
zuǒ yòu yì　ér guǎng shēn zì shè bǐ sān rén zhě

杀 其 二 人 ， 生 得 一 人 ， 果 匈 奴 射
shā qí èr rén　shēng dé yī rén　guǒ xiōng nú shè

雕 者 也 。 已 缚 之 上 马 ， 望 匈 奴 有
diāo zhě yě　yǐ fù zhī shàng mǎ　wàng xiōng nú yǒu

数 千 骑 。 见 广 ， 以 为 诱 骑 ， 皆 惊 ，
shù qiān jì　jiàn guǎng　yǐ wéi yòu jì　jiē jīng

上 山 陈 。 广 之 百 骑 皆 大 恐 ， 欲 驰
shàng shān zhèn　guǎng zhī bǎi jì jiē dà kǒng　yù chí

还 走 。 广 曰 ：「 吾 去 大 军 数 十 里 ；
huán zǒu　guǎng yuē　wú qù dà jūn shù shí lǐ

今如此以百骑走，匈奴追射我立
jīn rú cǐ yǐ bǎi jì zǒu xiōng nú zhuī shè wǒ lì

尽。今我留，匈奴必以我为大军
jìn jīn wǒ liú xiōng nú bì yǐ wǒ wèi dà jūn

诱之，必不敢击我。」广令诸骑曰：
yòu zhī bì bù gǎn jí wǒ guǎng lìng zhū jì yuē

「前！」前未到匈奴陈二里所，止。
qián qián wèi dào xiōng nú zhèn èr lǐ suǒ zhǐ

令曰：「皆下马解鞍！」其骑曰：
lìng yuē jiē xià mǎ jiě ān qí jì yuē

「虏多且近，即有急，奈何？」广
lǔ duō qiě jìn jí yǒu jí nài hé guǎng

曰：「彼虏以我为走；今皆解鞍以
yuē bǐ lǔ yǐ wǒ wéi zǒu jīn jiē jiě ān yǐ

示不走，用坚其意。」于是胡骑遂
shì bù zǒu yòng jiān qí yì yú shì hú jì suì

不敢击。
bù gǎn jí

有白马将出护其兵，李广上马
yǒu bái mǎ jiàng chū hù qí bīng lǐ guǎng shàng mǎ

与十余骑奔射杀胡白马将，而复
yǔ shí yú jì bēn shè shā hú bái mǎ jiàng ér fù

还至其骑中，解鞍，令士皆纵马
huán zhì qí jì zhōng jiě ān lìng shì jiē zòng mǎ

卧。是时会暮，胡兵终怪之，不敢
wò shì shí huì mù hú bīng zhōng guài zhī bù gǎn

击。夜半时，胡兵亦以为汉有伏
jí yè bàn shí hú bīng yì yǐ wéi hàn yǒu fú

军于旁欲夜取之，胡皆引兵而去。
jūn yú páng yù yè qǔ zhī hú jiē yǐn bīng ér qù

平旦，李广乃归其大军。
píng dàn lǐ guǎng nǎi guī qí dà jūn

# 27. Selection from the *Hanshu*

二十七．《汉书·循吏传》：龚遂传（节）
èr shí qī    hàn shū xún lì zhuàn    gōng suì zhuàn jié

渤 海 左 右 郡 岁 饥 ， 盗 贼 并 起 ，
bó hǎi zuǒ yòu jùn suì jī dào zéi bìng qǐ

二 千 石 不 能 禽 制 。 上 选 能 治 者 ，
èr qiān dàn bù néng qín zhì shàng xuǎn néng zhì zhě

丞 相 御 史 举 遂 可 用 ， 上 以 为 渤 海
chéng xiàng yù shǐ jǔ suì kě yòng shàng yǐ wéi bó hǎi

太 守 。 时 遂 年 七 十 余 ， 召 见 ， 形 貌
tài shǒu shí suì nián qī shí yú zhào jiàn xíng mào

短 小 。 宣 帝 望 见 ， 不 副 所 闻 ， 心 内
duǎn xiǎo xuān dì wàng jiàn bú fù suǒ wén xīn nèi

轻 焉 ， 谓 遂 曰 ：「 渤 海 废 乱 ， 朕 甚
qīng yān wèi suì yuē bó hǎi fèi luàn zhèn shèn

忧 之 。 君 欲 何 以 息 其 盗 贼 ， 以 称
yōu zhī jūn yù hé yǐ xī qí dào zéi yǐ chèng

朕 意 ？」 遂 对 曰 ：「 海 濒 遐 远 ， 不
zhèn yì suì duì yuē hǎi bīn xiá yuǎn bù

沾 圣 化 ， 其 民 困 于 饥 寒 而 吏 不 恤 ，
zhān shèng huà qí mín kùn yú jī hán ér lì bú xù

故 使 陛 下 赤 子 盗 弄 陛 下 之 兵 于 潢
gù shǐ bì xià chì zǐ dào nòng bì xià zhī bīng yú huáng

池 中 耳 。 今 欲 使 臣 胜 之 邪 ？ 将 安
chí zhōng ěr jīn yù shǐ chén shèng zhī yé jiāng ān

之 也 ？」 上 闻 遂 对 ， 甚 说 ， 答 曰 ：
zhī yě shàng wén suì duì shèn yuè dá yuē

「 选 用 贤 良 ， 固 欲 安 之 也 。」 遂 曰 ：
xuǎn yòng xián liáng gù yù ān zhī yě suì yuē

「臣闻治乱民犹治乱绳，不可急
chén wén zhì luàn mín yóu zhì luàn shéng bù kě jí

也；唯缓之，然后可治。臣愿丞相
yě wéi huǎn zhī rán hòu kě zhì chén yuàn chéng xiàng

御史且无拘臣以文法，得一切便
yù shǐ qiě wú jū chén yǐ wén fǎ dé yī qiè biàn

宜从事。」
yí cóng shì

上许焉，加赐黄金，赠遣乘传。
shàng xǔ yān jiā cì huáng jīn zèng qiǎn chéng zhuàn

至渤海界，郡闻新太守至，发兵
zhì bó hǎi jiè jùn wén xīn tài shǒu zhì fā bīng

以迎，遂皆遣还。移书敕属县：「悉
yǐ yíng suì jiē qiǎn huán yí shū chì shǔ xiàn xī

罢逐捕盗贼吏，诸持钼钩田器者
bà zhú bǔ dào zéi lì zhū chí chú gōu tián qì zhě

皆为良民，吏无得问，持兵者乃
jiē wéi liáng mín lì wú dé wèn chí bīng zhě nǎi

为盗贼。」遂单车独行至府，郡中
wéi dào zéi suì dān chē dú xíng zhì fǔ jùn zhōng

翕然，盗贼亦皆罢。渤海又多劫
xī rán dào zéi yì jiē bà bó hǎi yòu duō jié

掠相随，闻遂教令，即时解散，弃
lüè xiāng suí wén suì jiào lìng jí shí jiě sàn qì

其兵弩而持钩钼。盗贼于是悉平，
qí bīng nǔ ér chí gōu chú dào zéi yú shì xī píng

民安土乐业。
mín ān tǔ lè yè

## 28. Selection from the *Houhanshu* (No. 1)

二十八．《后汉书·酷吏列传》：董宣传（节）
èr shí bā   hòu hàn shū   kù lì liè zhuàn   dǒng xuān zhuàn   jié

宣 特 征 为 洛 阳 令 。 时 湖 阳 公 主
xuān tè zhēng wéi luò yáng lìng   shí hú yáng gōng zhǔ

苍 头 白 日 杀 人 ， 因 匿 主 家 ， 吏 不
cāng tóu bái rì shā rén yīn nì zhǔ jiā lì bù

能 得 。 及 主 出 行 ， 而 以 奴 骖 乘 ， 宣
néng dé jí zhǔ chū xíng ér yǐ nú cān shèng xuān

于 夏 门 亭 候 之 ， 乃 驻 车 叩 马 ， 以
yú xià mén tíng hòu zhī nǎi zhù chē kòu mǎ yǐ

刀 画 地 ， 大 言 数 主 之 失 ， 叱 奴 下
dāo huà dì dà yán shǔ zhǔ zhī shī chì nú xià

车 ， 因 格 杀 之 。 主 即 还 宫 诉 帝 ， 帝
chē yīn gé shā zhī zhǔ jí huán gōng sù dì dì

大 怒 ， 召 宣 ， 欲 箠 杀 之 。 宣 叩 头 曰 ：
dà nù zhào xuān yù chuí shā zhī xuān kòu tóu yuē

「 愿 乞 一 言 而 死 。 」 帝 曰 ： 「 欲 何
yuàn qǐ yī yán ér sǐ dì yuē yù hé

言 ？ 」 宣 曰 ： 「 陛 下 圣 德 中 兴 ， 而
yán xuān yuē bì xià shèng dé zhōng xīng ér

纵 奴 杀 良 人 ， 将 何 以 理 天 下 乎 ？
zòng nú shā liáng rén jiāng hé yǐ lǐ tiān xià hū

臣 不 须 箠 ， 请 得 自 杀 。 」 即 以 头 击
chén bù xū chuí qǐng dé zì shā jí yǐ tóu jī

楹 ， 流 血 被 面 。 帝 令 小 黄 门 持 之 ，
yíng liú xuě bèi miàn dì lìng xiǎo huáng mén chí zhī

使 宣 叩 头 谢 主 。 宣 不 从 ， 彊 使 顿
shǐ xuān kòu tóu xiè zhǔ xuān bù cóng qiǎng shǐ dùn

之 ， 宣 两 手 据 地 ， 终 不 肯 俯 。 主 曰 ：
zhī　　xuān liǎng shǒu jù dì　　zhōng bù kěn fǔ　　zhǔ yuē

「 文 叔 为 白 衣 时 ， 臧 亡 匿 死 ， 吏 不
wén shū wéi bái yī shí　　cáng wáng nì sǐ　　lì bù

敢 至 门 。 今 为 天 子 ， 威 不 能 行 一
gǎn zhì mén　　jīn wéi tiān zǐ　　wēi bù néng xíng yī

令 乎 ？ 」 帝 笑 曰 ： 「 天 子 不 与 白 衣
lìng hū　　dì xiào yuē　　tiān zǐ bù yǔ bái yī

同 。 」 因 敕 彊 项 令 出 ， 赐 钱 三 十 万 ，
tóng　　yīn chì jiàng xiàng lìng chū　　cì qián sān shí wàn

宣 悉 以 班 诸 吏 。 由 是 搏 击 豪 彊 ，
xuān xī yǐ bān zhū lì　　yóu shì bó jí háo qiáng

莫 不 震 慄 。 京 师 号 为 「 卧 虎 」 ， 歌
mò bù zhèn lì　　jīng shī hào wéi　　wò hǔ　　gē

之 曰 ： 「 枹 鼓 不 鸣 董 少 平 。 」
zhī yuē　　fú gǔ bù míng dǒng shào píng

🙙🙙🙙🙙🙙🙙🙙🙙🙙🙙🙙🙙🙙🙙🙙

## 29. Selection from the *Houhanshu* (No. 2)

二 十 九 . 《 后 汉 书 · 南 匈 奴 传 》 ： 昭 君 （ 节 ）
èr shí jiǔ　　hòu hàn shū　　nán xiōng nú zhuàn　　zhāo jūn　　jié

昭 君 字 嫱 ， 南 郡 人 也 。 初 ， 元 帝
zhāo jūn zì qiáng　　nán jùn rén yě　　chū　　yuán dì

时 以 良 家 子 选 入 掖 庭 。 时 呼 韩 邪
shí yǐ liáng jiā zǐ xuǎn rù yì tíng　　shí hū hán yé

来 朝 ， 帝 敕 以 宫 女 五 人 赐 之 。 昭
lái cháo　　dì chì yǐ gōng nǚ wǔ rén cì zhī　　zhāo

君 入 宫 数 岁 不 得 见 御 ， 积 悲 怨 ，
jūn rù gōng shù suì bù dé jiàn yù　　jī bēi yuàn

乃 请 披 庭 令 求 行 。 呼 韩 邪 临 辞 大
nǎi qǐng yì tíng lìng qiú xíng    hū hán yé lín cí dà

会 ， 帝 召 五 女 以 示 之 。 昭 君 丰 容
huì   dì zhào wǔ nǚ yǐ shì zhī   zhāo jūn fēng róng

靓 饰 ， 光 明 汉 宫 ， 顾 景 裴 回 ， 竦 动
jìng shì   guāng míng hàn gōng   gù yǐng péi huí   sǒng dòng

左 右 。 帝 见 大 惊 ， 意 欲 留 之 ， 而 难
zuǒ yòu   dì jiàn dà jīng   yì yù liú zhī   ér nán

于 失 信 ， 遂 与 匈 奴 。 生 二 子 。 及 呼
yú shī xìn   suì yǔ xiōng nú   shēng èr zǐ   jí hū

韩 邪 死 ， 其 前 阏 氏 子 代 立 ， 欲 妻
hán yé sǐ   qí qián yān zhī zǐ dài lì   yù qī

之 ， 昭 君 上 书 求 归 ， 成 帝 敕 令 从
zhī   zhāo jūn shàng shū qiú guī   chéng dì chì lìng cóng

胡 俗 ， 遂 复 为 后 单 于 阏 氏 焉 。
hú sú   suì fù wéi hòu chán yú yān zhī yān

## Reference Text I — Wang Anshi: "Ming Fei Song"

参 考 篇 章 一 —— 王 安 石 ：《 明 妃 曲 》
cān kǎo piān zhāng yī    wáng ān shí    míng fēi qǔ

明 妃 初 出 汉 宫 时 ，
míng fēi chū chū hàn gōng shí

泪 湿 春 风 鬓 脚 垂 。
lèi shī chūn fēng bìn jiǎo chuí

低 徊 顾 影 无 颜 色 ，
dī huí gù yǐng wú yán sè

尚 得 君 王 不 自 持 。
shàng dé jūn wáng bù zì chí

归 来 却 怪 丹 青 手 ，
guī lái què guài dān qīng shóu

入 眼 平 生 几 曾 有 ？
rù yǎn píng shēng jǐ céng yǒu

意 态 由 来 画 不 成 ，
yì tài yóu lái huà bù chéng

当 时 枉 杀 毛 延 寿 。
dāng shí wǎng shā máo yán shòu

一 去 心 知 更 不 归 ，
yī qù xīn zhī gèng bù guī

可 怜 着 尽 汉 宫 衣 。
kě lián zhuó jìn hàn gōng yī

寄 声 欲 问 塞 南 事 ，
jì shēng yù wèn sài nán shì

只 有 年 年 鸿 雁 飞 。
zhī yǒu nián nián hóng yàn fēi

家 人 万 里 传 消 息 ，
jiā rén wàn lǐ chuán xiāo xí

好 在 毡 城 莫 相 忆 。
hǎo zài zhān chéng mò xiāng yì

君 不 见 咫 尺 长 门 闭 阿 娇 ，
jūn bù jiàn zhǐ chǐ cháng mén bì ā jiāo

人 生 失 意 无 南 北 ！
rén shēng shī yì wú nán běi

# Reference Text II — Ouyang Xiu: "Ming Fei Song in Harmony with Wang Jiefu's Work"

参考 篇 章 二 — 欧 阳 修：《明 妃 曲 和 王 介 甫 作》
cān kǎo piān zhāng èr　　ōu yáng xiū　　míng fēi qǔ hè wáng jiè fǔ zuò

胡 人 以 鞍 马 为 家 ， 射 猎 为 俗 。
hú rén yǐ ān mǎ wéi jiā　　shè liè wéi sú

泉 甘 草 美 无 常 处 ， 鸟 惊 兽 骇 争 驰
quán gān cǎo měi wú cháng chù　　niǎo jīng shòu hài zhēng chí

逐 。 谁 将 汉 女 嫁 胡 儿 ？ 风 沙 无 情
zhú　　shéi jiāng hàn nǚ jià hú ér　　fēng shā wú qíng

貌 如 玉 。 身 行 不 遇 中 国 人 ， 马 上
mào rú yù　　shēn xíng bú yù zhōng guó rén　　mǎ shàng

自 作 思 归 曲 。 推 手 为 琵 却 手 琶 ，
zì zuò sī guī qǔ　　tuī shǒu wéi pí què shǒu pá

胡 人 共 听 亦 咨 嗟 。 玉 颜 流 落 死 天
hú rén gòng tīng yì zī jiē　　yù yán liú luò sǐ tiān

涯 ， 琵 琶 却 传 来 汉 家 。 汉 宫 争 按
yá　　pí pá què chuán lái hàn jiā　　hàn gōng zhēng àn

新 声 谱 ， 遗 恨 已 深 声 更 苦 。 纤 纤
xīn shēng pǔ　　yí hèn yǐ shēn shēng gèng kǔ　　xiān xiān

女 手 生 洞 房 ， 学 得 琵 琶 不 下 堂 。
nǚ shǒu shēng dòng fáng　　xué dé pí pá bú xià táng

不 识 黄 云 出 塞 路 ， 岂 知 此 声 能 断
bù shí huáng yún chū sài lù　　qǐ zhī cǐ shēng néng duàn

肠 ？
cháng

# 30. Tao Yuanming: "The Story of the Peach Blossom Stream"

三十．陶 渊 明：《桃 花 源 记》
sān shí táo yuān míng táo huā yuán jì

晋 太 元 中， 武 陵 人， 捕 鱼 为 业。
jìn tài yuán zhōng wǔ líng rén bǔ yú wéi yè

缘 溪 行， 忘 路 之 远 近。 忽 逢 桃 花
yuán xī xíng wàng lù zhī yuǎn jìn hū féng táo huā

林， 夹 岸 数 百 步， 中 无 杂 树， 芳 草
lín jiá àn shù bǎi bù zhōng wú zá shù fāng cǎo

鲜 美， 落 英 缤 纷； 渔 人 甚 异 之。 复
xiān měi luò yīng bīn fēn yú rén shèn yì zhī fù

前 行， 欲 穷 其 林。 林 尽 水 源， 便 得
qián xíng yù qióng qí lín lín jìn shuǐ yuán biàn dé

一 山。 山 有 小 口， 仿 佛 若 有 光， 便
yī shān shān yǒu xiǎo kǒu fǎng fú ruò yǒu guāng biàn

舍 船， 从 口 入。
shě chuán cóng kǒu rù

初 极 狭， 才 通 人； 复 行 数 十 步，
chū jí xiá cái tōng rén fù xíng shù shí bù

豁 然 开 朗。 土 地 平 旷， 屋 舍 俨 然。
huò rán kāi lǎng tǔ dì píng kuàng wū shè yǎn rán

有 良 田、 美 池、 桑、 竹 之 属。 阡 陌
yǒu liáng tián měi chí sāng zhú zhī shǔ qiān mò

交 通， 鸡 犬 相 闻。 其 中 往 来 种 作，
jiāo tōng jī quǎn xiāng wén qí zhōng wǎng lái zhòng zuò

男 女 衣 着， 悉 如 外 人， 黄 发 垂 髫，
nán nǚ yī zhuó xī rú wài rén huáng fà chuí tiáo

并 怡 然 自 乐。
bìng yí rán zì lè

见 渔 人 ，乃 大 惊 ，问 所 从 来 ；具
jiàn yú rén nǎi dà jīng wèn suǒ cóng lái jù

答 之 。便 要 还 家 ，设 酒 、杀 鸡 、作
dá zhī biàn yāo huán jiā shè jiǔ shā jī zuò

食 。村 中 闻 有 此 人 ，咸 来 问 讯 。自
shí cūn zhōng wén yǒu cǐ rén xián lái wèn xùn zì

云 ：「先 世 避 秦 时 乱 ，率 妻 子 邑 人
yún xiān shì bì qín shí luàn shuài qī zǐ yì rén

来 此 绝 境 ，不 复 出 焉 ；遂 与 外 人
lái cǐ jué jìng bù fù chū yān suì yǔ wài rén

间 隔 。」问 ：「今 是 何 世 ？」乃 不
jiàn gé wèn jīn shì hé shì nǎi bù

知 有 汉 ，无 论 魏 、晋 ！此 人 一 一 为
zhī yǒu hàn wú lùn wèi jìn cǐ rén yī yī wéi

具 言 所 闻 ，皆 叹 惋 。余 人 各 复 延
jù yán suǒ wén jiē tàn wǎn yú rén gè fù yán

至 其 家 ，皆 出 酒 食 。停 数 日 ，辞 去 。
zhì qí jiā jiē chū jiǔ shí tíng shù rì cí qù

此 中 人 语 云 ：「不 足 为 外 人 道 也 。」
cǐ zhōng rén yù yún bù zú wéi wài rén dào yě

既 出 ，得 其 船 ，便 扶 向 路 ，处 处
jì chū dé qí chuán biàn fú xiàng lù chù chù

志 之 。及 郡 下 ，诣 太 守 ，说 如 此 。
zhì zhī jí jùn xià yì tài shǒu shuō rú cǐ

太 守 即 遣 人 随 其 往 ，寻 向 所 志 ，
tài shǒu jí qiǎn rén suí qí wǎng xún xiàng suǒ zhì

遂 迷 不 复 得 路 。
suì mí bù fù dé lù

南 阳 刘 子 骥 ，高 尚 士 也 ，闻 之 ，
nán yáng liú zǐ jì gāo shàng shì yě wén zhī

欣 然 规 往 。 未 果 ， 寻 病 终 。 后 遂 无
xīn rán guī wǎng    wèi guǒ    xún bìng zhōng    hòu suì wú

问 津 者 。
wèn jīn zhě

## Reference Text — Wang Wei: "The Poem of the Peach Blossom Stream"

参 考 篇 章 — 王 维 ：《 桃 源 行 》
cān kǎo piān zhāng    wáng wéi    táo yuán xíng

渔 舟 逐 水 爱 山 春 ，
yú zhōu zhú shuǐ ài shān chūn

两 岸 桃 花 夹 去 津 。
liǎng àn táo huā jiá qù jīn

坐 看 红 树 不 知 远 ，
zuò kàn hóng shù bù zhī yuǎn

行 尽 青 溪 不 见 人 。
xíng jìn qīng xī bú jiàn rén

山 口 潜 行 始 隈 隩 ，
shān kǒu qián xíng shǐ wēi ào

山 开 旷 望 旋 平 陆 。
shān kāi kuàng wàng xuán píng lù

遥 看 一 处 攒 云 树 ，
yáo kàn yī chù zān yún shù

近 入 千 家 散 花 竹 。
jìn rù qiān jiā sàn huā zhú

樵 客 初 传 汉 姓 名 ，
qiáo kè chū chuán hàn xìng míng

居 人 未 改 秦 衣 服 。
jū rén wèi gǎi qín yī fú

居 人 共 住 武 陵 源 ，
jū rén gòng zhù wǔ líng yuán

还 从 物 外 起 田 园 。
huán cóng wù wài qǐ tián yuán

月 明 松 下 房 栊 静 ，
yuè míng sōng xià fáng lóng jìng

日 出 云 中 鸡 犬 喧 。
rì chū yún zhōng jī quǎn xuān

惊 闻 俗 客 争 来 集 ，
jīng wén sú kè zhēng lái jí

竞 引 还 家 问 都 邑 。
jìng yǐn huán jiā wèn dū yì

平 明 闾 巷 扫 花 开 ，
píng míng lǘ xiàng sǎo huā kāi

薄 暮 渔 樵 乘 水 入 。
bó mù yú qiáo chéng shuǐ rù

初 因 避 地 去 人 间 ，
chū yīn bì dì qù rén jiān

及 至 成 仙 遂 不 还 。
jí zhì chéng xiān suì bù huán

峡 里 谁 知 有 人 事 ，
xiá lǐ shéi zhī yǒu rén shì

世 中 遥 望 空 云 山 。
shì zhōng yáo wàng kōng yún shān

不 疑 灵 境 难 闻 见 ，
bù yí líng jìng nán wén jiàn

尘 心 未 尽 思 乡 县 。
chén xīn wèi jìn sī xiāng xiàn

出 洞 无 论 隔 山 水 ，
chū dòng wú lùn gé shān shuǐ

辞 家 终 拟 长 游 衍 。
cí jiā zhōng nǐ cháng yóu yǎn

自 谓 经 过 旧 不 迷 ，
zì wèi jīng guò jiù bù mí

安 知 峰 壑 今 来 变 。
ān zhī fēng huò jīn lái biàn

当 时 知 记 入 山 深 ，
dāng shí zhī jì rù shān shēn

青 溪 几 曲 到 云 林 。
qīng xī jǐ qū dào yún lín

春 来 遍 是 桃 花 水 ，
chūn lái biàn shì táo huā shuǐ

不 辩 仙 源 何 处 寻 。
bú biàn xiān yuán hé chù xún

🌀🌀🌀🌀🌀🌀🌀🌀🌀🌀🌀🌀🌀

# 31. Wang Xizhi: "Preface to the Lanting Gathering"

三 十 一 . 王 羲 之 : 《 兰 亭 集 序 》
sān shí yī wáng xī zhī lán tíng jí xù

永 和 九 年 ， 岁 在 癸 丑 ， 暮 春 之
yǒng hé jiǔ nián suì zài guǐ chǒu mù chūn zhī

初 ， 会 于 会 稽 山 阴 之 兰 亭 ， 修 禊
chū huì yú kuài jī shān yīn zhī lán tíng xiū xì

事 也 。 群 贤 毕 至 ， 少 长 咸 集 。 此 地
shì yě qún xián bì zhì shào zhǎng xián jí cǐ dì

有 崇 山 峻 岭 ， 茂 林 修 竹 ， 又 有 清
yǒu chóng shān jùn lǐng mào lín xiū zhú yòu yǒu qīng

流激湍，映带左右，引以为流觞
曲水，列坐其次。虽无丝竹管弦
之盛，一觞一咏，亦足以畅叙幽
情。是日也，天朗气清，惠风和畅，
仰观宇宙之大，俯察品类之盛，
所以游目骋怀，足以极视听之娱，
信可乐也。

夫人之相与，俯仰一世，或取
诸怀抱，晤言一室之内，或因寄
所托，放浪形骸之外。虽趣舍万
殊，静躁不同，当其欣于所遇，暂
得于己，快然自足，不知老之将
至。及其所之既倦，情随事迁，感
慨系之矣。向之所欣，俛仰之间，
已为陈迹，犹不能不以之兴怀；

况 修 短 随 化 ， 终 期 于 尽 。 古 人 云 ：
kuàng xiū duǎn suí huà zhōng qī yú jìn gǔ rén yún

「 死 生 亦 大 矣 。 」 岂 不 痛 哉 ！
sǐ shēng yì dà yǐ qǐ bù tòng zāi

每 览 昔 人 兴 感 之 由 ， 若 合 一 契 ，
měi lǎn xī rén xīng gǎn zhī yóu ruò hé yī qì

未 尝 不 临 文 嗟 悼 ， 不 能 喻 之 于 怀 。
wèi cháng bù lín wén jiē dào bù néng yù zhī yú huái

固 知 一 死 生 为 虚 诞 ， 齐 彭 殇 为 妄
gù zhī yī sǐ shēng wéi xū dàn qí péng shāng wéi wàng

作 ， 后 之 视 今 ， 亦 犹 今 之 视 昔 ， 悲
zuò hòu zhī shì jīn yì yóu jīn zhī shì xī bēi

夫 ！ 故 列 叙 时 人 ， 录 其 所 述 ， 虽 世
fú gù liè xù shí rén lù qí suǒ shù suī shì

殊 事 异 ， 所 以 兴 怀 ， 其 致 一 也 。 后
shū shì yì suǒ yǐ xīng huái qí zhì yī yě hòu

之 览 者 ， 亦 将 有 感 于 斯 文 。
zhī lǎn zhě yì jiāng yǒu gǎn yú sī wén

## 32. Han Yu: "Miscellaneous Essays No. 4"

三 十 二 . 韩 愈 ：《 杂 说 四 》
sān shí èr hán yù zá shuō sì

世 有 伯 乐 ， 然 后 有 千 里 马 。 千
shì yǒu bó lè rán hòu yǒu qiān lǐ mǎ qiān

里 马 常 有 ， 而 伯 乐 不 常 有 。 故 虽
lǐ mǎ cháng yǒu ér bó lè bù cháng yǒu gù suī

有 名 马 ， 只 辱 于 奴 隶 人 之 手 ， 骈
yǒu míng mǎ zhǐ rǔ yú nú lì rén zhī shǒu pián

死 于 槽 枥 之 间 ， 不 以 千 里 称 也 。
sǐ yú cáo lì zhī jiān bù yǐ qiān lǐ chēng yě

马 之 千 里 者 ， 一 食 或 尽 粟 一 石 。
mǎ zhī qiān lǐ zhě yī shí huò jìn sù yī dàn

食 马 者 ， 不 知 其 能 千 里 而 食 也 。
sì mǎ zhě bù zhī qí néng qiān lǐ ér sì yě

是 马 也 ， 虽 有 千 里 之 能 ， 食 不 饱 ，
shì mǎ yě suī yǒu qiān lǐ zhī néng shí bù bǎo

力 不 足 ， 才 美 不 外 见 ， 且 欲 与 常
lì bù zú cái měi bú wài xiàn qiě yù yǔ cháng

马 等 不 可 得 ， 安 求 其 能 千 里 也 。
mǎ děng bù kě dé ān qiú qí néng qiān lǐ yě

策 之 不 以 其 道 ， 食 之 不 能 尽 其 材 ，
cè zhī bù yǐ qí dào sì zhī bù néng jìn qí cái

鸣 之 而 不 能 通 其 意 ， 执 策 而 临 之
míng zhī ér bù néng tōng qí yì zhí cè ér lín zhī

曰 ： 「 天 下 无 马 。 」 呜 呼 ！ 其 真 无
yuē tiān xià wú mǎ wū hū qí zhēn wú

马 邪 ？ 其 真 不 知 马 也 ！
mǎ yé qí zhēn bù zhī mǎ yě

---

## 33.  Han Yu: "On Teachers"

三 十 三 . 韩 愈 ：《 师 说 》
sān shí sān hán yù shī shuō

古 之 学 者 必 有 师 。 师 者 ， 所 以
gǔ zhī xué zhě bì yǒu shī shī zhě suǒ yǐ

传 道 、 受 业 、 解 惑 也 。 人 非 生 而 知
chuán dào shòu yè jiě huò yě rén fēi shēng ér zhī

之 者 ， 孰 能 无 惑 ？ 惑 而 不 从 师 ， 其
zhī zhě shú néng wú huò huò ér bù cóng shī qí

为 惑 也 ， 终 不 解 矣 。
wéi huò yě zhōng bù jiě yì

生 乎 吾 前 ， 其 闻 道 也 ， 固 先 乎
shēng hū wú qián qí wén dào yě gù xiān hū

吾 ， 吾 从 而 师 之 。 生 乎 吾 后 ， 其 闻
wú wú cóng ér shī zhī shēng hū wú hòu qí wén

道 也 ， 亦 先 乎 吾 ， 吾 从 而 师 之 。 吾
dào yě yì xiān hū wú wú cóng ér shī zhī wú

师 道 也 ， 夫 庸 知 其 年 之 先 后 生 于
shī dào yě fú yōng zhī qí nián zhī xiān hòu shēng yú

吾 乎 ？ 是 故 无 贵 无 贱 ， 无 长 无 少 ，
wú hū shì gù wú guì wú jiàn wú zhǎng wú shào

道 之 所 存 ， 师 之 所 存 也 。
dào zhī suǒ cún shī zhī suǒ cún yě

嗟 乎 ！ 师 道 之 不 传 也 久 矣 ！ 欲
jiē hū shī dào zhī bù chuán yě jiǔ yì yù

人 之 无 惑 也 难 矣 ！ 古 之 圣 人 ， 其
rén zhī wú huò yě nán yì gǔ zhī shèng rén qí

出 人 也 远 矣 ， 犹 且 从 师 而 问 焉 。
chū rén yě yuǎn yì yóu qiě cóng shī ér wèn yān

今 之 众 人 ， 其 下 圣 人 也 亦 远 矣 ，
jīn zhī zhòng rén qí xià shèng rén yě yì yuǎn yì

而 耻 学 于 师 。 是 故 圣 益 圣 ， 愚 益
ér chǐ xué yú shī shì gù shèng yì shèng yú yì

愚 ， 圣 人 之 所 以 为 圣 ， 愚 人 之 所
yú shèng rén zhī suǒ yǐ wéi shèng yú rén zhī suǒ

以 为 愚 ， 其 皆 出 于 此 乎 ？
yǐ wéi yú qí jiē chū yú cǐ hū

爱其子，择师而教之，于其身也，则耻师焉，惑矣！彼童子之师，授之书而习其句读者，非吾所谓传其道、解其惑者也。句读之不知，惑之不解，或师焉，或不焉，小学而大遗，吾未见其明也。

巫、医、乐师、百工之人，不耻相师；士大夫之族，曰师、曰弟子云者，则群聚而笑之。问之，则曰：「彼与彼年相若也，道相似也。」位卑则足羞，官盛则近谀。呜呼！师道之不复可知矣。

巫、医、乐师、百工之人，君子不齿，今其智乃反不能及，其可怪也欤？！

圣 人 无 常 师 。 孔 子 师 郯 子 、 苌
shèng rén wú cháng shī kǒng zǐ shī tán zǐ cháng

弘 、 师 襄 、 老 聃 。 郯 子 之 徒 ， 其 贤
hóng shī xiāng lǎo dān tán zǐ zhī tú qí xián

不 及 孔 子 。 孔 子 曰 ： 「 三 人 行 ， 必
bù jí kǒng zǐ kǒng zǐ yuē sān rén xíng bì

有 我 师 。 」 是 故 弟 子 不 必 不 如 师 ，
yǒu wǒ shī shì gù dì zǐ bú bì bù rú shī

师 不 必 贤 于 弟 子 ， 闻 道 有 先 后 ，
shī bú bì xián yú dì zǐ wén dào yǒu xiān hòu

术 业 有 专 攻 ， 如 是 而 已 。
shù yè yǒu zhuān gōng rú shì ér yǐ

李 氏 子 蟠 ， 年 十 七 ， 好 古 文 ， 六
lǐ shì zǐ pán nián shí qī hào gǔ wén liù

艺 经 传 皆 通 习 之 。 不 拘 于 时 ， 学
yì jīng zhuàn jiē tōng xí zhī bù jū yú shí xué

于 余 ， 余 嘉 其 能 行 古 道 ， 作 师 说
yú yú yú jiā qí néng xíng gǔ dào zuò shī shuō

以 贻 之 。
yǐ yí zhī

# 34. Liu Zongyuan: "The Donkey from Qian"

三 十 四 . 柳 宗 元 ：《 黔 之 驴 》
sān shí sì liǔ zōng yuán qián zhī lú

黔 无 驴 ， 有 好 事 者 ， 船 载 以 入 ；
qián wú lú yǒu hào shì zhě chuán zài yǐ rù

至 则 无 可 用 ， 放 之 山 下 。 虎 见 之 ，
zhì zé wú kě yòng fàng zhī shān xià hǔ jiàn zhī

庞然大物也，以为神。蔽林间窥之，稍出近之，慭慭然莫相知。

他日，驴一鸣，虎大骇，远遁，以为且噬己也，甚恐！然往来视之，觉无异能者，益习其声，又近出前后，终不敢搏。稍近益狎，荡倚冲冒。驴不胜怒，蹄之。虎因喜，计之曰：「技止此耳！」因跳踉大阚，断其喉，尽其肉，乃去。

噫！形之庞也，类有德，声之宏也，类有能。向不出其技，虎虽猛，疑畏卒不敢取，今若是焉，悲夫！

## 35. Liu Zongyuan: "A Note on the Xiaoshicheng Hill"

三十五．柳宗元：《小石城山记》
sān shí wǔ　liǔ zōng yuán　　xiǎo shí chéng shān　jì

自 西 山 道 口 径 北 ， 踰 黄 茅 岭 而
zì xī shān dào kǒu jìng běi yú huáng máo lǐng ér

下 ， 有 二 道： 其 一 西 出 ， 寻 之 无 所
xià yǒu èr dào qí yī xī chū xún zhī wú suǒ

得 。 其 一 少 北 而 东 ， 不 过 四 十 丈 ，
dé qí yī shǎo běi ér dōng bù guò sì shí zhàng

土 断 而 川 分 ， 有 积 石 横 当 其 垠 。
tǔ duàn ér chuān fēn yǒu jī shí héng dāng qí yín

其 上 为 睥 睨 梁 欐 之 形 ， 其 旁 出 堡
qí shàng wéi bì nì liáng lì zhī xíng qí páng chū bǎo

坞 ， 有 若 门 焉 ， 窥 之 正 黑 。 投 以 小
wù yǒu ruò mén yān kuī zhī zhèng hēi tóu yǐ xiǎo

石 ， 洞 然 有 水 声 。 其 响 之 激 越 ， 良
shí dòng rán yǒu shuǐ shēng qí xiǎng zhī jī yuè liáng

久 乃 已 。 环 之 可 上 ， 望 甚 远 。
jiǔ nǎi yǐ huán zhī kě shàng wàng shèn yuǎn

无 土 壤 而 生 嘉 树 美 箭 ， 益 奇 而
wú tǔ rǎng ér shēng jiā shù měi jiàn yì qí ér

坚 。 其 疏 数 偃 仰 ， 类 智 者 所 施 设
jiān qí shū cù yǎn yǎng lèi zhì zhě suǒ shī shè

也 。
yě

噫 ！ 吾 疑 造 物 者 之 有 无 久 矣 。
yī wú yí zào wù zhě zhī yǒu wú jiǔ yǐ

及 是 愈 以 为 诚 有 。 又 怪 其 不 为 之
jí shì yù yǐ wéi chéng yǒu yòu guài qí bù wéi zhī

中 州 ， 而 列 是 夷 狄 ， 更 千 百 年 不
zhōng zhōu ér liè shì yí dí gēng qiān bǎi nián bù

得 一 售 其 伎 ， 是 固 劳 而 无 用 ， 神
dé yī shòu qí jì shì gù láo ér wú yòng shén

者 傥 不 宜 如 是 ， 则 其 果 无 乎 ？
zhě tǎng bù yí rú shì zé qí guǒ wú hū

或 曰 ： 「 以 慰 夫 贤 而 辱 于 此 者 。 」
huò yuē yǐ wèi fú xián ér rǔ yú cǐ zhě

或 曰 ： 「 其 气 之 灵 ， 不 为 伟 人 ， 而
huò yuē qí qì zhī líng bù wéi wěi rén ér

独 为 是 物 ， 故 楚 之 南 ， 少 人 而 多
dú wéi shì wù gù chǔ zhī nán shǎo rén ér duō

石 。 」 是 二 者 ， 余 未 信 之 。
shí shì èr zhě yú wèi xìn zhī

〰〰〰〰〰〰〰〰〰〰〰〰〰

# 36. Bo Juyi: "The Song of the Pipa" with the Preface

三 十 六 . 白 居 易 ：《 琵 琶 行 》并 序
sān shí liù bó jū yì pí pá xíng bìng xù

序
xù

元 和 十 年 ， 予 左 迁 九 江 郡 司 马 。
yuán hé shí nián yú zuǒ qiān jiǔ jiāng jùn sī mǎ

明 年 秋 ， 送 客 湓 浦 口 。 闻 船 中 夜
míng nián qiū sòng kè pén pǔ kǒu wén chuán zhōng yè

弹 琵 琶 者 ， 听 其 音 铮 铮 然 有 京 都
tán pí pá zhě tīng qí yīn zhēng zhēng rán yǒu jīng dū

声 。 问 其 人 ， 本 长 安 倡 女 ， 尝 学 琵
shēng wèn qí rén běn cháng ān chāng nǚ cháng xué pí

琵 于 穆 曹 二 善 才 。 年 长 色 衰 ，委
pá yú mù cáo èr shàn cái nián zhǎng sè shuāi wèi

身 为 贾 人 妇 。 遂 命 酒 使 快 弹 数 曲 。
shēn wéi gǔ rén fù suì mìng jiǔ shǐ kuài tán shù qǔ

曲 罢 悯 然 ， 自 叙 少 小 时 欢 乐 事 ；
qǔ bà mǐn rán zì xù shào xiǎo shí huān lè shì

今 漂 沦 憔 悴 ， 转 徙 于 江 湖 间 。 予
jīn piāo lún qiáo cuì zhuǎn xǐ yú jiāng hú jiān yú

出 官 二 年 ， 恬 然 自 安 ， 感 斯 人 言 ，
chū guān èr nián tián rán zì ān gǎn sī rén yán

是 夕 ， 始 觉 有 迁 谪 意 ， 因 为 长 句 ，
shì xī shǐ jué yǒu qiān zhé yì yīn wéi cháng jù

歌 以 赠 之 。 凡 六 百 一 十 六 言 ， 命
gē yǐ zèng zhī fán liù bǎi yī shí liù yán mìng

曰 ： 「 琵 琶 行 。 」
yuē pí pá xíng

《 琵 琶 行 》
pí pá xíng

浔 阳 江 头 夜 送 客 ，枫 叶 荻 花 秋
xún yáng jiāng tóu yè sòng kè fēng yè dí huā qiū

瑟 瑟 。 主 人 下 马 客 在 船 ， 举 酒 欲
sè sè zhǔ rén xià mǎ kè zài chuán jǔ jiǔ yù

饮 无 管 弦 ； 醉 不 成 欢 惨 将 别 ， 别
yǐn wú guǎn xián zuì bù chéng huān cǎn jiāng bié bié

时 茫 茫 江 浸 月 。 忽 闻 水 上 琵 琶 声 ，
shí máng máng jiāng jìn yuè hū wén shuǐ shàng pí pá shēng

主 人 忘 归 客 不 发 。 寻 声 暗 问 弹 者
zhǔ rén wàng guī kè bù fā xún shēng àn wèn tán zhě

谁（shéi）？琵（pí）琶（pá）声（shēng）停（tíng）欲（yù）语（yǔ）迟（chí）。移（yí）船（chuán）相（xiāng）近（jìn）

邀（yāo）相（xiāng）见（jiàn），添（tiān）酒（jiǔ）回（huí）灯（dēng）重（chóng）开（kāi）宴（yàn）。千（qiān）呼（hū）

万（wàn）唤（huàn）始（shǐ）出（chū）来（lái），犹（yóu）抱（bào）琵（pí）琶（pá）半（bàn）遮（zhē）面（miàn）。

转（zhuǎn）轴（zhóu）拨（bō）弦（xián）三（sān）两（liǎng）声（shēng），未（wèi）成（chéng）曲（qǔ）调（diào）先（xiān）有（yǒu）

情（qíng）；弦（xián）弦（xián）掩（yǎn）抑（yì）声（shēng）声（shēng）思（sī），似（sì）诉（sù）平（píng）生（shēng）

不（bù）得（dé）意（yì）。低（dī）眉（méi）信（xìn）手（shǒu）续（xù）续（xù）弹（tán），说（shuō）尽（jìn）

心（xīn）中（zhōng）无（wú）限（xiàn）事（shì），轻（qīng）拢（lǒng）慢（màn）捻（niǎn）抹（mǒ）复（fù）挑（tiāo），

初（chū）为（wéi）霓（ní）裳（cháng）后（hòu）六（liù）幺（yāo）。大（dà）弦（xián）嘈（cáo）嘈（cáo）如（rú）急（jí）

雨（yǔ），小（xiǎo）弦（xián）切（qiè）切（qiè）如（rú）私（sī）语（yǔ），嘈（cáo）嘈（cáo）切（qiè）切（qiè）

错（cuò）杂（zá）弹（tán），大（dà）珠（zhū）小（xiǎo）珠（zhū）落（luò）玉（yù）盘（pán）。间（jiān）关（guān）

莺（yīng）语（yǔ）花（huā）底（dǐ）滑（huá），幽（yōu）咽（yè）泉（quán）流（liú）水（shuǐ）下（xià）滩（tān）；

水（shuǐ）泉（quán）冷（lěng）涩（sè）弦（xián）凝（níng）绝（jué），凝（níng）绝（jué）不（bù）通（tōng）声（shēng）暂（zàn）

歇（xiē）。别（bié）有（yǒu）幽（yōu）愁（chóu）暗（àn）恨（hèn）生（shēng），此（cǐ）时（shí）无（wú）声（shēng）

胜（shèng）有（yǒu）声（shēng）。银（yín）瓶（píng）乍（zhà）破（pò）水（shuǐ）浆（jiāng）迸（bèng），铁（tiě）骑（jì）

突（tú）出（chū）刀（dāo）枪（qiāng）鸣（míng）。曲（qǔ）终（zhōng）收（shōu）拨（bō）当（dāng）心（xīn）画（huà），

四 弦 一 声 如 裂 帛 。 东 船 西 舫 悄 无
sì xián yī shēng rú liè bó dōng chuán xī fǎng qiǎo wú

言 ， 唯 见 江 人 秋 月 白 。 沉 吟 放 拨
yán wéi jiàn jiāng rén qiū yuè bái chén yín fàng bō

插 弦 中 ， 整 顿 衣 裳 起 敛 容 。 自 言 ：
chā xián zhōng zhěng dùn yī cháng qǐ liǎn róng zì yán

「 本 是 京 城 女 ， 家 在 虾 蟆 陵 下 住 ，
běn shì jīng chéng nǚ jiā zài há má líng xià zhù

十 三 学 得 琵 琶 成 ， 名 属 教 坊 第 一
shí sān xué dé pí pá chéng míng shǔ jiào fāng dì yī

部 。 曲 罢 曾 教 善 才 服 ， 妆 成 每 被
bù qù bà céng jiào shàn cái fú zhuāng chéng měi bèi

秋 娘 妒 ； 武 陵 年 少 争 缠 头 ， 一 曲
qiū niáng dù wǔ líng nián shào zhēng chán tóu yī qù

红 绡 不 知 数 ； 钿 头 银 篦 击 节 碎 ， 血
hóng xiāo bù zhī shù diàn tóu yín bì jī jié suì xuè

色 罗 裙 翻 酒 污 。 今 年 欢 笑 复 明 年 ，
sè luó qún fān jiǔ wū jīn nián huān xiào fù míng nián

秋 月 春 风 等 闲 度 。 弟 走 从 军 阿 姨
qiū yuè chūn fēng děng xián dù dì zǒu cóng jūn ā yí

死 ， 暮 去 朝 来 颜 色 故 。 门 前 冷 落
sǐ mù qù zhāo lái yán sè gù mén qián lěng luò

车 马 稀 ， 老 大 嫁 作 商 人 妇 ！ 商 人
chē mǎ xī lǎo dà jià zuò shāng rén fù shāng rén

重 利 轻 离 别 ， 前 月 浮 梁 买 茶 去 ；
zhòng lì qīng lí bié qián yuè fú liáng mǎi chá qù

去 来 江 口 守 空 船 ， 绕 船 月 明 江 水
qù lái jiāng kǒu shǒu kōng chuán rào chuán yuè míng jiāng shuǐ

寒 。 夜 深 忽 梦 少 年 事 ， 梦 啼 妆 泪
hán yè shēn hū mèng shào nián shì mèng tí zhuāng lèi

红阑干。」我闻琵琶已叹息，又闻
hóng lán gān　　　　wǒ wén pí pá yǐ tàn xí　　yòu wén

此语重唧唧！同是天涯沦落人，
cǐ yǔ chóng jī jī　tóng shì tiān yá lún luò rén

相逢何必曾相识！我从去年辞帝
xiāng féng hé bì céng xiāng shí　wǒ cóng qù nián cí dì

京，谪居卧病浔阳城；浔阳地僻
jīng　zhé jū wò bìng xún yáng chéng　xún yáng dì pì

无音乐，终岁不闻丝竹声。住近
wú yīn yuè　zhōng suì bù wén sī zhú shēng　zhù jìn

湓江地低湿，黄芦苦竹绕宅生；
pén jiāng dì dī shī　huáng lú kǔ zhú rào zhái shēng

其间旦暮闻何物？杜鹃啼血猿哀
qí jiān dàn mù wén hé wù　dù juān tí xuè yuán āi

鸣。春江花朝秋月夜，往往取酒还
míng　chūn jiāng huā zhāo qiū yuè yè　wǎng wǎng qǔ jiǔ huán

独倾。岂无山歌与村笛？呕哑嘲哳
dú qīng　qǐ wú shān gē yǔ cūn dí　ōu yǎ zhāo zhā

难为听。今夜闻君琵琶语，如听仙
nán wéi tīng　jīn yè wén jūn pí pá yǔ　rú tīng xiān

乐耳暂明。莫辞更坐弹一曲，为君
yuè ěr zàn míng　mò cí gèng zuò tán yī qǔ　wèi jūn

翻作琵琶行。感我此言良久立，却
fān zuò pí pá xíng　gǎn wǒ cǐ yán liáng jiǔ lì　què

坐促弦弦转急；凄凄不似向前声，
zuò cù xián xián zhuǎn jí　qī qī bú sì xiàng qián shēng

满座重闻皆掩泣。座中泣下谁最
mǎn zuò chóng wén jiē yǎn qì　zuò zhōng qì xià shéi zuì

多？江州司马青衫湿。
duō　jiāng zhōu sī mǎ qīng shān shī

# 37. Fan Zhongyan: "A Note on the Yueyang Pavilion"

三十七．范仲淹：《岳阳楼记》
sān shí qī　fàn zhòng yān　　yuè yáng lóu　jì

庆 历 四 年 春 ， 滕 子 京 谪 守 巴 陵
qìng lì sì nián chūn　téng zi jīng zhé shǒu bā líng

郡 。 越 明 年 ， 政 通 人 和 ， 百 废 具 兴 ，
jùn　yuè míng nián　zhèng tōng rén hé　bǎi fèi jù xīng

乃 重 修 岳 阳 楼 ， 增 其 旧 制 ， 刻 唐
nǎi chóng xiū yuè yáng lóu　zēng qí jiù zhì　kè táng

贤 今 人 诗 赋 于 其 上 ； 属 予 作 文 以
xián jīn rén shī fù yú qí shàng　zhǔ yú zuò wén yǐ

记 之 。
jì zhī

予 观 夫 巴 陵 胜 状 ， 在 洞 庭 一 湖 。
yú guān fū bā líng shèng zhuàng　zài dòng tíng yī hú

衔 远 山 ， 吞 长 江 ， 浩 浩 汤 汤 ， 横 无
xián yuǎn shān　tūn cháng jiāng　hào hào shāng shāng　héng wú

际 涯 ； 朝 晖 夕 阴 ， 气 象 万 千 ； 此 则
jì yá　zhāo huī xī yīn　qì xiàng wàn qiān　cǐ zé

岳 阳 楼 之 大 观 也 ， 前 人 之 述 备 矣 。
yuè yáng lóu zhī dà guān yě　qián rén zhī shù bèi yǐ

然 则 北 通 巫 峡 ， 南 极 潇 湘 ， 迁 客
rán zé bèi tōng wū xiá　nán jí xiāo xiāng　qiān kè

骚 人 ， 多 会 于 此 ， 览 物 之 情 ， 得 无
sāo rén　duō huì yú cǐ　lǎn wù zhī qíng　dé wú

异 乎 ？
yì hū

若 夫 霪 雨 霏 霏 ， 连 月 不 开 ； 阴
ruò fú yín yǔ fēi fēi　lián yuè bù kāi　yīn

风(fēng) 怒(nù) 号(háo)，浊(zhuó) 浪(làng) 排(pái) 空(kōng)；日(rì) 星(xīng) 隐(yǐn) 耀(yào)，山(shān)
岳(yuè) 潜(qián) 形(xíng)；商(shāng) 旅(lǚ) 不(bù) 行(xíng)，樯(qiáng) 倾(qīng) 楫(jí) 摧(cuī)，薄(bó)
暮(mù) 冥(míng) 冥(míng)，虎(hǔ) 啸(xiào) 猿(yuán) 啼(tí)；登(dēng) 斯(sī) 楼(lóu) 也(yě)，则(zé)
有(yǒu) 去(qù) 国(guó) 怀(huái) 乡(xiāng)，忧(yōu) 谗(chán) 畏(wèi) 讥(jī)，满(mǎn) 目(mù) 萧(xiāo)
然(rán)，感(gǎn) 极(jí) 而(ér) 悲(bēi) 者(zhě) 矣(yǐ)！

至(zhì) 若(ruò) 春(chūn) 和(hé) 景(jǐng) 明(míng)，波(bō) 澜(lán) 不(bù) 惊(jīng)，上(shàng)
下(xià) 天(tiān) 光(guāng)，一(yī) 碧(bì) 万(wàn) 顷(qǐng)；沙(shā) 鸥(ōu) 翔(xiáng) 集(jí)，锦(jǐn)
鳞(lín) 游(yóu) 泳(yǒng)，岸(àn) 芷(zhǐ) 汀(tīng) 兰(lán)，郁(yù) 郁(yù) 青(qīng) 青(qīng)。而(ér)
或(huò) 长(cháng) 烟(yān) 一(yī) 空(kōng)，皓(hào) 月(yuè) 千(qiān) 里(lǐ)，浮(fú) 光(guāng) 跃(yuè)
金(jīn)，静(jìng) 影(yǐng) 沉(chén) 壁(bì)，渔(yú) 歌(gē) 互(hù) 答(dá)，此(cǐ) 乐(lè) 何(hé)
极(jí)！登(dēng) 斯(sī) 楼(lóu) 也(yě)，则(zé) 有(yǒu) 心(xīn) 旷(kuàng) 神(shén) 怡(yí)，宠(chǒng)
辱(rǔ) 皆(jiē) 忘(wàng)、把(bǎ) 酒(jiǔ) 临(lín) 风(fēng)，其(qí) 喜(xǐ) 洋(yáng) 洋(yáng) 者(zhě)
矣(yǐ)！

嗟(jiē) 夫(fú)！予(yú) 尝(cháng) 求(qiú) 古(gǔ) 仁(rén) 人(rén) 之(zhī) 心(xīn)，或(huò)
异(yì) 二(èr) 者(zhě) 之(zhī) 为(wéi)，何(hé) 哉(zāi)？不(bù) 以(yǐ) 物(wù) 喜(xǐ)，不(bù)

以 己 悲 ， 居 庙 堂 之 高 ， 则 忧 其 民 ；
yǐ jǐ bēi jū miào táng zhī gāo zé yōu qí mín

处 江 湖 之 远 ， 则 忧 其 君 。 是 进 亦
chǔ jiāng hú zhī yuǎn zé yōu qí jūn shì jìn yì

忧 ， 退 亦 忧 ； 然 则 何 时 而 乐 耶 ？ 其
yōu tuì yì yōu rán zé hé shí ér lè yé qí

必 曰 ： 「 先 天 下 之 忧 而 忧 ， 后 天 下
bì yuē xiān tiān xià zhī yōu ér yōu hòu tiān xià

之 乐 而 乐 欤 ？ 」 噫 ！ 微 斯 人 ， 吾 谁
zhī lè ér lè yú yī wēi sī rén wú shéi

与 归 ！ 时 六 年 九 月 十 五 日 。
yǔ guī shí liù nián jiǔ yuè shí wǔ rì

# 38. Ouyang Xiu: "A Note on the Zuiweng Pavillion"

三 十 八 . 欧 阳 修 ：《 醉 翁 亭 记 》
sān shí bā ōu yáng xiū zuì wēng tíng jì

环 滁 皆 山 也 。 其 西 南 诸 峰 ， 林
huán chú jiē shān yě qí xī nán zhū fēng lín

壑 尤 美 。 望 之 蔚 然 而 深 秀 者 ， 琅
hè yóu měi wàng zhī wèi rán ér shēn xiù zhě láng

琊 也 。 山 行 六 七 里 ， 渐 闻 水 声 潺
yé yě shān xíng liù qī lǐ jiàn wén shuǐ shēng chán

潺 ， 而 泻 出 于 两 峰 之 间 者 ， 酿 泉
chán ér xiè chū yú liǎng fēng zhī jiān zhě niàng quán

也 。 峰 回 路 转 ， 有 亭 翼 然 临 于 泉
yě fēng huí lù zhuǎn yǒu tíng yì rán lín yú quán

上 者 ， 醉 翁 亭 也 。 作 亭 者 谁 ？ 山 之
shàng zhě zuì wēng tíng yě zuò tíng zhě shéi shān zhī

僧 智 僊 也 。 名 之 者 谁 ？ 太 守 自 谓
sēng zhì xiān yě míng zhī zhě shéi tài shǒu zì wèi

也 。 太 守 与 客 来 饮 于 此 ， 饮 少 辄
yě tài shǒu yǔ kè lái yǐn yú cǐ yǐn shǎo zhé

醉 ， 而 年 又 最 高 ， 故 自 号 曰 「 醉 翁 」
zuì ér nián yòu zuì gāo gù zì hào yuē zuì wēng

也 。 醉 翁 之 意 不 在 酒 ， 在 乎 山 水
yě zuì wēng zhī yì bú zài jiǔ zài hū shān shuǐ

之 间 也 。 山 水 之 乐 ， 得 之 心 而 寓
zhī jiān yě shān shuǐ zhī lè dé zhī xīn ér yù

之 酒 也 。
zhī jiǔ yě

若 夫 日 出 而 林 霏 开 ， 云 归 而 岩
ruò fú rì chū ér lín fēi kāi yún guī ér yán

穴 暝 ， 晦 明 变 化 者 ， 山 间 之 朝 暮
xué míng huì míng biàn huà zhě shān jiān zhī zhāo mù

也 。 野 芳 发 而 幽 香 ， 佳 木 秀 而 繁
yě yě fāng fā ér yōu xiāng jiā mù xiù ér fán

阴 ， 风 霜 高 洁 ， 水 落 而 石 出 者 ， 山
yīn fēng shuāng gāo jié shuǐ luò ér shí chū zhě shān

间 之 四 时 也 。 朝 而 往 ， 暮 而 归 ， 四
jiān zhī sì shí yě zhāo ér wǎng mù ér guī sì

时 之 景 不 同 ， 而 乐 亦 无 穷 也 。
shí zhī jǐng bù tóng ér lè yì wú qióng yě

至 于 负 者 歌 于 涂 ， 行 者 休 于 树 ，
zhì yú fù zhě gē yú tú xíng zhě xiū yú shù

前 者 呼 ， 后 者 应 ， 伛 偻 提 携 ， 往 来
qián zhě hū hòu zhě yìng yǔ lǔ tí xié wǎng lái

而 不 绝 者 ， 滁 人 游 也 。 临 溪 而 渔 ，
ér bù jué zhě chú rén yóu yě lín xī ér yú

溪 深 而 鱼 肥 ； 酿 泉 为 酒 ， 泉 香 而
xī shēn ér yú féi niàng quán wéi jiǔ quán xiāng ér

酒 冽 ； 山 肴 野 蔌 ， 杂 然 而 前 陈 者 ，
jiǔ liè shān yáo yě sù zá rán ér qián chén zhě

太 守 宴 也 。 宴 酣 之 乐 ， 非 丝 非 竹 ，
tài shǒu yàn yě yàn hān zhī lè fēi sī fēi zhú

射 者 中 ， 弈 者 胜 ， 觥 筹 交 错 ， 起 坐
shè zhě zhòng yì zhě shèng gōng chóu jiāo cuò qǐ zuò

而 喧 哗 者 ， 众 宾 谨 也 。 苍 颜 白 发 ，
ér xuān huá zhě zhòng bīn huān yě cāng yán bái fà

颓 然 乎 其 间 者 ， 太 守 醉 也 。
tuí rán hū qí jiān zhě tài shǒu zuì yě

已 而 夕 阳 在 山 ， 人 影 散 乱 ， 太
yǐ ér xī yáng zài shān rén yǐng sǎn luàn tài

守 归 而 宾 客 从 也 。 树 林 阴 翳 ， 鸣
shǒu guī ér bīn kè cóng yě shù lín yīn yì míng

声 上 下 ， 游 人 去 而 禽 鸟 乐 也 。 然
shēng shàng xià yóu rén qù ér qín niǎo lè yě rán

而 禽 鸟 知 山 林 之 乐 ， 而 不 知 人 之
ér qín niǎo zhī shān lín zhī lè ér bù zhī rén zhī

乐 ； 人 知 从 太 守 游 而 乐 ， 而 不 知
lè rén zhī cóng tài shǒu yóu ér lè ér bù zhī

太 守 之 乐 其 乐 也 。 醉 能 同 其 乐 ，
tài shǒu zhī lè qí lè yě zuì néng tóng qí lè

醒 能 述 其 文 者 ， 太 守 也 。 太 守 谓
xǐng néng shù qí wén zhě tài shǒu yě tài shǒu wèi

谁 ？ 庐 陵 欧 阳 修 也 。
shéi lú líng ōu yáng xiū yě

# 39. Wang Anshi: "A Note on My Visit to Mt. Baochan"

三十九．王安石：《游褒禅山记》
sān shí jiǔ wáng ān shí yóu bāo chán shān jì

褒禅山，亦谓之华山。唐浮图慧
bāo chán shān yì wèi zhī huá shān táng fú tú huì

褒始舍于其址，而卒葬之，以故其
bāo shǐ shè yú qí zhǐ ér zú zàng zhī yǐ gù qí

后名之曰褒禅。今所谓慧空禅院
hòu míng zhī yuē bāo chán jīn suǒ wèi huì kōng chán yuàn

者，褒之庐冢也。距其院东五里，
zhě bāo zhī lú zhǒng yě jù qí yuàn dōng wǔ lǐ

所谓华阳洞者，以其在华山之阳
suǒ wèi huá yáng dòng zhě yǐ qí zài huá shān zhī yáng

名之也。距洞百余步，有碑仆道，
míng zhī yě jù dòng bǎi yú bù yǒu bēi pū dào

其文漫灭，独其为文犹可识，曰：
qí wén màn miè dú qí wéi wén yóu kě shí yuē

「花山。」今言「华」如「华实」之
huā shān jīn yán huá rú huá shí zhī

「华」者，盖音谬也。其下平旷，
huá zhě gài yīn miù yě qí xià píng kuàng

有泉侧出，而记游者甚众，所谓前
yǒu quán cè chū ér jì yóu zhě shèn zhòng suǒ wèi qián

洞也。由山以上五六里，有穴窈然，
dòng yě yóu shān yǐ shàng wǔ liù lǐ yǒu xué yǎo rán

入之甚寒，问其深，则其好游者不
rù zhī shèn hán wèn qí shēn zé qí hào yóu zhě bù

能穷也，谓之后洞。
néng qióng yě wèi zhī hòu dòng

予 与 四 人 拥 火 以 入 ， 入 之 愈 深 ，
yú yǔ sì rén yōng huǒ yǐ rù rù zhī yù shēn

其 进 愈 难 ， 而 其 见 愈 奇 。 有 怠 而
qí jìn yù nán ér qí jiàn yù qí yǒu dài ér

出 者 ， 曰 ： 「 不 出 ， 火 且 尽 。 」 遂
chū zhě yuē bù chū huǒ qiě jìn suì

与 之 俱 出 。 盖 予 所 至 ， 比 好 游 者
yǔ zhī jù chū gài yú suǒ zhì bǐ hào yóu zhě

尚 不 能 十 一 ， 然 视 其 左 右 ， 来 而
shàng bù néng shí yī rán shì qí zuǒ yòu lái ér

记 之 者 已 少 。 盖 其 又 深 ， 则 其 至
jì zhī zhě yǐ shǎo gài qí yòu shēn zé qí zhì

又 加 少 矣 。 方 是 时 ， 予 之 力 尚 足
yòu jiā shǎo yǐ fāng shì shí yú zhī lì shàng zú

以 入 ， 火 尚 足 以 明 也 。 既 其 出 ， 则
yǐ rù huǒ shàng zú yǐ míng yě jì qí chū zé

或 咎 其 欲 出 者 ， 而 予 亦 悔 其 随 之 ，
huò jiù qí yù chū zhě ér yú yì huǐ qí suí zhī

而 不 得 极 乎 游 之 乐 也 。
ér bù dé jí hū yóu zhī lè yě

于 是 予 有 叹 焉 。 古 人 之 观 于 天
yú shì yú yǒu tàn yān gǔ rén zhī guān yú tiān

地 、 山 川 、 草 木 、 虫 鱼 、 鸟 兽 ， 往
dì shān chuān cǎo mù chóng yú niǎo shòu wǎng

往 有 得 ， 以 其 求 思 之 深 而 无 不 在
wǎng yǒu dé yǐ qí qiú sī zhī shēn ér wú bú zài

也 。 夫 夷 以 近 ， 则 游 者 众 ； 险 以 远 ，
yě fú yí yǐ jìn zé yóu zhě zhòng xiǎn yǐ yuǎn

则 至 者 少 。 而 世 之 奇 伟 瑰 怪 非 常
zé zhì zhě shǎo ér shì zhī qí wěi guī guài fēi cháng

之观，常在于险远，而人之所罕至焉。故非有志者不能至也。有志矣，不随以止也，然力不足者，亦不能至也。有志与力，而又不随以怠，至于幽暗昏惑，而无物以相之，亦不能至也。然力足以至焉而不至，于人为可讥，而在己为有悔。尽吾志也，而不能至者，可以无悔矣。其孰能讥之乎？此予之所得也！

余于仆碑，又以悲夫古书之不存，后世之谬其传而莫能名者，何可胜道也哉？此所以学者不可以不深思而慎取之也。

四人者：庐陵萧君圭君玉，长

乐 王 回 深 父 ， 余 弟 安 国 平 父 、 安
lè wáng huí shēn fù yú dì ān guó píng fù ān

上 纯 父 。 至 和 元 年 七 月 某 日 ， 临
shàng chún fù zhì hé yuán nián qī yuè mǒu rì lín

川 王 某 记 。
chuān wáng mǒu jì

## 40. Su Shi: "On the Marquis of Liu"

四 十 . 苏 轼 ：《 留 侯 论 》
sì shí sū shì liú hóu lùn

古 之 所 谓 豪 杰 之 士 者 ， 必 有 过
gǔ zhī suǒ wèi háo jié zhī shì zhě bì yǒu guò

人 之 节 。 人 情 有 所 不 能 忍 者 ， 匹
rén zhī jié rén qíng yǒu suǒ bù néng rěn zhě pǐ

夫 见 辱 ， 拔 剑 而 起 ， 挺 身 而 斗 ， 此
fū jiàn rǔ bá jiàn ér qǐ tǐng shēn ér dòu cǐ

不 足 为 勇 也 。 天 下 有 大 勇 者 ， 卒
bù zú wéi yǒng yě tiān xià yǒu dà yǒng zhě cù

然 临 之 而 不 惊 ， 无 故 加 之 而 不 怒 ，
rán lín zhī ér bù jīng wú gù jiā zhī ér bú nù

此 其 所 挟 持 者 甚 大 ， 而 其 志 甚 远
cǐ qí suǒ xié chí zhě shèn dà ér qí zhì shèn yuǎn

也 。
yě

夫 子 房 受 书 于 圯 上 之 老 人 也 ，
fū zǐ fáng shòu shū yú yí shàng zhī lǎo rén yě

其 事 甚 怪 ； 然 亦 安 知 其 非 秦 之 世 ，
qí shì shèn guài rán yì ān zhī qí fēi qín zhī shì

有 隐 君 子 者， 出 而 试 之 。 观 其 所
yǒu yǐn jūn zǐ zhě chū ér shì zhī guān qí suǒ

以 微 见 其 意 者， 皆 圣 贤 相 与 警 戒
yǐ wēi xiàn qí yì zhě jiē shèng xián xiāng yǔ jǐng jiè

之 义 ； 而 世 不 察， 以 为 鬼 物， 亦 已
zhī yì ér shì bù chá yǐ wéi guǐ wù yì yǐ

过 矣 。 且 其 意 不 在 书 。
guò yǐ qiě qí yì bú zài shū

当 韩 之 亡， 秦 之 方 盛 也， 以 刀
dāng hán zhī wáng qín zhī fāng shèng yě yǐ dāo

锯 鼎 镬 待 天 下 之 士 。 其 平 居 无 罪
jù dǐng huò dài tiān xià zhī shì qí píng jū wú zuì

夷 灭 者， 不 可 胜 数 。 虽 有 贲 、 育，
yí miè zhě bù kě shēng shǔ suī yǒu bēn yù

无 所 复 施 。 夫 持 法 太 急 者， 其 锋
wú suǒ fù shī fú chí fǎ tài jí zhě qí fēng

不 可 犯， 而 其 末 可 乘 。 子 房 不 忍
bù kě fàn ér qí mò kě chéng zǐ fáng bù rěn

忿 忿 之 心， 以 匹 夫 之 力 而 逞 于 一
fèn fèn zhī xīn yǐ pǐ fū zhī lì ér chěng yú yì

击 之 间， 当 此 之 时， 子 房 之 不 死
jī zhī jiān dāng cǐ zhī shí zǐ fáng zhī bù sǐ

者， 其 间 不 能 容 发， 盖 亦 已 危 矣 。
zhě qí jiān bù néng róng fà gài yì yǐ wēi yǐ

千 金 之 子 不 死 于 盗 贼 。 何 者？ 其
qiān jīn zhī zǐ bù sǐ yú dào zéi hé zhě qí

身 之 可 爱， 而 盗 贼 之 不 足 以 死 也 。
shēn zhī kě ài ér dào zéi zhī bù zú yǐ sǐ yě

子 房 以 盖 世 之 材， 不 为 伊 尹 、 太
zǐ fáng yǐ gài shì zhī cái bù wéi yī yǐn tài

公 之 谋 ， 而 特 出 于 荆 轲 、 聂 政 之
gōng zhī móu ér tè chū yú jīng kē niè zhèng zhī

计 ， 以 侥 幸 于 不 死 ， 此 圯 上 老 人
jì yǐ jiǎo xìng yú bù sǐ cǐ yí shàng lǎo rén

之 所 为 深 惜 者 也 。 是 故 倨 傲 鲜 腆
zhī suǒ wèi shēn xī zhě yě shì gù jù ào xiān tiǎn

而 深 折 之 ， 彼 其 能 有 所 忍 也 ， 然
ér shēn zhé zhī bǐ qí néng yǒu suǒ rěn yě rán

后 可 以 就 大 事 ， 故 曰 ：「 孺 子 可 教
hòu kě yǐ jiù dà shì gù yuē rú zǐ kě jiāo

也 。」
yě

楚 庄 王 伐 郑 ， 郑 伯 肉 袒 牵 羊 以
chǔ zhuāng wáng fá zhèng zhèng bó ròu tǎn qiān yáng yǐ

逆 ， 庄 王 曰 ：「 其 主 能 下 人 ， 必 能
nì zhuāng wáng yuē qí zhǔ néng xià rén bì néng

信 用 其 民 矣 。」 遂 舍 之 。 句 践 之 困
xìn yòng qí mín yǐ suì shě zhī gōu jiàn zhī kùn

于 会 稽 ， 而 归 臣 妾 于 吴 者 ， 三 年
yú kuài jī ér guī chén qiè yú wú zhě sān nián

而 不 倦 。 且 夫 有 报 人 之 志 ， 而 不
ér bú juàn qiě fú yǒu bào rén zhī zhì ér bù

能 下 人 者 ， 是 匹 夫 之 刚 也 。 夫 老
néng xià rén zhě shì pǐ fū zhī gāng yě fú lǎo

人 者 ， 以 为 子 房 才 有 余 ， 而 忧 其
rén zhě yǐ wéi zǐ fáng cái yǒu yú ér yōu qí

度 量 之 不 足 ， 故 深 折 其 少 年 刚 锐
dù liàng zhī bú zú gù shēn zhé qí shào nián gāng ruì

之 气 ， 使 之 忍 不 忿 而 就 大 谋 。 何
zhī qì shǐ zhī rěn bú fèn ér jiù dà móu hé

则 ？ 非 有 生 平 之 素 ， 卒 然 相 遇 于
zé       fēi yǒu shēng píng zhī sù     cù rán xiāng yù yú

草 野 之 间 ， 而 命 以 仆 妾 之 役 ， 油
cǎo yě zhī jiān   ér mìng yǐ pú qiè zhī yì   yóu

然 而 不 怪 者 ， 此 固 秦 皇 之 所 不 能
rán ér bú guài zhě   cǐ gù qín huáng zhī suǒ bù néng

惊 ， 而 项 籍 之 所 不 能 怒 也 。
jīng   ér xiàng jí zhī suǒ bù néng nù yě

观 夫 高 祖 之 所 以 胜 ， 而 项 籍 之
guān fú gāo zǔ zhī suǒ yǐ shèng   ér xiàng jí zhī

所 以 败 者 ， 在 能 忍 与 不 能 忍 之 间
suǒ yǐ bài zhě   zài néng rěn yǔ bù néng rěn zhī jiān

而 已 矣 。 项 籍 唯 不 能 忍 ， 是 以 百
ér yǐ yǐ   xiàng jí wéi bù néng rěn   shì yǐ bǎi

战 百 胜 ， 而 轻 用 其 锋 ； 高 祖 忍 之 ，
zhàn bǎi shèng   ér qīng yòng qí fēng   gāo zǔ rěn zhī

养 其 全 锋 ， 以 待 其 弊 ， 此 子 房 教
yǎng qí quán fēng   yǐ dài qí bì   cǐ zǐ fáng jiāo

之 也 。 当 淮 阴 破 齐 ， 而 欲 自 王 ， 高
zhī yě   dāng huái yīn pò qí   ér yù zì wàng   gāo

祖 发 怒 ， 见 于 词 色 。 由 此 观 之 ， 犹
zǔ fā nù   jiàn yú cí sè   yóu cǐ guān zhī   yóu

有 刚 强 不 能 忍 之 气 ， 非 子 房 其 谁
yǒu gāng qiáng bù néng rěn zhī qì   fēi zǐ fáng qí shéi

全 之 ？
quán zhī

太 史 公 疑 子 房 以 为 魁 梧 奇 伟 ，
tài shǐ gōng yí zǐ fáng yǐ wéi kuí wú qí wěi

而 其 状 貌 乃 如 妇 人 女 子 ， 不 称 其
ér qí zhuàng mào nǎi rú fù rén nǚ zǐ   bù chèn qí

志 气 。 而 愚 以 为 此 其 所 以 为 子 房
zhì qì ér yú yǐ wéi cǐ qí suǒ yǐ wéi zǐ fáng

欤 ？
yú

# Vocabulary Index

Each entry lists the vocabulary item, its corresponding pinyin, and the lesson number in which the vocabulary item appears. (An asterisked lesson number refers to the reference text in the lesson.) The entries are placed in alphabetical order by the initials of their pinyin. Within each initial the entries are ordered by the main vowel (a, e, i, o, u) in the final, and within each main vowel the entries are ordered by the four tones (1st tone through 4th tone).

**A**

| | | |
|---|---|---|
| 阿嬌 | Ā jiāo | 29* |
| 哀 | āi | 9（乙） |
| 埃 | āi | 14 |
| 安 | ān | 1（丁） |
| 安 | ān | 4（甲） |
| 安 | ān | 10 |
| 鞍 | ān | 26 |
| 安事死馬 | ān shì sǐ mǎ | 22 |
| 安土樂業 | ān tǔ lè yè | 27 |
| 鰲 | áo | 14 |

**B**

| | | |
|---|---|---|
| 巴陵 | Bālíng | 37 |
| 班 | bān | 28 |
| 包茅 | bāo máo | 17 |
| 褒禪山 | Bāochánshān | 39 |
| 拔 | bá | 23 |
| 白馬將 | bái mǎ jiàng | 26 |
| 白衣 | bái yī | 28 |
| 把 | bǎ | 37 |
| 百廢 | bǎi fèi | 37 |
| 百工 | bǎi gōng | 33 |
| 寶 | bǎo | 9（甲） |
| 堡塢 | bǎo wù | 35 |
| 罷 | bà | 15 |
| 霸 | bà | 23 |
| 罷 | bà | 27 |
| 罷中山 | bà Zhōngshān | 15 |
| 拜 | bài | 11 |
| 敗 | bài | 23 |

| | | |
|---|---|---|
| 敗績 | bài jī | 16 |
| 敗績 | bài jī | 18 |
| 報 | bào | 22 |
| 報 | bào | 22 |
| 報 | bào | 40 |
| 報讎 | bào chóu | 22 |
| 卑 | bēi | 8 |
| 卑 | bēi | 22 |
| 卑 | bēi | 33 |
| 碑 | bēi | 39 |
| 賁 | Bēn | 40 |
| 崩 | bēng | 18 |
| 北 | běi | 23 |
| 北 | běi | 35 |
| 北海 | Běihǎi | 12 |
| 本紀 | Běnjì | 23 |
| 備 | bèi | 14 |
| 被 | bèi | 23 |
| 被 | bèi | 28 |
| 備 | bèi | 37 |
| 迸 | bèng | 36 |
| 濱 | bīn | 17 |
| 瀕 | bīn | 27 |
| 賓 | bīn | 38 |
| 繽紛 | bīn fēn | 30 |
| 兵 | bīng | 10 |
| 兵 | bīng | 23 |
| 兵符 | bīng fú | 25 |
| 鄙 | bǐ | 16 |
| 比 | bǐ | 21 |
| 鄙臣 | bǐ chén | 20 |

| | | | | | |
|---|---|---|---|---|---|
| 正 | zhèng | 3 (丁) | 製 | zhì | 18 |
| 政 | zhèng | 9 (乙) | 致 | zhì | 19 |
| 政 | zhèng | 19 | 制 | zhì | 27 |
| 鄭 | Zhèng | 40 | 誌 | zhì | 30 |
| 鄭伯 | Zhèng Bó | 40 | 制 | zhì | 37 |
| 正黑 | zhèng hēi | 35 | 志 | zhì | 40 |
| 政通 | zhèng tōng | 37 | 志氣 | zhì qì | 40 |
| 正言若反 | zhèng yán ruò fǎn | 10 | 至若 | zhì ruò | 37 |
| 之 | zhī | 1 (甲) | 至於 | zhì yú | 38 |
| 之 | zhī | 1 (甲) | 治裝 | zhì zhuāng | 21 |
| 卮 | zhī | 1 (丁) | 至和 | Zhìhé | 39 |
| 知 | zhī | 3 (甲) | 智僊 | Zhìxiān | 38 |
| 之 | zhī | 5 (甲) | 終 | zhōng | 1 (丁) |
| 知 | zhī | 11 | 忠 | zhōng | 3 (乙) |
| 脂 | zhī | 19 | 忠 | zhōng | 16 |
| 織 | zhī | 19 | 終 | zhōng | 30 |
| 之 | zhī | 21 | 忠臣 | zhōng chén | 10 |
| 之 | zhī | 21 | 中貴人 | zhōng guì rén | 26 |
| 之 | zhī | 32 | 終歲 | zhōng suì | 36 |
| 支子 | zhī zǐ | 19 | 中興 | zhōng xīng | 28 |
| 知足 | zhī zú | 21 | 中州 | zhōng zhōu | 35 |
| 直 | zhí | 14 | 中山 | Zhōngshān | 15 |
| 直 | zhí | 23 | 舟 | zhōu | 2 (乙) |
| 直 | zhí | 24 | 周室 | Zhōu shì | 17 |
| 執 | zhí | 32 | 冢 | zhǒng | 39 |
| 止 | zhǐ | 2 (乙) | 眾 | zhòng | 8 |
| 止 | zhǐ | 20 | 中 | zhòng | 14 |
| 祇 | zhǐ | 32 | 眾 | zhòng | 17 |
| 芷 | zhǐ | 37 | 種 | zhòng | 19 |
| 址 | zhǐ | 39 | 眾 | zhòng | 23 |
| 咫尺 | zhǐ chǐ | 29* | 中 | zhòng | 24 |
| 志 | zhì | 4 (甲) | 中 | zhòng | 38 |
| 至 | zhì | 7 | 眾人 | zhòng rén | 33 |
| 置 | zhì | 8 | 重死 | zhòng sǐ | 10 |
| 識 | zhì | 9 (乙) | 仲尼 | Zhòngní | 5 (乙) |
| 至 | zhì | 10 | 株 | zhū | 1 (丙) |
| 智 | zhì | 11 | 諸 | zhū | 4 (乙) |
| 質 | zhì | 13 | 諸 | zhū | 5 (甲) |
| 知 | zhì | 14 | 諸 | zhū | 8 |
| 志 | zhì | 14 | 諸 | zhū | 21 |
| 治 | zhì | 18 | 諸侯 | zhū hóu | 17 |